A LINGERING FEAR

EAST SUSSEX HOSPITALS
AND THE WORKHOUSE LEGACY

By the same author:

A Guide to Hospital Careers
(Museum Press)

The Strongest Enemy
(A novel: Alvin Redman)

Out of the Shadows: A History of Newhaven Downs Hospital, 1836-1996
(South Downs Health NHS Trust)

Brighton's County Hospital, 1828-2007

The Alex Story: A Portrait of Brighton's Children's Hospital, 1868-2007

A Lingering Fear

East Sussex Hospitals
And The Workhouse Legacy

Harry Gaston

BA (Hons), MHSM, Dip.MHSM, D.Phil

Southern Editorial Services

2009

2009
Published by
SOUTHERN EDITORIAL SERVICES
34 Hillcrest Road,
Newhaven, East Sussex, BN9 9EG

ISBN 978-0-9558467-2-4

Typeset in Garamond 12/14 pt and Bell 12/14.5
by Southern Editorial Services, Australia,
28 Herbert Street, Albert Park, Melbourne, VIC 3206
Printed by 4edge, Hockley. www.4edge.co.uk

Dedicated to the memory of
Dr A.N.G. (Tony) Clark

We occasionally disagreed on the means
But never on the end
The best possible care of older people in hospital

Contents

Illustrations

Photos 2, 3, 9, 25, 37, 44, 45, 46, 50, 53,54, 58, 59, 67, 69, 72, 80, 81, 82, 86, 91, 96, 97, 99, 100, 101, 102 from the author's collection; 6, 8, 21, 49, 56, 57, 63, 64, 65, 66, 68, 70, 71A, 71B, 74A, 74B, 75, 76, 77, 77, 78, 79, 83, 84, 85, 87, 88, 89, 90, 98 Brighton and Sussex University Hospitals Bulletin archive; 16, 36, 51, 62 Cuckfield Hospital archive; 1 East Sussex County Record Office; 29, 33 C. Farrant; 11, 18,48, 55, A and R Hibbs; 5, 10, 12, 13 © P.Higginbotham (www.workhouses.org.uk); 17, 47, 72 Marie Lewis; 19, 20, 22, 23, 38, 42, 43, 61, 92, 93, 94, 95 R G Martin; 4 Sarah-Anne Morley; 26, 30 D.J. Poole; 24, 25, 34, 35 M Roberts; 39 B Sprague; 28, 32, 32A, 40, 41 K H Thomas; 31, 60 Don Valentine.

Acknowledgements

I would have normally begun by acknowledging the help so kindly given to me by a number of people during the past couple of years while I worked on *A Lingering Fear*. However, perhaps they will forgive me if I first publicly acknowledge those who made possible the original research for my doctoral thesis which forms the basis of this book. That was undertaken some twenty years ago and their names are all recorded in the Preface to the thesis which is available at the University of Sussex and the library in the Audrey Emerton Building at the Royal Sussex County Hospital.

My thanks to the late Dr A.N.G. Clark, consultant geriatrician to Brighton and Cuckfield hospitals. To David Bowden of Brighton Health Authority, the general managers and chief executives of Hastings, Eastbourne and Mid-Downs health authorities, and to Hastings Borough Council, who allowed me to consult their closed records at East and West Sussex county records offices and, of course, to the records offices staff of both.

Similarly, I received much appreciated help from the inter-library loans staff at the University of Sussex, from Judy Lehmann and her colleagues at the library, then based at the Sussex Postgraduate Medical Centre, and from Peter Merry and his editorial staff at the Health and Social Service Journal who welcomed me to their London office and allowed me to peruse the journal's archives.

I am grateful, too, to the trustees of the Open University's Crowther Fund for providing some financial assistance during the early stages of my research and last, but by no means least, to my supervisors at the University of Sussex, initially Dr Stephen Yeo and later Dr Eileen Yeo.

Using the material from the thesis as the basis of a book that I hoped would reach a wider audience has been challenging but made easier by the help given by a number of people.

Firstly, my thanks to those who provided the photos, their names appear on the previous page. Ron Martin was especially helpful by letting me have access to his articles and numerous photographs of the former Sussex workhouses. Southlands Hospital only features in the earlier part of the book and I am grateful to Malcolm Brett, chairman of the League of Friends and to Martin Booker for their help in locating material about that hospital. For material on Eastbourne, I must thank Jacqui of Eastbourne Reference Library, Zoë Edwards, Information Librarian East Sussex County Council and Mrs K. Thomas (nee Jenner). Jean Sullivan has been a tremendous help with information about St Helen's Hospital. Thanks, too, Simon Meredith and Joyce Worts who accessed the old Cuckfield photo archive for me.

I would like to acknowledge, also, those who have helped in various ways to make the production of this book possible, especially Andy Morley who read through the initial drafts, David Arscott, Kim Leslie of West Sussex County Record Office, Lynn Gaylor and Pam Lelliott of Worthing and Southlands NHS Trust, Mrs Masters, Margaret Gearing, Rena Crook, Philip Bye of East Sussex County Record Office and Frankie Gee. My apologies if I have missed anyone: work on the book has been carried out over a two year period, interrupted by the need to meet a promised deadline on previous book, *The Alex Story*.

However, I cannot forget the debt I owe to Sarah-Anne Morley. This is the fourth book we have worked on together. She has once again been responsible for typesetting, page and cover design and on this occasion she has also acted as editor, a service she is now providing for academics and authors in Australia. My sincere thanks, Sarah-Anne.

Abbreviations

CMO	Chief Medical Officer (Ministry of Health)
CMOH	County Medical Officer of Health
COHSE	Confederation of Health Service Employees
EMS	Emergency Medical Service
ESCC	East Sussex County Council
ESCRO	East Sussex County Record Office
HAS	Hospital (later Health) Advisory Service
HMC	Hospital Management Committee
HMSO	Her Majesty's Stationery Office
H of C	House of Commons
H of L	House of Lords
LCC	London County Council
MO	Medical Officer
MOH	Medical Officer of Health
NOPWC	National Old People's Welfare Committee
OPWC	Old People's Welfare Committee
PAC	Public Assistance Committee
PLI	Poor Law Institution
RCN (or RCn)	Royal College of Nursing
RHB	Regional Hospital Board
SAMO	Senior Administrative Medical Officer
SWC	Social Welfare Committee
WI	Women's Institute
WVS/WRVS	Women's (Royal) Voluntary Service
WSCRO	West Sussex County Record Office

Preface

In the early 1970s, not long after the new tower block at the Royal Sussex County Hospital opened, my father-in-law, Harry Randall, was admitted for emergency surgery. At that time, the procedure was for patients to be moved to a ward in the original nineteenth century building as soon as possible after surgery. To reach the ward, patients were pushed in their beds down a long, bare brick corridor. As he was being moved along this corridor, accompanied by my wife and I, he looked up at us and said: "They are not taking me to the workhouse, are they?"

Workhouses officially ceased to exist some sixty years earlier, in 1912. Since then, two major pieces of legislation should have severed once and for all the Poor Law connections of these institutions. The most recent of these is the National Health Service Act of 1946 which, incidentally my father-in-law, at that time Member of Parliament for Clitheroe in Lancashire, had spent sleepless nights attending debates in the House ensuring that the Bill became law. Two years later the NHS was born and yet, a quarter of a century later, here he was, now in his early seventies, expressing concern that he might be going into the workhouse.

All the evidence points to the fact that his was not an uncommon fear among older people. On the one hand, hospitals for the elderly had not thrown off their Poor Law origins. In 1952, for example, the house committee formulated proposals to upgrade Pouchlands Hospital 'which is still regarded in the locality as a workhouse.'[1] Writing in 1959, the organiser of a garden fete at Newhaven Downs Hospital observed: 'There can be no doubt that present impressions of our chronic sick hospitals, for example, are too often coloured by past associations.'[2]

One reason for the lingering fear of the former workhouses was the belief that anyone entering these institutions would never see the outside world again – a view not confined just to the elderly patients themselves and their relatives according to one geriatric consultant:

> The consultant saw relatives in his office once weekly on an 'open door' basis … At these interviews, a gentle examination of the prospects for discharge was made and discussed should recovery occur. It was made clear that the patient had not been admitted for the rest of his or her life. Much valuable information was obtained at this discussion and one common exclamation was: "the general practitioner said mother would never come out of hospital again" – so reminiscent of the old municipal hospital attitude.'[3]

Taking the two periods 1930 – 1948, following the abolition of the Poor Law Boards of Guardians, and 1948 – 1974, the first period of the National Health Service when the former workhouse hospitals came under the control of local hospital management committees, this book explores the reasons why hospitals in East Sussex in particular (they were by no means exceptional, of course) failed the throw off their former workhouse associations and how they dealt with the large numbers of elderly chronic sick patients who were incarcerated in their wards.

It is unusual, perhaps, that this book is not based solely on academic research. The starting point was my Open University honours project on the development of hospital services for the elderly chronic sick in East Sussex. This owed much to the encouragement of Dr A.N.G. (Tony) Clark, formerly geriatric consultant for Brighton and Mid Sussex, who originally suggested I should write a history of the old Newhaven workhouse.[4] Next, this work was expanded and set in the context of the national situation together with the development of the specialty of geriatric medicine in my doctoral thesis for the University of Sussex.[5]

Thirdly, the history of Newhaven Downs Hospital commissioned by South Downs NHS Trust to mark its closure in 1996 and the opening of a new facility on site adds another dimension – the testimony of former members of staff obtained mainly from interviews carried out by my colleague Sarah-Anne Morley and myself.[6]

This work also contained, like the present volume, personal recollections of my years at the hospital to which I was first appointed in 1950, later becoming hospital secretary. Brighton General, Pouchlands and Newhaven Downs hospitals, were all former workhouses, for which I was administratively responsible at the time of my early retirement in 1983.

Introduction

The Fear of the Workhouse

Even today the term 'workhouse' is still used by the older generation, sometimes jocularly — 'we're not in the workhouse yet' — and all too often with dread. For the old buildings still remain, their exteriors a grim reminder that the architects of 'less eligibility' were the designers of prisons too ... the buildings still stand and with them their memories. — J.C. Brocklehurst, 'Textbook of Geriatric Medicine', 1973

In 1948, with the introduction of the National Health Service, the hospitals in East Sussex included some that had their origins as workhouses established in the years following the Poor Law Amendment Act of 1834 – Battle, Brighton General, Cuckfield, Newhaven Downs, Pouchlands (Chailey), St Helen's (Hastings) and St Mary's (Eastbourne). An eighth hospital, Southlands (Shoreham), formerly administered by East Sussex County Council, was one of the former workhouses that joined others administered by hospital management committees in West Sussex.

Workhouses had existed prior to 1834, of course. Following the dissolution of the monasteries, responsibility for caring for the poor during Elizabethan times had fallen upon the parishes and some 'poor houses', many of them previously church houses, were already in existence. During the eighteenth century, however, some of the larger parishes and unions of smaller parishes developed these houses into more elaborate institutions.

In Brighton, for example, a tenement was set aside in East Street in 1690 to act as a poor house. A new poor house was erected in Market Street in 1727 for sick, aged people and poor children, enlarged in 1733 and again in1800. Then, having grown too small for the purpose, it was demolished in 1823. It was replaced by a larger workhouse opened in September 1822, celebrated by a procession of ninety-five inmates from the old workhouse.[1]

A workhouse was established in Cuckfield during the eighteenth century when a property in South Street called the Bull Inn was used by the churchwardens to help the poor. It was rebuilt in the early 1800s.[2] Eastbourne's first poor house was believed to be in what is now Grove Road but prior to 1817 was in Pillory Place, now part of Bradford

Street.[3] At Hastings a workhouse serving three parishes, St Clements', All Saints' and St Mary-in-the-Castle, was established in George Street in 1754.[4] There are records in 1777 of a small workhouse in Steyning and a larger one at Battle. It is not clear when a poor house was established at Newhaven, but it probably existed during the eighteenth century. It is recorded that the first meeting on the new board of guardians was held there in 1835 before adjourning to the Bridge Inn.[5]

Before 1834, however, much of the assistance to destitute people was given primarily in the form of allowances. These were funded from a compulsory poor rate levied on every inhabitant and occupier of land. The system had many critics. Some argued that the poor laws encouraged early marriage between those who had little or no prospect of supporting a family and this intensified the very thing the poor laws were intended to deal with – the problem of the relief of widespread poverty. Critics also argued that the laws tended to eradicate the spirit of independence and self-help that would have otherwise existed among the poor.

1834 marked a turning point in workhouse history. Relief now centred largely on the workhouse which, it was believed, would distinguish the deserving from the undeserving. The test was a simple one: anyone who accepted relief in an institution as repellent as a workhouse must lack the moral determination to survive outside it.

Following a report by the Poor Law Commission in 1832, the new Act established a system centrally controlled by three Poor Law Commissioners at Somerset House assisted by their Secretary, Edwin Chadwick. 15,000 parishes were combined into some 600 unions. Their purpose was to administer the new poor law and provide the new workhouses which were to be administered by boards of guardians elected by the ratepayers in each parish.

The Cuckfield Union, for example, combined the parishes of Cuckfield, Lindfield, Ardingly, Horsted Keynes, Balcombe, Slaugham, Hurstpierpoint, Twineham, Albourne, Newtimber, Cowfold, Bolney, Keymer, Clayton and Pyecombe. All apart from Slaugham and Cowfold, which was to join the Horsham Union, gave their names to wards in Cuckfield Hospital and later, following its closure, to wards in the new hospital that replaced it, the Princess Royal at Haywards Heath.

The Newhaven Union consisted of the parishes of Newhaven itself with a population of 900, Blatchington, Bishopstone, Denton, Tarring, Heighton, Piddinghoe, Southease, Telscombe, Rodmell, Rottingdean,

1. One of the earliest workhouses built in Sussex after 1834 at Newhaven. Designed by the noted workhouse architect Sampson Kempthorne it opened on 5 February 1836. This engraved view of the church and workhouse (ref P426/7/17/3) is reproduced with the permission of the County Archivist of East Sussex, copyright reserved.

Ovingdean, Falmer and Stanmer. The stables used for the horses of the guardians riding from the outlying parishes were later used, in the twentieth century, by the workhouse master to garage his car. Neighbouring Seaford was included in the Eastbourne Union. This covered an area along the coast as far as Wallers Haven on the Pevensey Marshes, northwards to Whelpley, just south of Hailsham, and included the parishes of Alfriston, East Dean, Folkington, Friston, Jevington, Litlington, Lullington, Pevensey, West Dean, Westham, Willingdon and Wilmington.[6]

The workhouses built following the Poor Law Amendment Act, 1834, were intended to deter the able-bodied poor, with conditions that had to be inferior to those of the lowest paid labourer outside. They were grim places that earned the name of 'bastiles'[7][sic], where men were separated from women and discipline was harsh. If, as a result, the labouring classes became self-reliant, it was believed, this would lead to a substantial reduction in the poor rates.

It was never intended that the aged should suffer under this system but rather that they should 'enjoy their indulgences without torment from the boisterous'[8]. However, for some reason the original intention to provide separate institutions – for the aged and for children, for example – failed to materialise. As a result, old people were admitted into largely mixed workhouses that also catered for the 'undeserving' destitute, and it was inevitable that they too suffered hardships in the same way.

Cuckfield possibly provides the most graphic illustration of why the poor, even under the most desperate circumstances, feared the new regime after 1834.

The great snowstorm of Christmas 1836 blocked all road communications and flattened cottages, killing eight people and injuring many more.[9] On the fifth day after the snow had set in, 149 able bodied labourers thrown out of work and suffering distress applied for relief at the board meeting of the Cuckfield guardians. A few of the labourers, considered 'urgent cases of necessity' were given flour. Entry to the workhouse was offered to 118 of the labourers. Only six accepted. At the next board meeting, sixty applications for relief were made. Only five agreed to enter the workhouse in the evening and three of them left the next morning rather than being put to work on the corn-grinding mill.[10]

Not surprisingly, there was considerable opposition to the 1834 Poor Law Act. The first organised protest took place in Eastbourne in the spring of 1835 when the new board of guardians announced that married paupers would be separated in the Union workhouses. Tradespeople and agricultural labourers joined together to resist the new regulations and the authorities responded by drafting troops and the Metropolitan police into the area.

The separation of married couples was one of the factors contributing to growing popular fear of the workhouses that was to continue to exist more than a century later.

The nature of the work undertaken by the able-bodied inmates also contributed to the public perceptions of these institutions – and with good reason. This work had to be hard, or dull and disagreeable, although not so much so that the paupers would refuse to undertake it. Picking oakum was one of the onerous tasks the inmates had to perform. This involved untwisting and picking old hemp ropes to obtain the loose fibres. A common task, incidentally, for both paupers and convicts.

Other tasks for the men included digging previously untilled ground, stone-breaking and operating a corn-grinding mill. This involved a group of men trudging round in a circle pushing the bars of a capstan for hour after hour. The most notorious, possibly, was bone-crushing.

Bone-crushing could be both heavy and unpleasant work. The Poor Law Commission had recommended special apparatus for the task: a long iron bar or rammer weighing twenty or thirty pounds and an iron-bound wooden box with sides which lifted off to enable the dust of the bones to be taken out, the dust being used for manure. In some workhouses men – and even boys of nine or ten working in pairs – pounded as much as 96 lbs of bones daily, the dust of which had to pass through a sieve. Where farmers demanded finer dust, a quarter-inch sieve was used and in this case it was not possible to pound more than 30 or 40 lbs a day.

As well as these unpleasant tasks, inmates were also subject to harsh punishments for what were sometimes relatively trivial offences. To help maintain strict discipline, the workhouse master had authority to punish certain offences committed by 'refractory or disorderly' inmates. These and more serious offences which he was not empowered to deal with were entered into a book. This was regularly examined by the guardians and, in the more serious cases, they recorded their decisions regarding the punishment.[11]

Two punishment books for the Newhaven workhouse are preserved in the county record office. The earlier entries in the first of these covering the period 1864 to 1912 show the type of offences punished during the mid-nineteenth century.

In December 1864 Charles Dyer broke ten windows and in January he broke two more. His punishment was to be confined in a room by himself. William Hale escaped over a wall in August 1865. He was 'kept without dinner and caused to pick 3 lbs of oakum'. John Peace, who refused to sweep the dormitories, was sent to Lewes Jail for ten days!

Drunkenness was the most frequently recorded offence, followed by fighting, absconding (escaping over the wall), refusing to obey the master's orders and, for the children, being late for school. Corporal punishment was also inflicted on the younger inmates. 'Two stripes of the cane over his breech outside his clothes' were ordered for Albert Fuller and Richard Moore for fighting each other. Albert Fuller again and George Parker were given four stripes of the cane on the hands for stealing gooseberries.[12]

At Steyning, seven men were sentenced to hard labour for climbing the fence separating the men from the women in the workhouse. As late as 1905, an inmate who absconded was sentenced to fourteen days imprisonment with hard labour while one inmate was sentenced to two months with hard labour for assaulting another inmate.[13] At Eastbourne in 1835, the governor was authorised to punish misbehaviour by keeping inmates on bread and water 'for such number of days as he may think necessary'.[14]

But no doubt it was the scandals, mostly occurring during the early years following 1834, that were the major factor accounting for the long-lasting public fear of the workhouse – and bone crushing featured in what was probably the most notorious of these. Apart from the heaviness of the work and the danger of scarring caused by flying fragments of bone, there was the unpleasantness. Often the bones delivered to the workhouse were green and gave off an offensive smell, which made many of the inmates ill. It was bones in this condition that paupers in Andover workhouse were forced to gnaw to relieve their hunger, in one of the worst scandals that came to light in the mid 1880s.

Earlier, in 1839, the master of Bath workhouse had locked up a woman believed to be pregnant who, it was later claimed, had miscarried in a 'damp, black hole' in November without bedding. Other proven cases included the master of Blean workhouse who locked a little girl overnight in the mortuary as a punishment, and the master at Hoo who indecently flogged women and children.

Bone-crushing also featured in a less well-known case although it was widely publicised in a pamphlet, *The Murder Den and its Means of Destruction*. This concerned William Smith, an agricultural labourer from Wilmington, who petitioned the House of Commons in protest against his 'cruel and inhuman treatment' in Eastbourne workhouse. He claimed he had been locked with other men in a room only eight feet by fourteen for seven hours a day pounding bones collected from local butchers and private houses. Any human bones included, however, were disposed of 'down the privy hole.'[15]

Historians have argued that examples like these contributed to the 'myth of the workhouse'; that some were merely sensationalised unconfirmed press reports or propaganda by the anti-Poor Law campaigners and that the majority of the institutions were not like those featuring in the scandals. It is even claimed, no doubt correctly, that unlike at Andover inmates were often better fed than those living outside. Clearly, conditions in the workhouses varied enormously, but that did nothing to lessen the fear these places engendered in the popular imagination.

Writing as a journalist, Charles Dickens referred to a visit he made to Wapping workhouse, which he described as well and kindly run as it could be, given the inadequate building and the poverty of the ratepayers. In another workhouse article, written in 1866, he argued that the poor would rather creep in corners to die, than rot in such infamous places.

Nevertheless, it is not as a journalist but as a novelist, the author of *Oliver Twist* first published in 1837, that he created what was to remain a lasting image of the workhouse as a place to be feared.

Part I

1930-1948:

The Local Authority Years

1. The Survival of the Guardians

The new authorities under the Poor Law have in many instances co-opted on to the Public Assistance Committees old members of the Boards of Guardians, so that the experience of those who have for years been in touch with the poor, as well as the Poor Law, need not be lost. — Editorial in the Sussex Daily News, April 1930.

Towards the end of the nineteenth century, things had certainly improved for old people in the workhouse infirmaries. Local Government Board circulars, for example, laid down the principles for workhouse administration for the elderly. They were to be given 'a better diet, tobacco and more privacy in sleeping arrangements. There were certainly improvements … committees visiting workhouses were enjoined to see that the aged were specially attended to.'[1]

In 1913, the union workhouses *officially* ceased to exist and it was decreed that in future they should be named poor law institutions. Nevertheless, the name workhouse continued to be used in academic

NEWHAVEN UNION.

REGULATIONS RELATING TO
VISITING OF INMATES.

All Visitors before passing the Lodge to give their names and purport of visit.

Sundays and Wednesdays are the days on which Inmates may be visited, between the hours of 2 and 4 p.m.

No Inmate may be allowed to have more than TWO visitors in the Ward at one time, subject to the discretion of the Master.

Whereas the Guardians are empowered by Articles 47 and 51 of the Poor Law Institutions Order, 1913, to make regulations relating to gifts to Inmates.

The following articles are permitted :— Tobacco, Tea, Sugar, Sound Fruit, Biscuits, Eggs, Sweets and Jam.

These to be left with the Porter.

The following Rules to be observed :

No materials whatever to provide occupation for Inmates are to be introduced.

Visitors are not to pass from one Ward to another.

No gratuity is on any account whatsoever allowed to be given to anyone in the Institution.

Anyone introducing Spirituous or Fermented Liquor into the Institution is liable to a fine of £10 or 2 months imprisonment.

All changes of address of Inmates' friends to be notified to the Porter.

The above Regulations were adopted by the Guardians at a Meeting held on the 27th March, 1914.

H. W. COUPE,

CERTIFICATE FOR DETENTION.

3. the undersigned, MEDICAL OFFICER of the Workhouse of the County [Borough] of *East Sussex*

at *Newhaven*, HEREBY CERTIFY that it is necessary that the Rate-aided Person referred to in the foregoing Order, dated the *18th* day of *September* 1935, should be detained as a Patient in the said Workhouse.

Dated this *18th* day of *September* 1935

(Signed) *J.O.S.*

Medical Officer of the Workhouse

2. *A notice to visitors dated 1914 shows that the term 'workhouse' had officially ceased to exist by then.*

3. *More than 20 years after poor law institutions had ceased being known as workhouses, official workhouse forms, like this certificate, were still being used.*

works and, more importantly, by the general public for whom they remained places in which many of the aged and infirm were condemned to spend the rest of their days. Changing the name in itself was not enough. What was required was an end to the poor law and the abolition of the boards of guardians.

The opportunity to achieve both these objectives was provided by the reform of the poor law during the 1920s. During the passage of the Bill in 1928, the Minister of Health, Neville Chamberlain, made it clear that the intention was that the boards of guardians would be abolished and their functions taken over by the local authorities. However, it emerged that, despite Labour Party opposition, local authorities would only be enabled, not compelled, to take hospitals out of the poor law. The Labour opposition also warned that the new system made it possible for 'reactionary' guardians to be co-opted and continue to work in poor law administration. Events, not least in East Sussex, were to prove their fears were well founded.

The result, in the eyes of the members of the general public, was that despite the promise of the new law, so far as the workhouses were concerned, it was very much business as usual. Press reports at the time illustrated why this came about.

The abolition of the guardians was described by the Ministry of Health's chief medical officer (CMO) as 'the long deferred fruit of the Royal Commission on the Poor Laws, 1905-1909'[2] Effectively this meant that 37,000 beds in separate infirmaries and 84,000 beds for the sick in mixed workhouses were to be transferred from the control of 650 union areas to 62 county and 83 county borough authorities.

Whilst the immediate effect was to transfer control from the guardians to their local authority successors, in fact often these were largely the same people now serving as members of the new public assistance committees (PACs) or as co-opted members of institutional house committees.

However, it was not anticipated that this situation would be other than temporary for, as the CMO pointed out: ' . . . the Local Government Act will fail in its purpose if its operation is limited to the transfer of Poor Law powers *en bloc* to Public Assistance Committees'.[3]

Once local authorities had taken stock of the situation, it was hoped they would, wherever possible, transfer services and institutions to the control of appropriate committees – that is, to those set up other than by virtue of the Poor Law Act.

Despite the dislike, even loathing, of the poor law and, in particular, the workhouses, especially among the poorer sections of the community, the abolition of the boards of guardians was not greeted with public acclamation. Daily and weekly papers in Sussex, for example, contained numerous photos of groups of workhouse staff and reports of staff functions in the period leading up to April 1st and these clearly were meant as a celebration of what had passed rather than of what was to come. Even the guardians themselves appeared to exhibit considerable emotion at their final meetings:

> The final meeting of the Newhaven Board of Guardians yesterday provided one of the most memorable scenes ever witnessed in the Board Room at the Poor Law Institution. The Chairman's references to long years of association with the Board, and the fact that the end is in sight, had a marked effect on two of the officials who were almost unable to restrain their feelings.[4]

According to another press report, emotions also ran high at Eastbourne:

> Alderman Prior – a former chairman – said the moment was one of the most tragic moments in his life . . . this transference need not have occurred. (*Hear, hear*). It would not be a change for the better, but they had to face facts and make the best of a bad job.[5]

Brighton guardians made their 'Exeunt With Flying Colours' according to the headline of the *Brighton and Hove Herald* report, with a farewell dinner attended by 120 people at the Old Ship Rooms: 'Officially it was a farewell dinner, but never were funereal baked meats more cheerily taken'.[6]

Despite the cheerful atmosphere, however, several speakers referred to the good work the board had done and of the members' sense of loss and the master of the Institution assured the members 'when your work is viewed in the light of history, you will probably be found to have left a monument of service that will last for many generations to come'[6].

Nor were such sentiments confined to the guardians and their officers. An editorial in a Brighton newspaper commented:

> It is impossible to escape a certain feeling of emotion in bidding farewell to the Brighton Board of Guardians. . . . They have kept personal watch over every detail of that huge institution, a town in itself, on the top of the hill, with its aged, its infirm, its bedridden, its sick, the leavening of difficult, even dangerous characters among those who have either broken every rule of life or have been broken by life.[7]

The *Sussex Daily News* also devoted a leader to the subject:

> The old Boards of Guardians . . . exist no more. We need not lament their passing, in spite of the excellent work they have done and the high esteem in which they stood with all who were affected by their work, for they have been replaced by a system which is expected to show greater efficiency. Nor must it be thought that the 'human touch' . . . will be lost as the price to be paid for greater efficiency. The new authorities under the Poor Law have in many instances co-opted on to the Public Assistance Committees old members of the Boards of Guardians, so that the experience of those who have for years be in touch with the poor as well as the Poor Law need not be lost.[8]

Little wonder, then, that many of the guardians went on to serve on the new public assistance committees either in their capacities as councillors or aldermen or as co opted members or on the house committees attached to the various hospitals, infirmaries and institutions. Eastbourne provides a good example of the extent to which former guardians continued to play a part in the control of the transferred institutions. Five of the PAC's ten members were former guardians; they also formed the majority of the institutional house committee – six of the nine councillors and aldermen, and all four of the co-opted members.

Examining the records of the various public assistance committees reveals that parsimony was often an overwhelming feature of the proceedings. This is not always so, however, when the house committee minutes and reports are examined. Many of the former guardians serving on these bodies, possibly a majority, appear to have possessed a genuine concern for the inmates. But was the man in the street really aware of this?

So far as the fear of the workhouse was concerned, to him the continued existence of public assistance committees and the guardians guaranteed that this fear, irrational or not, was certain to continue.

2. The East Sussex Inheritance

I have taken out the particulars and the nature of the persons who happened to be in one particular institution on one night this month ... this institution contained seven acutely sick persons, 55 infirm and senile, six epileptics, eight certified lunatics, 18 certified mental deficients [sic], one able-bodied man and healthy infants ... Nobody can consider that it is a satisfactory state of things when you get brought together in a single institution so many cases which, obviously, required treatment so diverse — Health Minister Neville Chamberlain on the undesirability of mixed institutions speaking during the Second Reading of the 1929 Local Government Bill.

On 1st April 1930, the former workhouses became public assistance institutions. Almost certainly they still had the same masters and matrons and other officials in charge but were now controlled by the local authorities, not the boards of guardians established almost one hundred years before.

Twelve institutions were transferred to East Sussex County Council as a result of the 1929 Local Government Act. Eight were situated entirely within the boundaries of the administrative county; the four others in which the council had an interest were Eastbourne, Hastings, Ticehurst and Steyning. A thirteenth institution, at Brighton, the only parish not incorporated in a union with other parishes as a result of the 1834 Act and so outside the jurisdiction of East Sussex, was transferred directly to the County Borough of Brighton.

For its part, East Sussex handed over its interest in the Eastbourne and Hastings institutions to the county boroughs in which they were situated. Eastbourne received a compensatory payment of £4,450 and Hastings received £4,500. At the same time, Kent County Council relinquished its interest in Ticehurst and received £3,412. The ownership of Steyning, it was decided, should remain vested in East Sussex. In return, West Sussex received a capital payment of £70,000 and access to 165 beds, for which East Sussex was to receive an annual payment of £3,000 plus maintenance costs at the current rate.[1]

At times of organisational change, it is by no means uncommon for the new authority to blame any shortcomings, in part at least, on the failings of its predecessor. The situation in 1930 was no exception and the comment by three senior officials in a report to the county's public assistance committee (PAC) was probably typical: 'The council is handicapped at the

4. Former workhouses in East Sussex in 1930.

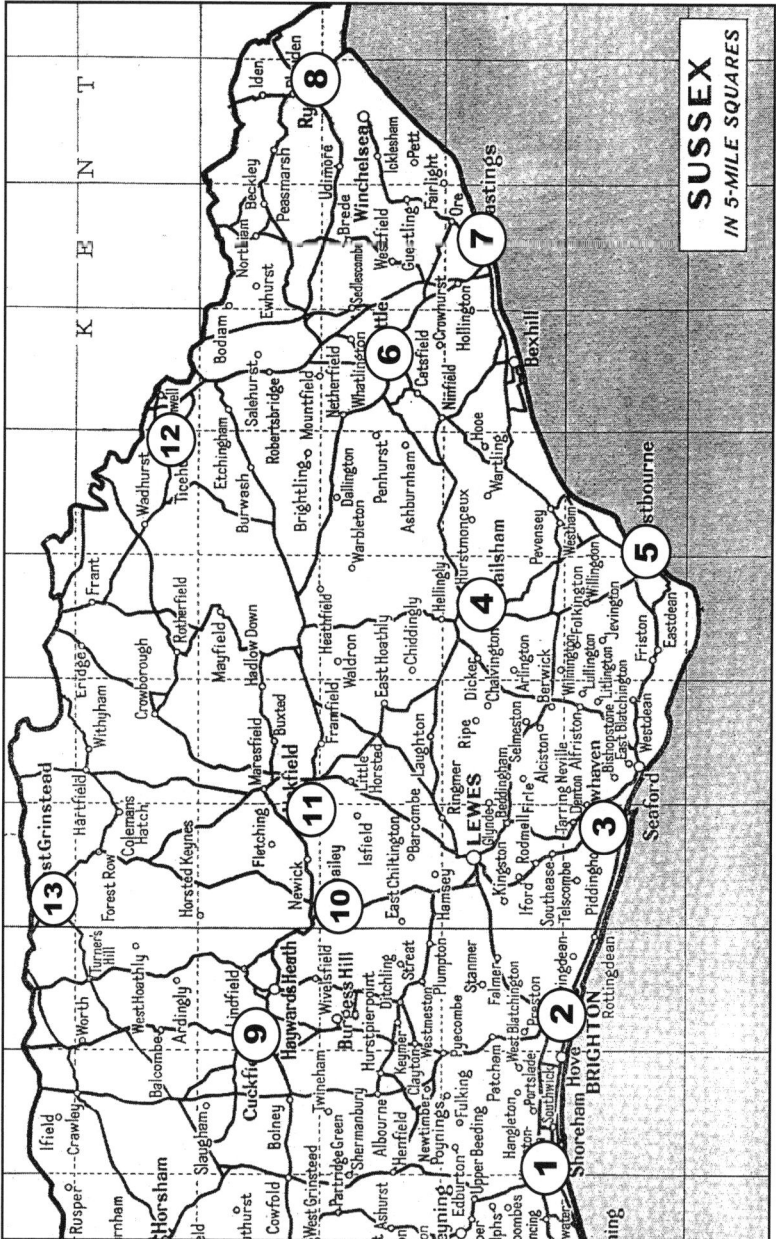

1. Shoreham (Steyning)
2. Brighton
3. Newhaven
4. Hailsham
5. Eastbourne
6. Battle (Stone House)
7. Hastings
8. Rye
9. Cuckfield
10. Chailey
11. Uckfield
12. Ticehurst
13. East Grinstead

5. The old Steyning Workhouse building in the early 1900s.

6. Pouchlands Hospital, the former Chailey Workhouse, pictured from the north.

outset in East Sussex ... by the structural condition of the majority of the Institutions which are their inheritance from the Boards of Guardians'[2] which were described in this and another memorandum as follows:

Steyning Institution, situated outside the boundary of administrative county, was the only one of modern construction throughout. The House was built in 1901, the infirmary built in 1906 lying to the east and separated from the Institution by a dividing wall. Steyning was provisionally classified by East Sussex county council as a combined hospital and infirmary.

Chailey Institution was described as situated in rural surroundings about five miles to the north of Lewes on a site of about 25 acres.

Until 1871, there were three workhouses in central East Sussex situated in the parishes of Chailey, Ditchling and Ringmer. In an effort to save money, these three were amalgamated to form the Chailey Union Workhouse. The three existing buildings were closed and a new, larger workhouse was built on a site in the village of East Chiltington at a cost of £10,489. Originally a lower tender of £9,600 had been accepted but then the contractor withdrew claiming he hadn't added his figures correctly.

In 1898, it was decided to merge the Lewes and Firle Unions with Chailey. As a result, all their work was transferred to Chailey. By 1930, the House block, erected in 1872, had been adapted for male and female mental defectives and was approached by a drive through grounds laid out as a garden. The infirmary buildings, erected between 1901 and 1929, consisted of a two-storied building with a large ward at each end, a maternity ward, two day rooms, a service kitchen and small wards in the centre and a second small block erected for cancer patients. The reports to the council initially recommended that the whole institution should be adapted for medium- and low-grade mental defectives.

Cuckfield Institution had been built on a site about ten acres to the north-east of Cuckfield with a main entrance through Union Lane. It was more than a quarter of a mile from the main road through the village and was almost two miles west from Haywards Heath station. The House block had been erected in 1844 (or perhaps 1845, when the old parish workhouse in Ockenden Lane merged with Hurstpierpoint workhouse)[3] and a new wing with 30 beds added in 1873. This was a three-storied building, said by the county council to be unsuitable for the reception of the sick. The infirmary at the rear was built in 1894 with additions in

7. Cuckfield Union, 1908 and 8. Cuckfield House block and Infirmary, 1908.

9. The House block at Newhaven.

1924 and 1929. It consisted of two pavilions of two storeys 'each of good construction'. Heating was by open fires and there was electric lighting throughout. A nurses' home had been provided in 1924 (the casual wards were rebuilt in 1933). It was suggested that ultimately the institution should be used for the acute and chronic sick, maternity and the infirm, if generally bedridden. Like many workhouses, **Newhaven Institution** was not easily accessible, being built either in the heart of the country (like Chailey), well away from the town (Hastings workhouse was built in Ore, then known as Oare) or, as in this case, at the top of a hill between Newhaven Road and Brighton Road.

The three storey House block opened in 1836 was considered to be obsolete, badly designed and, because there was no damp course in its walls, it was damp 'unless fires were maintained' and was 'quite unsuitable for the purpose.' The two storey infirmary block, on the other hand, erected in 1892, was well built and contained two large wards for men with 17 beds on each (one on the ground floor and one on the first floor) and two 13-bedded wards for women.

Battle Institution, originally Stone House, was described as 'old fashioned, but still serviceable'. The Institution stood on an excellent site of about five and a half acres including two of steep sloping woodland. Described as being 'of an old-fashioned workhouse type, but with pleasing exterior appearance', it had been designed and built by architect Frederick Thatcher, who later became famous for churches he built in New Zealand. Work began in 1840 using soldiers stationed nearby as a precaution against a feared French invasion. The first patients were admitted on 13 November 1840. The infirmaries in three of the other inherited former workhouses – **East Grinstead** (erected 1865 according to the council's report, but probably in 1859) situated about 100 yards from the railway station, **Rye** (built between 1840 and 1850 on a site of about seven acres about a mile north of the borough) and **Uckfield** (1837) – were said to be structurally less satisfactory than the House accommodation, 'which, however, leaves much to be desired in all of them.' **Ticehurst** (1836) situated at Flimwell about half a mile to the west of the village was described as 'not well adapted to modern needs either in the House or the Infirmary'. **Hailsham** (1835) was 'structurally unsatisfactory, not suitable for modern requirements.'

Not surprisingly, the county council gave serious consideration to the closure of some of its older properties in order to effect economies in

10. Battle Workhouse c.1908.

1931, particularly Ticehurst and possibly East Grinstead. However, two other closely related considerations probably weighed more heavily in the eventual development of hospital services during the 1930s: the desire to develop modern general hospitals and the need to classify hospitals (in the counties) and wards and even patients (in both the counties and the county boroughs.)

A complaint sometimes made against the guardians was that, knowing it was only a matter of time before they were taken over by the local authorities, they failed to undertake any significant expenditure during their final years. However, this was not always the case. Despite the undoubted antiquity of much of the accommodation in East Sussex, at Battle Institution improvements had recently been carried out and a report noted that it was the only one that could properly be used as an infirmary.

Considerable work had also been undertaken on at least one of the three institutions taken over by the county boroughs. At **Eastbourne** the guardians believed they were handing over 'an institution of which they could be proud'.[4]

Originally built as cavalry barracks in the Peninsular War of 1809-1815 (possibly some parts were built even earlier in 1793), it was sold

11. The former Eastbourne workhouse pictured shortly before the closure of the hospital.

by the War Office to two landowners who then rented the barrack buildings to the Eastbourne guardians who needed to replace the existing workhouse in Bradford Street that was too small. An additional block had been built in 1889 on the east side of the hospital area for the use of non-infectious patients. In 1920 the sick wards were designated as a poor law hospital and a new group of wards, the Centre Block, was officially opened in 1928 when the former boardroom was converted into a theatre and anaesthetic room[5].

Like Chailey, the original workhouse in **Hastings** situated at 42 George Street, had served three parishes. In 1836, having become too small, a replacement was built on the east side of Cackle Street, so named because of the chicken farms situated in the neighbourhood. It was renamed after the chairman of the guardians, Alderman Frederick Tuppenney, and became Frederick Road in November 1904. In the meantime, in 1868, wards had been added to the original building that had opened on 10 July 1837. Later, in April 1900, Ald. Tuppenney formally laid the foundation stone of a new workhouse built on the opposite side of Cackle Street.

12. Hastings Workhouse from the south east, early 1900s. 13. Hastings south and east wings from the south east.

As in Eastbourne, some improvements had taken place during the 1920s. Using redundant accommodation for casuals (more commonly known, perhaps, as vagrants or tramps), a pharmacy was established south of the main gate, while lifts were installed in two dormitory blocks replacing flights of stone stairs.

Brighton had built a new workhouse in 1865 with a detached infirmary. Two additional blocks were added in 1891 and a third one in 1898. Much of the 1920s were dominated by debates about building a home for the nursing staff eventually opened at the end of 1929. An X-ray and Therapeutic Department opened in the basement of E Block in 1926. Apart from these two examples there is little evidence of expenditure on the buildings of the institution. In fact, the master was to report to the House committee in 1932 that no redecoration had taken place in A and F blocks and again in 1933 that it was twelve years since J Block had been painted.

Classification in East Sussex

Classification was seen as a means of ridding the system of the 'evils of the mixed workhouse.' According to Sidney and Beatrice Webb, the one positive recommendation with regard to children and the aged in the report of the 1905-1909 Royal Commission on the Poor Law was the repeated demand that care should be provided in entirely separate buildings under independent management.

Not surprisingly, the influential Minority Report, whose signatories included Mrs Webb and George Lansbury, condemned the continued existence of the mixed institutions, which had a 'depressing, degrading and positively injurious effect on the character of all classes of their inmates'[6]

In his annual report for 1931/2, the Minister for Health listed the main classes into which inmates might be grouped: the sick, the aged, mental cases (including mental defectives), children and casuals. However, classification was not needed simply to separate the young from the old, or the deserving from the undeserving. Because of the increasing complexity of medical treatment another differentiation began to evolve: separating the acute from the chronic sick, the chronic sick from the so-called infirm.

In East Sussex the process of classification offered the opportunity to close some of the inherited institutions that were in poor condition,

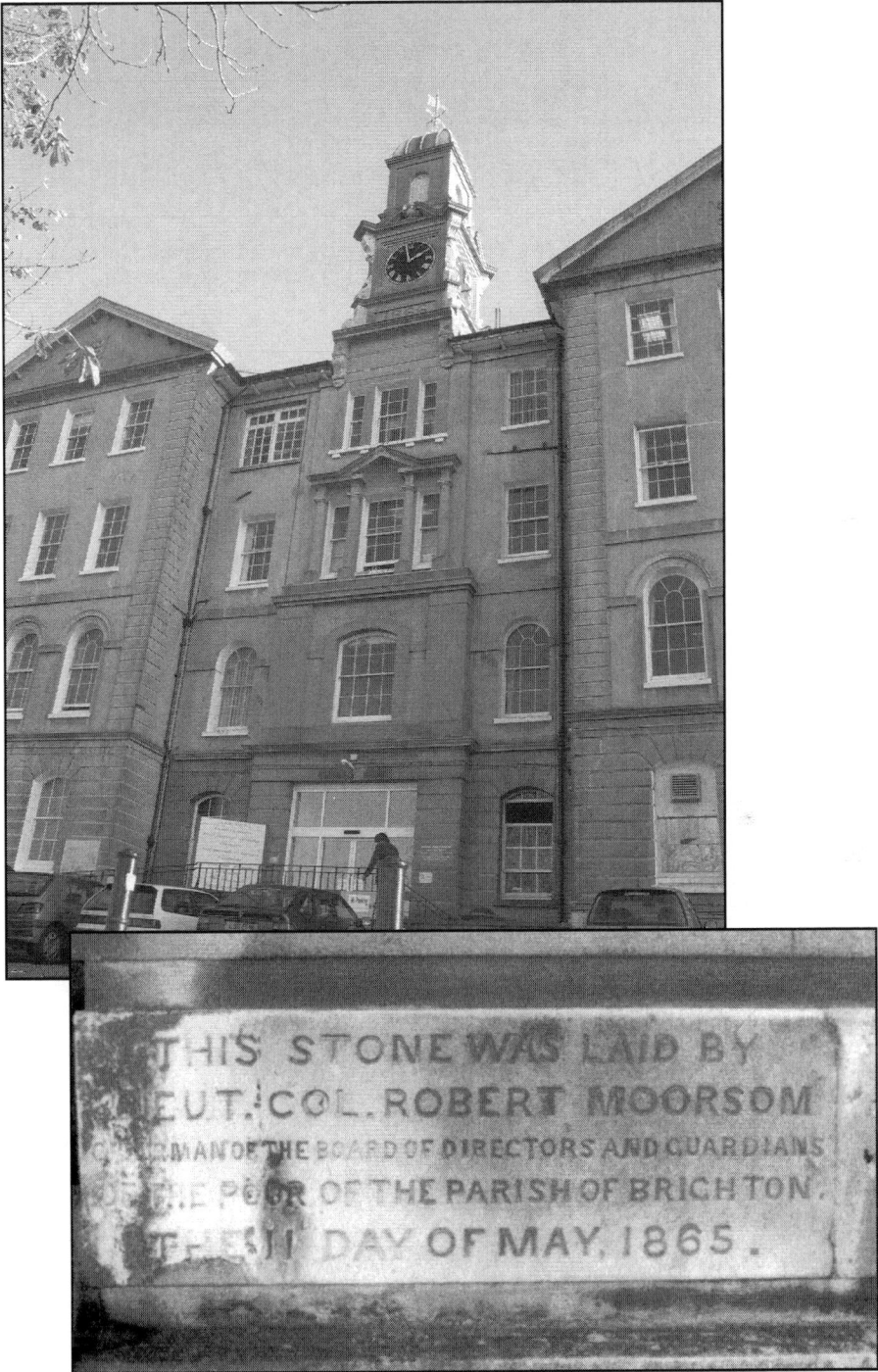

14. A Block at Brighton General Hospital, the former House block; and 15. The foundation stone of Brighton Workhouse.

which would both increase efficiency and reduce the burden on the rates. A sub-committee was appointed to consider the best use that could be made of the transferred institutions and whether or not they could be closed. This last point was stressed in a memorandum that quoted from Chamberlain's speech on the Second reading of the 1928 Bill.

> When this Bill becomes law there will be one single Health Authority in each area whose duty and function it will be to survey the whole institutional needs of that area. They will have the opportunity of reclassifying their institutions, *of closing such as are no longer suitable for modern requirements at all,* [joint authors' original emphasis] of altering and adapting others and using one for one purpose and another for another purpose.[7]

Classification may have been regarded as panacea for the ills of the mixed workhouse, but there was a price to be paid by the inmates and their friends and relatives. The joint memorandum by the East Sussex officials recognised that old people applying for admission to the House should be accommodated 'on more homely lines than is possible in the barrack system' and that nothing should be done that would perpetuate mixed workhouses. But to provide for proper classification within each of the county's ten institutions would require 'prohibitive expenditure.'

> ... classification ... cannot be brought about without widening the area over which the service is administered. This would involve the removal of individuals to a greater distance than under the present system, and, consequently, some hardship so far as visiting by relatives is concerned.[8]

For areas such as East Sussex this constituted a considerable problem: later policy, in fact,was that they should be cared for as close to home as possible. In the 1930s, moving patients some distance away from home, family and friends was the price that had to be paid for doing away with the mixed workhouse. The authors of the East Sussex joint memorandum believed, however, that modern transport reduced the disadvantages and they suggested that financial help could be given to visiting relatives who were in receipt of poor relief.

Following the abolition of guardians, East Sussex had been divided into four geographical areas for the purposes of public assistance. It was suggested that each area should possess a fully equipped hospital (or have an arrangement with a voluntary hospital) for the treatment of acute illness, accommodation for the isolation and treatment of infectious disease, an infirmary for cases of chronic sickness and the aged and infirm, special provision for maternity, a nursery for children under three, accommodation for those who were not sick or infirm but who needed institutional care, and, finally, casual wards.

The areas were: *North*, the sanitary districts of East Grinstead, Cuckfield, Burgess Hill and Uckfield; *East*, Bexhill, Rye and Battle; *South*, Lewes, Newhaven, Seaford, Hailsham and Chailey; *West*, Hove and Portslade-by-Sea.

To a large extent this formed the basis for the county council's development of its hospital and other institutional services during the 1930s. Progress was not particularly rapid although, to be fair, the period was sandwiched between the financial crisis of 1931 and the outbreak of war in 1939. Moreover, there had been a four year blight on institutional developments between 1928 and 1932 – the guardians had suspended their policy of carrying out improvements from 1928 when the Local Government Bill was published and the county council having undertaken little capital expenditure since April 1930. There was, therefore, considerable leeway to make up.

The plan for the Northern Area envisaged using Cuckfield Institution as the hospital and infirmary including arrangements for the reception of maternity cases and children under the age of three. Uckfield was favoured to care for ordinary inmates.

In the Eastern Area, the council favoured Battle Institution, at which improvements had recently been carried out, as the one in which all infirm and chronic cases were to be accommodated as well as maternity cases and children under three. For acute cases, 12 beds were to be reserved at Eastbourne Poor Law Institution and a further 10 in Hastings Municipal Hospital.

In the Southern Area it was recommended that Chailey should be appropriated as a mental deficiency institution and, providing they were not wholly required for mental defectives, the excellent infirmary and nurses' home should serve the area for infirmary purposes. Newhaven, having its modern infirmary building, was proposed as the general hospital for the area although it would be necessary to provide a small operating theatre, a maternity home, nursery and dispensary.

In the Western Area there was no alternative to Steyning Institution, which would become the hospital and infirmary for that part of the county.

By 1934, the council was providing 899 beds in the sick wards and 843 other beds. The sick beds were made up of 303 at Shoreham (including

75 reserved for West Sussex), 94 at Battle, Chailey 86, Cuckfield 143, East Grinstead 48, Newhaven 67, Rye 41, Ticehurst 41, and Uckfield 54. 12 beds were reserved at St Mary's Eastbourne and 10 at Hastings Municipal Hospital. In addition there were 25 beds for tubercular patients (Chailey 15, Cuckfield 4, Ticehurst 2, Uckfield 2).

A report to the county council by the Committee on Hospital Policy and Accommodation submitted on 31 December 1935[9] detailed the progress made since 1930 and suggested plans for the future. Pride of place went to Southlands Hospital that had been developed 'very considerably' and dealt with the needs of the whole of the Hove .district and was receiving an increasing number of urgent cases. Interestingly, in view of later post-war proposals for developing hospital facilities in Hove the report continued:

> This Hospital deals with the population of the large and very valuable area from a rate producing point of view of Hove and its surrounding Parishes, and I think no reasonable complaint is to be expected from that part of the County. If such a thing happened, rather than building more Wards at Southlands Hospital, and so upset the balance of the place completely, I think the Committee should explore the possibility of the reservation of accommodation at the existing voluntary hospitals in Brighton and Hove.

The desire to appease Hove ratepayers by developing Southlands Hospital probably accounts for the complaints by other East Sussex masters, expressed later by the master of Newhaven, who felt their institutions were suffering as a result.[10] So far as Newhaven was concerned in the report, it was argued that the old workhouse was fit for nothing but demolition. It was recommended that the inmates should be accommodated in the infirmary block and that a new infirmary for 50 to 75 aged and infirm patients should be built (but this never materialised because of the outbreak of war).

Among the other recommendations made following consideration of the report were that at some future date the House wards should be demolished and replaced with more suitable, modern buildings, that 50 beds for chronic sickness should be provided at Uckfield and that two wards each accommodating 20 additional patients should meet the immediate needs at Battle.

The evidence is that East Sussex dealt quite conscientiously with the question of classification, but the process did occupy a considerable period of time. It was not until 1938 that real progress was evident when a five-year capital programme was adopted but because of the war this was never completed.

In some respects this was a mixed blessing: among the casualties was a scheme to concentrate accommodation for the chronic sick in the Southern Area in a new block in Uckfield. This would have undoubtedly caused hardship to its elderly patients and their relatives and resulted in a post-war legacy of inconveniently placed accommodation. However, the end result was that at the outbreak of war in 1939 all their institutions were eventually destined to become NHS hospitals. Battle, Newhaven, Chailey and Cuckfield, were mixed institutions which Neville Chamberlain ten years earlier had described as an unsatisfactory situation and something his Local Government Act had been intended to rectify.

3. Farewell to the Poor Law

With the abolition of the Guardians, the interaction of poverty and disease was finally given statutory recognition. It was laid down by the Government and accepted by the Council that the ultimate policy should be to provide medical care under the Public Health Acts and not as Poor Relief — CRV Bell, A History of East Sussex County Council, 1889-1974.

If Section 5 of the 1929 Act was the licence that enabled those responsible to take steps to remove the care of the sick from the opprobrium of Poor Law, why wasn't it more successful?

The institutions situated within the county and the one outside the administrative boundary were all general mixed workhouses. The immediate effect of the Act was to place all of these under the control of the public assistance committee. But the ultimate aim, as the clerk to the council pointed out at an early stage, was that ultimately they should all be dealt with by the appropriate council committee.[1] And this committee, of course, although he did not specify it in the case of the chronic sick, was the public health committee.

At an early stage, only two institutions situated within the county were believed by the council to be suitable for ultimate appropriation – that is appropriately transferred to the control of the public health committee. They were West Hylands at Cuckfield and Newhaven, both of which possessed modern infirmaries built 'within the last 34 years'[2].

In both institutions, the majority of beds were in the sick wards, 132 out of 261 at Cuckfield and 70 out of 125 at Newhaven. The three 'adjacent to but outside the county boundary' at Eastbourne, Hastings and Shoreham also appeared to the county medical officer to be very suitable for use as general hospitals.[3]

The committee agreed that Cuckfield Institution was suitable for conversion to a 'county public hospital' and that it should be possible to appropriate the infirmary part of Steyning (Shoreham) Institution. However, nothing was done until 1932 when, renamed as Southlands Hospital, it was classified as a Public Assistance Hospital in accordance with Part IV of the Public Assistance Act, 1930. This still left it under the control of the public assistance committee.

The matter was revived in 1934 when a letter from the Ministry was

16. The ward block at Cuckfield Institution.

referred to the Committee on Hospital Accommodation and resulted in a report by the county medical officer of health the following May. In this, Dr Glegg summarised in some detail the advantages and disadvantages of providing hospital accommodation for *recoverable sickness* (his emphasis, in other words acute cases, not the chronic sick) under poor law or otherwise.

Among his principal points was an acknowledgement that 'the stigma of pauperism' would be retained under poor law. Appropriation, he believed, would result in a more willing acceptance of treatment 'with consequent better provision for the restoration of working capacity of the people.' On the other hand, the power of recovery of contributions towards the cost of treatment was wider under poor law. In appropriated hospitals this would be restricted to relatives generally considered liable at common law.[4]

Dr Glegg came down clearly in favour of appropriation. His only reservation concerned the recovery of contributions and it may well be that this was the deciding factor for the six members of the Committee on Hospital Accommodation – three from the finance committee, three from the PAC – who recommended that, after comparing the advantages and disadvantages, no steps should be taken 'with such an end in view'.[5]

The Ministry of Health also used its annual reports to urge local authorities to make the change. However, this was not reflected in its official dealings on the ground with the individual authorities. There was only one brief attempt to persuade Hastings to transfer its hospital's control to the public health committee, but neighbouring Eastbourne fought a running battle with the Ministry over a period of ten years or so.

Eastbourne v the Ministry of Health

In Eastbourne the PAC transferred some of its functions as early as 1931 – for example, domiciliary assistance to sighted dependents of blind persons to the Blind Persons Act Relief Sub Committee and the maintenance of certain poor children to the Maternity and Child Welfare Sub Committee.

However, the first reference to appropriation of hospital services does not appear in the PAC minutes until 1934 when a report on 'the suggested appropriation of St. Mary's Hospital' was considered.

The minutes of Eastbourne's various committees reflect a high degree of civic pride, which included the local poor law infirmary, St. Mary's. In a newspaper article, 'Passing of the Guardians', Col. F.S. Garwood wrote:

> One thing on which the outgoing board have the right to pride themselves is that the last five years have shown very considerable improvements in their Institution in Green Street ... especially is this the case in the new wing which has been added to St Mary's Hospital. It has all cost money, but the conversion of the old out of date infirmary into a modern well equipped hospital proves that the money has been well spent.[6]

17. *Workhouse relic exhibited at St Mary's Hospital.*

This view was reflected in the comments of another guardian at the board's final meeting: 'They were handing over an institution of which they could be proud'.[7] Not surprisingly, perhaps, Eastbourne's guardians regretted their passing but Alderman Prior was appointed to the new PAC and Councillor West became its chairman. Both were appointed to St Mary's house committee whilst Col. Garwood became a co-opted member.

The continuing strong guardian presence, and the attitude of the former guardians to the hospital they helped to create, appears to have been tacitly acknowledged in the campaign waged by the Ministry over the appropriation of St Mary's. This opened in December 1933 with a letter that referred to a survey by Ministry officials and paid tribute to the 'reasonable, in some cases high, standard of efficiency and progress in the discharge of public health functions'. It continued with a detailed reference to 'the appropriation of accommodation for the purposes of the Public Health Acts':

> The Minister observes that since the Council took over ... the hospital work ... has increased both in volume and in proportion of cases needing active medical or surgical treatment ... the hospital has recently been approved provisionally as a complete training school for probationer nurses. ... While the actual extent of the Infirmary to be appropriated requires consideration, there need be no obstacles to the appropriation of the hospital portion... [8]

Following consideration of the letter, the council requested the PAC to form a sub committee consisting of the town clerk, the medical officer of health, the borough treasurer, the public assistance officer and the medical officer of St Mary's. They discussed not only appropriation but also the possibility of declaring the infirmary a hospital under Part IV of the Public Assistance Act, 1930 – an attractive alternative that enabled the council to reclaim the cost of treatment under what were generally considered to be the wider ranging powers of the poor law. In the event the special sub committee rejected appropriation and the alternative, largely, it appears, because of the borough treasurer's argument that to do so would involve the cost of maintaining two record keeping systems, one for the hospital, one for the institution. Thus the PAC not only decided against appropriating the hospital but also that the 'present time is not opportune' for it to be declared a hospital under Part IV of the Public Assistance Act 1930.

But the Ministry did not let the matter rest. In December 1934 the town clerk received another letter requesting a visit by council officials to discuss the suggested appropriation 'more fully'. As well as dealing with the suggestion that the recovery of the costs of treatment would be restricted by the 1929 Act the letter also referred to the dual role of public assistance committees: the administration of out relief and the administration of indoor institutional out relief:

> The former duty, to which was added in 1931 the administration of transitional benefit, has in many respects been distasteful and unpopular. It is therefore to the institutional side that the keenest members of the Committees have looked for their opportunities of performing some tangible constructive work and of maintaining personal contact with those needing assistance, without most of the disadvantages which have in their eyes come to be attached to the administration of outdoor relief. Moreover the Public Assistance committees have tended to attract those members of the Council who had previously served as Guardians while the adoption of co opted members often served to strengthen this association between the past and present regimes. The Public Assistance Committee started, therefore, with a strong inherited interest in the administration of the institution, which many of their members had assisted in building up over a number of years, and the improvements which they rightly viewed with considerable pride. The thought that ... this most constructive aspect of their work should be taken out of their hands and passed over to another Committee has naturally been distasteful...[9]

Interestingly, Eastbourne PAC was at this time putting together a scheme of major improvements for the hospital which the full council had

18. The exterior of St Mary's pictured after the closure of the hospital.

deferred pending the outcome of the consultations with the Ministry. It is also interesting to note that a year earlier the Ministry had commented adversely on the 'apparently excessive [out] relief granted by Eastbourne guardians in a number of cases.'[10]

A few weeks later the two sides met in London. In his report to the Sanitary and Public Health Committee, the town clerk said the Minister had 'very strongly urged the appropriation of St. Mary's Hospital as a public health hospital'.

They were reminded that it was the intention of the 1929 Act to take the treatment of sick persons out of poor law. It was most desirable to separate the hospital from the institution from a medical point of view to remove the taint of poor law; patients and their relatives should not have to use the same entrance as 'vagrants, epileptics, lunatics etc'.[11] If the hospital was properly administered running costs need not increase, the Ministry officials argued. And, finally, by making St. Mary's an appropriated hospital, or a hospital under Part IV of the Public Assistance Order, 1930, the present superintendent nurse could be made matron of the hospital and would no longer be under control of the matron of the institution, thus removing 'the friction which must obviously exist where a qualified nurse is under the control of a Lay Matron'.[12]

The first three arguments clearly demonstrate the Ministry's desire to persuade the council to move its hospital out of poor law and, in order that medicine should not be tainted by the stigma of poor law, to do away with the almost symbolic entrance (necessary to secure control over the inmates) through which passed not only the sick, but 'undesirables' too.

Despite the Ministry's lengthy appeal to the guardians, the council's response appears to have been largely built around arguments put forward by the borough treasurer. Using figures from the Ministry's own reports he showed that the cost of treating patients was higher in general hospitals than in poor law hospitals, higher still than in poor law institutions.[13] There would also be additional costs of separating kitchens and stores and providing a separate entrance. Extra medical and nursing staff would be needed to cope with acutely ill patients attracted from voluntary hospitals.

Eastbourne's resistance was based almost entirely on financial grounds. The borough treasurer asked the Ministry officials to give an assurance that appropriation would not entail extra expenditure. He also suggested that the town's voluntary hospitals provided sufficient accommodation for local needs, apart from destitute sick persons, a point apparently not supported by his colleague, the medical officer of health. He referred to the impossibility of recovering costs from patients who were settled in other areas (the Ministry officials insisted that suitable 'machinery' could be devised to overcome this difficulty) and to the question of recovering charges from relatives.

The influence of the borough treasurer appears to have been a critical factor in Eastbourne's resistance to the implementation of Section 5. After the visit to London, and following a report to the council from the treasurer on the additional costs, the Ministry was informed that 'the Council is not at present prepared to appropriate St Mary's ... owing to the expense'.[14]

When the issue was revived less than a year later, the compromise of administering the sick wards as a poor law hospital was again opposed by the borough treasurer. Now, however, the balance of argument appears to have moved against him. The medical officer supported the change insisting that no extra medical or nursing staff would be needed. The treasurer responded that if later on it was decided that a whole time medical superintendent was needed, that a separate entrance was required and the ground should be divided, 'the extra annual cost would be considerable and extra capital expenditure would be necessary'. However:

> If any change must be made, the extra burden on the ratepayers would be less if the Hospital is administered as a Poor Law Hospital under Part IV of the Public Assistance Order than as a General Hospital under the Public Health Acts, as all the existing power of recovery from relatives and others would be preserved.[15]

And, in spite of the treasurer's contention that even this would place a 'considerable extra burden on the rates', the committee decided to apply to the Minister for the recognition of the sick wards as a hospital under the 1930 Public Assistance Order from April 1st, 1937.

But this was not the end of the saga. The borough treasurer continued his attempts to keep down the town's rates. Two months later he suggested that the hospital and maternity home should be concentrated on one site so that it could be administered as one establishment. The Ministry of Health, on the other hand, appeared to be playing for time. An 'unofficial' letter to the MOH suggested that the council should do away with the maternity block at St. Mary's 'especially in light of the intention of the Local Government Act, 1929'. In January the council requested the Ministry to expedite its decision on the application for the sick wards to be administered as a poor law hospital.

A compromise was reached on maternity cases: St. Mary's would be used only 'in very exceptional cases of necessity'. The Minister then recognised St Mary's as 'a separate establishment for the reception and maintenance of the sick or persons requiring maternity treatment' – but only for a period of two years from April 1, 1937.

Early in 1939 the council asked the Ministry to extend this recognition for a further period. The Ministry then requested the council should give further consideration to the question of appropriation and suggested another meeting in London.

The PAC, displaying a marked shift in attitude, responded that whilst members were in agreement in principle to taking the treatment of the sick out of poor law and were, in fact, having the site of the Hospital and Institution replanned with the ultimate object of its being used for hospital purposes only, they felt that 'the present is an inopportune time'.[16] The Ministry repeated its request for a meeting in London 'at an early date'; the PAC suggested a meeting in Eastbourne but the Ministry officials were not agreeable to this.

Eventually the Ministry called a halt to the exchange: 'In view of the existing emergency [the outbreak of the Second World War] the Minister has decided to defer further consideration of the question of appropriation,' the public assistance officer reported to his committee in November.[17]

Despite the problems posed by the war, the Ministry did not let the matter drop completely. Twice more Eastbourne was asked to consider appropriating St Mary's Hospital but when the war ended it still functioned as a poor law hospital (although the PAC had by then been renamed the Social Welfare Committee).

However, in the interim the White Paper on the future of the health services had been published and the establishment of the National Health Service looked certain, so the question of appropriation was by then purely academic.

This somewhat detailed examination of the Eastbourne experience illustrates how tenacious the Ministry could be in pursuit of its goal and how a local authority determined to keep down the local rates could fight to delay the procedure even when by its own admission the battle was as good as lost.

19. The administrative block and 20. The North lodge at St Helen's Hospital.

Hastings and Brighton

In Hastings, as early as 1930, the infirmary had been renamed the Municipal Hospital following a request from the maternity and child welfare committee which was concerned about 'the disinclination of poor persons to be admitted to the Frederick Road Infirmary ... for the purpose of confinements.'[18] However, it never became a municipal hospital in the fullest sense, administered by the public health committee.

The only reference to appropriation in the public assistance committee minute books appears in 1934 when a letter from the Ministry requesting the council to consider the matter was referred to a special sub committee but the conclusions reached by that committee were never recorded.

The case of the remaining county borough, Brighton, is somewhat different. Brighton had earned itself a reputation as a forward looking authority: it was one of the first to set up birth control clinics, for example. But it was by no means among the first to embrace the idea of appropriation although the matter was certainly considered as early as 1931 when the medical officer of health reported: 'although many advantages would result from separating the administration of the sick wards from the Institution as a whole, this is not practical with due regard to economy...'[19]

Nevertheless, Brighton was relatively quick off the mark. In October 1933 the Ministry requested the council to consider appropriating the sick wards and the council approved a resolution from the health committee that appropriation should take place 'at the earliest date'.[20]

However, the decision was not taken without some pressure. The letter considered by the health committee said the Ministry was 'most concerned' over the delay in the conversion of the sick wards into a municipal hospital. According the medical officer the need was the more urgent in so far as 'our Sick Wards at present constitute a fairly up to date hospital of some 700 beds' although administered as an adjunct to the House with some 300 inmates. In order that the medical work could be done more satisfactorily, the wards should be recognised at least as a poor law hospital and placed under a medical superintendent, which could be done 'without interfering in any way with finance.'

Furthermore, 'appropriation ... would lead to closer working arrangements with the Voluntary Hospitals ... the work done in the Municipal Hospitals would be complementary to that done in the Voluntary Hospitals and thus an efficient and co ordinated hospital service could be made available for Brighton residents'.[21]

21. The view of Brighton Municipal Hospital from Elm Grove. Buildings to the right of the entrance were administered by the public health committee while those to left (including the main block) became Elm Grove Home, still under poor law. 22. Dyke Block, part of the Municipal Hospital from 1937. 23. J. Block, still under poor law administration after 1937.

This part of the Ministry's letter and the MOH's response should perhaps be considered in the light of the fact that the Brighton division of the British Medical Association had established a committee to discuss the local implications of the 1929 Act. By 1932, the committee's proposals, which included a suggestion that the needs of Brighton, Hove and district would best be served by one general hospital, were adopted by the local medical profession and issued in a pamphlet 'for the consideration of expert and layman alike'.[22]

> All fresh accommodation should be provided by building on sites provided at this general hospital, to which all the other hospitals in the district should be affiliated ... the use of some of the existing hospitals as recovery homes would set free beds in the general hospital for acute cases – at present in the Brighton district from ten days to three months are needed to remove a patient from the waiting list...[23]

The Ministry's letter also dealt with the financial aspects of appropriation. Interestingly (especially in light of the way the situation was to develop in Eastbourne) the Ministry did not press the need for 'actual physical separation' of House and Infirmary and was therefore able to give an assurance 'that appropriation will not involve any heavy capital expenditure'.

In making his recommendation urging appropriation, however, the MOH argued that his decision was not based solely on the request to meet the obligations of the 1929 Act 'but more particularly in order to provide a better hospital service for the inhabitants of the town'.[24]

In January 1935 representatives of the house and health committees attempted to work out the details of a scheme of appropriation. Like their Eastbourne counterparts, they discussed the question of recovery of charges and other financial matters; unlike them, they do not appear to have considered these to be a problem and the borough accountant pointed out that the 'sick wards and the institution wards were already costed separately'.

The question of a separate entrance gate and lodge was not seen as an insurmountable difficulty and it was decided to consider this later if it was found to be desirable. Appropriation, it was decided, should take effect 'at the earliest possible date',[25] and following to receipt of the Ministry's sanction of the scheme it was agreed that Brighton Municipal Hospital should function as a public health hospital from the 1st January, 1936.[26]

Despite this change, the hospital (later to become Brighton General Hospital) was not able to throw off its workhouse reputation locally.

Although all building to the right of the roadway leading up from the Elm Grove entrance, Blocks C. D and E together with Blocks F and H were under the control of the public health committee, most of the site, including the dominant central building, A Block, retained their poor law associations and became known as Elm Grove Home.

Conditions in the buildings forming the Home, almost certainly without exception, were far inferior to those comprising the municipal hospital. A Block contained a mix of men and women (no doubt kept quite separate). In 1936 it contained 49 able-bodied and 133 aged and infirm men. J Block housed 118 women and L Block 74 men described as 'chronic'.

All toilet facilities in A Block were out of doors. J Block had only one inside toilet.

4. Institutional Life

It was not violence, but the unrelieved tedium of institutional life, which probably afflicted the inmates most. — M. Crowther, *The Workhouse System, 1834-1929*, Batsford, 1981.

So who were the inhabitants and what was life like for them in the former workhouses now bearing a new identity as public assistance institutions? A son of the master at Chailey who lived in the institution from 1921 to 1935 said:

> They were a mixed group with an occasional well educated, well spoken person among them. The majority were able bodied men 'down on their luck' for one reason or another. Women came in due to some domestic upheaval or being 'left in the lurch' when a baby was expected ... Babies under three years of age were kept in the workhouse. Over that age they went to a children's home in Lewes, part of the old Lewes workhouse situated in the Wallands area. The chronic sick in the infirmary were mostly long-stay inmates, about an equal number of men and women. Occasionally one or two came in for a few weeks to 'dry out' before returning to the road and the bottle.[1]

Almost certainly the able-bodies inmates would have worn some sort of uniform. According to the matron's maid at Newhaven, whose sister worked in the sewing room 'patching and looking after the inmates', the women were dressed the same in white calico. 'They had a chemise and it was sort of gathered. And their drawers were two legs pinned together at the top, and they wore a half petticoat.' The master and matron's daughter who also visited the sewing room recalled the women being dressed in striped blue or grey white dresses (not plain white) with white pinafores, although the dresses may have changed slightly over the years.[2]

At Brighton, according to a nurse who started work there in 1936, the men were dressed in blue with a white shirt and red tie. 'It wasn't very nice, and the ladies used to wear blue skirts, white blouses and a blue tippet, a little blue cape, and boots.'[3] At Steyning, the records give little information about the women's dress except for a reference to a new type of bonnet for the elderly infirm in 1921, while the men were dressed in 'Drabbett' jackets and vests, or cord sleeve vests and cord trousers.[4]

In one of the few published accounts of life on a hospital ward in the late twenties and early thirties by a former patient, the author, Bella Aranovitch, wrote: 'There was nothing to do. The only break in the deadly monotony were the two visiting periods, Wednesday and Sunday.'[5]

Monotony was referred to in another patient's account:

> The days were monotonous, the routine unvarying, and the rules and regulations in their number and inhumanity might have been devised for an institution for the punishment of criminals. My crime, and that of hundreds like me, was that of being a young chronic.[6]

The account, published in 1966, was written by Michelle Gilbert who, as a sixteen year-old, was admitted in 1943 to what she described as a 'geriatric ward of the Chronic Hospital' and which, 23 years later, was still her home. Describing her first night in the hospital where she was woken at 3 a.m. for a wash, she wrote:

> I felt like a character in Dickens novel, and in the days that followed I came to realise more and more that the social evils that aroused Dickens had not all been left behind in the darkness of the nineteenth century.

Probably the first contemporary account of institutional life to appear in a national newspaper was given in a letter to the Manchester Guardian published during the Second World War. The letter, *A Workhouse Visit* by X.Y.Z, appeared in March 1943 – the same year that Michelle Gilbert was admitted. It painted a graphic picture of life in what was probably a ward for the elderly infirm and set in train a lengthy series of letters from a variety of readers including a hospital chaplain and a member of a public assistance committee. The letters appeared almost daily, sometimes two or three a day for almost a month and were followed by a special report by an official of the Ministry of Health.

X.Y.Z, in a lengthy and moving account of life for twenty old ladies on the top storey of a large institutional building, was critical of the system rather than individuals.

> The ward was clean, warm, rigidly tidy, the nurse kind, the food adequate. But down each side of the ward were ten beds, facing one another. Between each bed and its neighbour was a small locker and a straight-backed, wooden, uncushioned chair. On each chair sat an old woman in workhouse dress, upright, unoccupied. No library books or wireless. Central heating, but no open fire. No easy chairs. No pictures on the walls. And no common room in which these deficiencies are made good.[44]

X.Y.Z. went away after her visit 'with an unforgettable picture … lines of old women sitting like figures on a mantelpiece, on hard chairs, facing one another, and waiting without occupation for death.'

For the first dozen or so years following the abolition of the guardians, very little was written about the elderly chronic sick living in the workhouses. Correspondence like that initiated by X.Y.Z. was meant to throw a light on and help to alleviate the situation and indeed bring about some improvements in the institution she had visited. In fact, 'immense, although hidden, efforts ... produced a few ameliorations' but 'no library books, no easy chairs, no privacy and no relief from crushing monotony.'

The picture painted by X.Y.Z. would not have applied to every public assistance institution, but it was a picture that can only have contributed to public perceptions of them, still remembered as workhouses, as places to be feared.

For their part, the institutions in East Sussex all provide evidence, to a greater or lesser extent, of the shortcomings enumerated by Aranovitch, Gilbert, X.Y.Z. and the *Manchester Guardian* correspondents: crushing monotony, lack of privacy, unsuitable buildings, inadequate equipment, and food dumped on lockers, to name a few.

The East Sussex experience

An examination of existing records for the East Sussex institutions and infirmaries helps to provide a fuller picture of ward life in the pre-NHS era. On the credit side, East Sussex records show there were attempts to alleviate the monotonous existence of the patients with references to gramophone recitals, visiting and staff concert parties, film shows and other entertainments. At Chailey, preparations for Christmas in the early part of the 1930s included rehearsals for plays and songs by some of the women inmates. In the evening, entertainment was provided by the inmates and staff.[7] In 1946, regular 16 mm regular film shows were given to inmates on 'the old side' at Hastings with sometimes a second performance on a hospital ward.[8]

From time to time, patients who were fit enough left the wards to go on outings and excursions. At Hastings, for example, 118 inmates were taken to see the Fol-de-Rols in August 1930 and later in the month sixteen infirm men attended a garden party in Fairlight.[9] Twenty four St Mary's inmates were invited to the RAOB annual dinner in 1933.[10] No doubt the frequency of entertainments and outings such as these varied considerably from institution to institution and from ward to ward but they did at least provide some break from the monotony between the twice weekly visiting hours during which at least a few fresh faces appeared on the wards.

As for the wards themselves, too often they reflected the state described, for example, by Michelle Gilbert: 'the usual institutional dark brown and green, relived occasionally by dingy cream'. At Battle Institution, for example, the visiting committee noted in 1934 that 'the dark day made the female wards and especially the day room look gloomy' and emphasised 'the need for redecoration with lighter/brighter paint'.[11] In an earlier report, this same committee had noted there was a 'very comfortless' stone floor in the men's infirmary day room.[12] Even after the end of the Second World War St Mary's presented the same décor everywhere:

24. A group of staff perform at a concert for patients at Newhaven in the 1930s and 25. The Newhaven Institution staff concert party with the Master, Edward Milnes, on the left and the Labour Master, Frank Dean, on the right.

brown or dirty green for the lower half of the walls, separated by a black stripe from a dull, institutional cream colour on the upper half, painted directly onto the brick walls.[13]

At Brighton the public assistance officer reported that in J Block bathing accommodation on the ground floor was inadequate and patients who got up had to use outside lavatories. Also, no day room accommodation was provided for them. Most of the patients in the ward were in bed for the greater part of the day but they were able to get up and wash and go to the lavatory. In addition to problems with ventilation, the medical officer of health criticised room 6, 'a long, depressing ward with no outlook ... and undesirable for permanent bed cases'. Rooms 2 and 3 were satisfactory but room 5 was 'again ... a long, narrow room which certainly lacks any essence of cheerfulness.' The report noted that the sanitary arrangements were especially inadequate:

> ... only one water closet placed in a room where there are only wash basins and this room is also used for storing bed pans which are at present placed on the floor. Other WCs are available, but can only be reached by going outside.[14]

There was no bath on this floor and patients had to be taken up to the first floor, while bed pans had also to be carried to a sluice halfway up a flight of stairs.

The problems arising from stairs – often narrow and twisting – were to plague chronic sick hospitals and wards for years. In Brighton Municipal Hospital, for example, patients in F Block had to be carried up and down staircases 'which had such narrow bends that these journeys were always hazardous and often depressing.'[15]

There were few lifts in this type of hospital in the 1930s but there is evidence of attempts to secure their installation. As early as 1932, the new medical officer at Newhaven Institution requested that a lift should be provided in the infirmary because of the dangers of carrying patients upstairs to the upper wards.

At Brighton, a Ministry of Health inspector's report made following a visit to Elm Grove Home noted there were no lifts in blocks for the chronic sick. However, the master observed that in one block, L, there was only one upper floor so a lift there was 'hardly necessary' whilst in the other case, J Block, it would have to be erected outside the building and the committee, presumably following his advice, decided that lifts should not be provided.[16]

At Battle during wartime in 1943, a House Visitor, R.C. Evernden JP, expressed concern about the stairs leading to the upper floors of the infirmary believing it to be 'a miracle' if no accidents occurred, adding 'I shudder to think of the results should incendiaries be dropped'.[17]

Straw mattresses and collapsing beds

The absence of lifts meant that many patients were, in effect, condemned to spend the rest of their stay, often until the end of their lives, within the four walls of the upper floor wards. Moreover, most of them would have been confined to bed, and hospital beds were not always the most comfortable, as a Ministry inspector observed after her Brighton visit.

> The majority of beds are made of straw. Mattresses are gradually being provided, 72 were obtained last year but none this far. Many sheets and draw sheets on the beds were dirty. It would be an advantage, and help to facilitate the difficulties of nursing, if straw beds were done away with and good hair mattresses provided, also straw pillows replaced by flock, or feather ones.[18]

Apart from the general discomfort, one of the more serious problems arising from straw mattresses, according to the inspector, was that it was difficult to keep the bed linen under the patients smooth. This could, of course, have given rise to bed sores, a perennial problem with bedfast patients.

Commenting on the report, the master said there were 73 beds on L Block and 104 on J. The actual number of straw mattresses was 19 on L Block and 36 on J Block. Provision had been made for their replacement in the current year's estimates, costing £122 9s 6d. The patients already had top feather pillows, he said, the lower ones made mostly of straw. It was a 'matter of opinion' whether it was desirable to replace the lower ones with flock for the many incontinent cases on J Block and he blamed the infrequent change of bed linen on inadequate ward stocks. To put this right would entail heavy expenditure, £345 6s 7d, which was placed in the draft estimates for 1939/40.[19] Throughout the 1930s there were quite frequent references to the need for bedside lockers and bed screens while at Hastings the medical officer reported that on the sick wards 'many of the old beds keep collapsing from time to time.'[20]

Inadequate heating, lighting and domestic hot water supplies brought forth even more recommendations in the official records of the institutions between 1930 and 1948. It is true that probably the majority of homes during this time relied on open coal fires and kitchen ranges and gas lighting was by no means uncommon. Nevertheless, these were not necessarily suitable for institutional use.

Brighton Municipal Hospital, for example, had long, draughty wards in one block warmed only by coal stoves which were not replaced until 1937 when they were removed to make space available for cubicles.

At Newhaven in 1930 the wards were lit by gas produced by the institution's own rather inefficient petrol gas plant. The new medical officer lost no time complaining about this and two years later the PAC allocated £271 to install electric light. However, it was not until 1943 (the PAC had decided the year before to defer the matter until after the war) that the Ministry of Health installed wall fittings for bed lights in the wards, a benefit gained from being a wartime EMS hospital.

At Chailey Institution the lighting was so poor that even in 1948 the medical officer was unable to examine patients after four o'clock on a winter afternoon. However, the problem here was not the lack of electricity or electrical fittings. It was because of the cost-conscious master who would only allow 25 watt lamps to be installed in the ward lights.[21]

Ward heating was another problem at Newhaven and one that took much longer to resolve than the deficient ward lighting. Although there were radiators in the corridors and four small side wards, the four principal wards were heated only by two open coal fires in each and these continued in use until the 1960s when central heating was at last installed.

The hot water supply posed similar problems: for example, nurses who washed 30 patients in the early morning had to heat kettles on the kitchen stove and actually carry the water into the wards.

Eastbourne also reported inadequacies with heating. In 1931, following a report by the house committee visitors, the master was instructed for fires to be lit in the bedrooms of the infirm ward during the winter evenings and there was further reference to complaints about heating in 1942.

Food, glorious food?

Another facet of daily life which meant a great deal to hospital patients – and one which concerned Aranovitch in the early 1930s – was food. 'People in hospital think and talk a great deal about food,' she wrote, 'even if they are unable to eat very much. They would wistfully mention all manner of choice dishes they would eat in large quantities, if only it was available. Such conversation often passed the time of day'.[22]

Aranovitch found the general attitude towards food strange:

There were no heated trolleys at that time, so the nurses carried the plates of food into the ward from the adjoining kitchen and because of the vast amount of work they had to get through, there was no time for civilized eating. Meals were regarded as a necessary evil, to be surmounted as quickly as possible so that, from start to finish, speed was the watchword.[23]

These comments were no doubt meant to apply equally to both local authority and voluntary hospitals (Aranovitch was a patient in two voluntary hospitals before her transfer to a chronic sick hospital) but the situation would have been worse in a ward for elderly patients, many of whom would have been unable to feed themselves.

Certainly she did not think there was a great deal to choose between catering standards in the two different types of hospital. In the two voluntary hospitals the food was so poor in quality and little in quantity, that it was impossible to be reasonably fed without patients' friends or families bringing food to the hospital, she recorded. There was actually more food in the poor law hospital, but of such poor quality and so badly cooked, most of it was uneatable.

The daily routine for patients on ordinary diet in both was more or less:

6 a.m.	Early morning cup of tea.
8 a.m. Breakfast:	Porridge, tea, two half slices of bread, egg if available; sometimes bacon, but never with egg; occasional surprise items (two undersized sardines).
Mid morning drink:	Ovaltine, milk, coffee.
Noon Lunch.	Meat, vegetable, 'undercooked' potatoes, 'thin, watery gravy. A limited amount of chicken for the very ill. Sweet: mostly semolina or rice.
3 p.m.	Afternoon tea:. Bread, butter, jam with a small cake on Sundays.
6.30 p.m. Evening Meal:	Usually mince, sometimes fish, followed by a drink.[24]

It seems likely that meal times probably varied from place to place, sometimes an earlier start to the day (much earlier in some, as Gilbert reported) and an earlier evening meal, too, often with a milky drink later in the evening. But the long gap between supper and breakfast was to remain a problem for years to come. So, too, was the question of waste, which occurred according to Aranovitch, was because the food was monotonous and unappetising.

In East Sussex, the Chailey workhouse master's son described the food, apart from Christmas, as 'plain, rather monotonous, catering for basic needs, but there was always a hot mid-day meal.'

The daily routine for the able-bodied was: Get-up 6.45 am; breakfast 7.30 am; morning tea-break 10 am; mid-day meal 12 noon; tea 5 pm; bed 8 pm. A bell was rung for each occasion. The men were given tobacco, from one to three ounces a week, depending on what work they did.[25]

Evidence from East Sussex confirms that institutional diets left much to be desired. From time to time efforts were made to bring about improvements. At Newhaven, cake was issued twice weekly in 1931 and golden syrup was allowed with porridge. Hastings was one of a number of institutions which replaced margarine with butter in the early 1930s (at an estimated additional weekly cost of £2). In 1932, the medical officer told Eastbourne PAC that there was great difficulty in keeping the hospital's dinners hot.

Also in 1932, a sub committee submitted a report on dietary tables to East Sussex PAC in response to a memorandum from the Ministry of Health. These not only stated what food was to be supplied to institutional inmates, they also specified the quantities to be issued as ingredients in cooked dishes in accordance with the number of meals to be provided. 'There is,' the report stated, 'no doubt in the minds of your Sub Committee that the diets at present laid down are unsatisfactory ... the introduction of Standard Dietary Tables, providing a variation in the meals provided, is of utmost importance'.[26]

The estimated cost of the changes was about £1,000 at a time when the provisionally estimated total running costs of all the county's institutions was approximately £57,000. A start was recommended in April 1933. It was feared this might necessitate a reduction of expenditure in other directions although the sub committee hoped this would not mean 'curtailing essential services'.[27]

The recommendations also included the adoption of the principle that inmates should be fed in accordance with appetite instead of being given prescribed quantities; also that meals should be served at tables laid with table cloths. The PAC's decision, which was to become an almost predictable response to innovative suggestions, was that the adoption of the new tables should be deferred for twelve months although the sub committee was asked to see whether some revisions could be undertaken in the meantime without additional expenditure. Only the suggestion that inmates should be fed in accordance with appetite was accepted. It was believed that this change would lead to the prevention of waste.

A year later, the PAC was told that the modified diets approved by the sub committee had involved extra expenditure which 'can and will be met by economies in other directions'. (The full male diet was reduced from about 5s weekly to approximately 4s 7d). Once again the 'utmost importance' of introducing dietary scales that provided a reasonable variation of meals was stressed and on this occasion the PAC decided to implement the recommendations with effect from April, 1934.[28] The decision was taken only days before the Ministry of Health again issued a circular, reiterating its advice on the subject of criticism and improvement of diets.

Official visitors to Southlands Hospital on April 13th received comments on the new dietary – and a complaint about the lack of meat in the shepherd's pie which the visitor examined but could find no fault. 'I also examined steam pudding which seemed to me to be excellent'.[29]

In July, there was a fairly detailed report about the 'very large bowls of soup' served to the old people in the House about which there were complaints, and two from the hospital block, regarding the lack of meat in the soup.[30]

At Newhaven the new dietary was reported by the master to be 'very popular' but five years later he recorded that, although the dietary was satisfactory, further improvements were under consideration.[31]

Throughout this period the institution's visiting committee made a number of comments on the food. In this and the following years there are several references by visiting committees to the inspection and sampling of meals. In the more rarefied atmosphere of the PAC, however, parsimony still appeared to prevail. The Sub Committee on Dietaries considered, for example, that one egg or some other form of protein should be provided weekly and also recommended that an ounce of fish or meat paste should be issued once a week (when half an ounce less of margarine would be issued). However, learning that this might cost £485 a year to implement throughout the county, the PAC invited the PAO to confer with the masters with a view to 'a less expensive suggestion being put forward'.[32]

Brighton PAC also reviewed its dietaries in 1934 but in the sick wards diets were only amended to replace margarine with butter. Subject to this, the medical officer advised, 'dietaries at present in force form a perfectly sound basis for the satisfactory feeding of the inmates.'[33]

Overcrowded wards

Life on the wards was also affected by the mix of patients which was made worse on occasions by overcrowding. Aranovitch was astounded by the size of the ward in the poor law hospital to which she was admitted:

It was simply enormous. It was not only long but exceptionally wide. There were four rows of beds very close together, with only just enough room between each row to move around. At one end of the ward was a long row of cot beds with the adjustable sides drawn up. These cot beds had frightening associations with old age, senility and incontinence, where life had turned full cycle and people returned to their childhood ... I was put into a bed along one of the inner rows, far away from the light of any of the windows. My spirits sank and I felt overwhelmed as I looked round this sea of beds and faces.[34]

At Southlands Hospital in 1934, a house committee visitor reported that there were 16 maternity cases when only eight beds were available. The surplus patients were transferred to the sterilising room in another block. But this was not all:

D Block overcrowded, infection of wounds where septic appendicitis cases have to be nursed in close proximity to clean bladder cases... In some Wards I found children mixed with old and dying people, this is undesirable. [35]

The following year, another visitor commented on the effect of overcrowding:

There were 21 Maternity cases in the Hospital, thirteen confinements, eight ante natal with complications, besides five patients suffering with septicemia with their babies, three of whom were being treated for Ophthalmia neonatorium, owing to the present lack of accommodation these patients were scattered through the wards...[36]

A report by the medical officer at to the Brighton infirmary in 1931 referred to overcrowding during the 'busy season' – usually the first three months of the year – in 1930. There was overcrowding in every ward, he said, when beds were not only placed more closely together, but extra beds were placed in the centre of the wards. 'It cannot be said that this is a good thing. Patients naturally dislike obvious overcrowding and it adds greatly to nursing difficulties'[37]

The Frederick Road Infirmary at Hastings also experienced problems with overcrowding. The management and house committee were told in 1930 that owing to the shortage of beds 'quite unsuitable cases' had been occupying the maternity ward beds and sick women had been placed in the nursery. Dr S.J. Firth, the newly appointed medical officer, stressed the need for classification of the wards which 'now contain a very mixed type of case' and which he intended 'to rectify as far as possible under existing conditions'.[38] One unexpected consequence was that complaints were made to the house committee that patients occupying adjoining beds for long periods had become separated. No doubt there were many similar casualties.

The medical officer's report for 1932 revealed no improvement. 'The wards are still too full ... the two wards C and G, where senile and slightly confused patients are treated, are particularly congested.'[39] At neighbouring Eastbourne there was a similar situation, the MOH reported in 1932 that there was pressure on the accommodation at St Mary's Hospital. In fact, the records of the various East Sussex institutions and infirmaries contain quite frequent references to problems with overcrowding throughout the inter war period and these were even worse when wartime pressures were added.

Individual accounts of the effects of overcrowding or patient mix are mainly from the perspective of young patients or medical staff or visiting members of the house committees and not surprisingly concentrate on the effects on young patients and the acute sick. But elderly chronic patients were affected, too, not only by overcrowding but also because they had to live alongside other patients who made their lives difficult, not least those patients suffering from mental illness.

The nature of the mixed cases treated in infirmaries in the 1930s can be illustrated by statistics from two East Sussex institutions:

At Hastings on 8 April 1930 there were 200 patients on the sick wards including 15 surgical, 24 acute medical, 8 tuberculosis, 3 midwifery, 8 paying patients and one infectious case. Six months later the medical officer reported:

> There are now 4 cases of Pulmonary Tuberculosis who are occupying the same ward as acute medical cases. Again, chronic cases have to sleep on this ward and owing to their becoming noisy have on several occasions disturbed acutely ill people. This mixing of cases is prejudicial to the patients' welfare...[40]

Hastings contained its share of mental patients and, although they caused considerable problems for the medical and nursing staff, they appeared to have been cared for separately at the time and there is no reference to any adverse effects on other patients. It was not the same at all institutions, especially the smaller, mixed institutions like Newhaven.

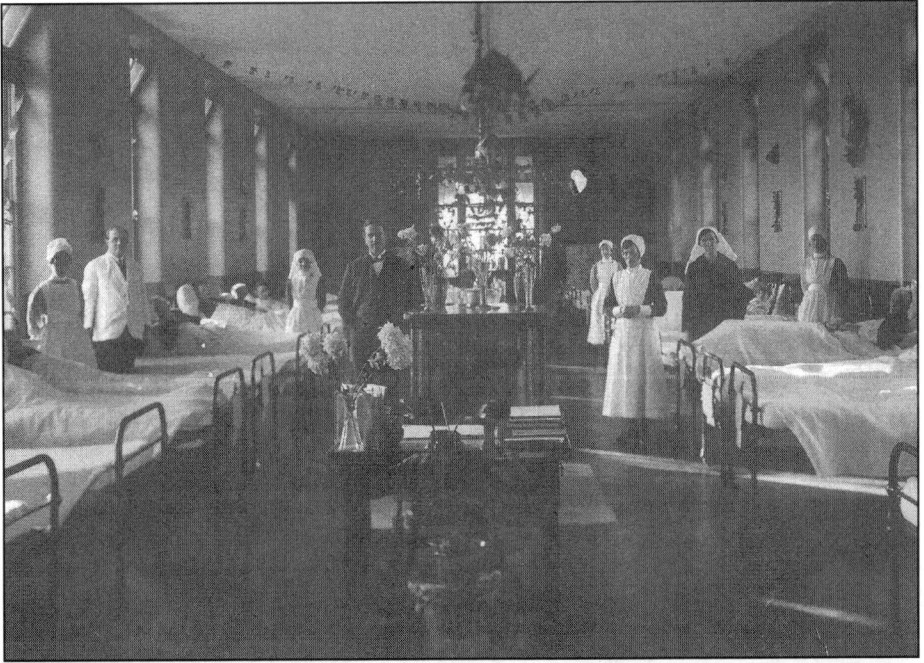

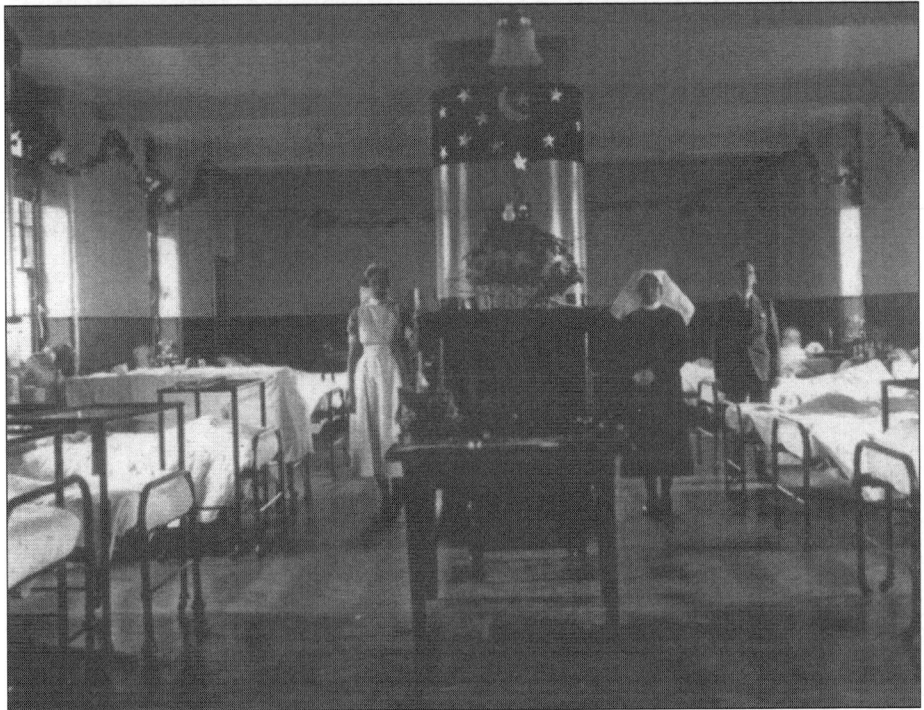

26. *A ward at Brighton Institution in 1926, clearly posed at or immediately after Christmas for a postcard.* 27. *A 1930s ward at Newhaven with Matron and the Master prominent, again taken at Christmas time.*

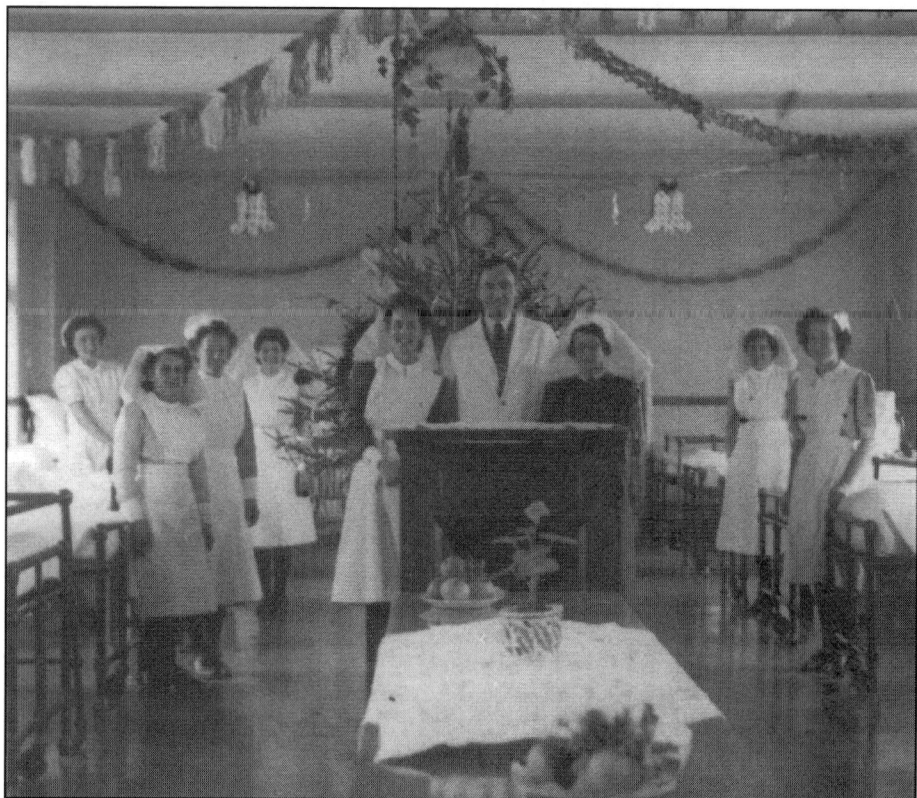

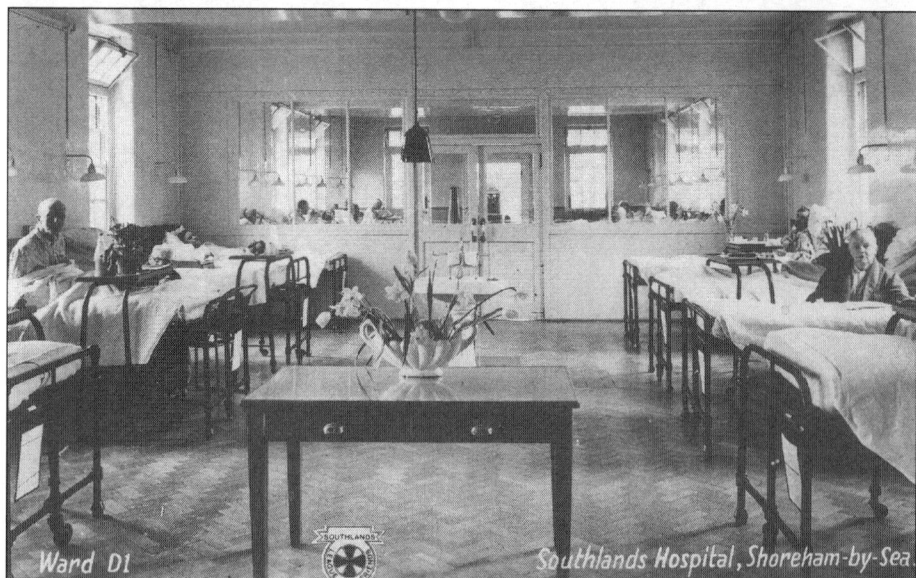

28. *A ward at Eastbourne, probably in the 1940s, photographed, as at Brighton and Newhaven, during the festive season.* 29. *A carefully posed photograph taken for a postcard of ward D1 at Southlands Hospital.*

Newhaven Institution. Beds occupied on the infirm and sick wards on 4 May 1929, excluding casual wards and maximum occupied at any one time in 1928.

Type of case	4.5.1929	Maximum 1928
Maternity	4	2
Acute	8	14
Chronic	8	40
Epileptic	1	2
Mental	2	2
Total (available beds, 71)	53	60

Source: ESCRO C/C11/64/1

In the years which followed there were frequently mental patients on the wards of Newhaven's infirmary. From time to time there was overcrowding, especially during the winter months when patients were admitted with pneumonia and other respiratory illnesses during influenza epidemics. The often noisy mental cases who were admitted included some who made distressing suicide attempts.

The problems arising from the admission of mental patients were particularly serious at Hastings. As a former Poor Law hospital, the Municipal Hospital was compelled to admit four classes of mental patients: on a three-day detention order; for observation; from other hospitals in the town; and those sent in by the police for observation. This, reported the medical officer, meant there was an urgent need for a padded room. Its absence meant that dealing with violent patients was a danger to both patients sleeping in the same room and to staff. In his report, he gave a graphic illustration of the difficulties:

> One evening last week a young woman sent in for observation by the police became violent. She was standing on the bed, adopting a threatening attitude and there were only a couple of young probationers on the ward. I arrived in time to prevent her swallowing some rosary beads and, in the struggle that ensued, one of the nurses was kicked and I myself was bitten. The patient had to be held down until drugs could produce their desired effect.[44]

Four years later the hospital was still experiencing problems, the medical officer telling a meeting of a sub-committee dealing with accommodation for mental patients that on that very day there were four male and eight mental patients on the general wards who were noisy and troublesome and causing considerable annoyance and worry to the other patients. But at least there was hope for the future because, it was reported, there were plans to adapt the old casual wards for approximately fourteen male and female mental patients.[41]

5. The Chronic Sick and their Nurses

We had a temporary nurse … she was not satisfactory in her work, I asked the acting master to get rid of her. She said she was 'not going to pamper the poor patients,' got them out of bed against orders, one heart case was very bad after this, and others complained. — Dr Summerhayes, medical officer, Newhaven Institution, 1934.

Confidence in the institutions and hospitals for the chronic sick will not have been helped by the criticisms of the nurses that emerged during the 1940s. Michelle Gilbert, for example, wrote in the *Manchester Guardian* about an aspect of nursing care that still gives rise to criticisms right up until the present day.

> After the early wash came the early breakfast – at 6 a.m. This was simply dumped on the locker and there it remained until someone had time to feed it to the helpless patient. Many a time I have fallen asleep while waiting and been rudely awakened by someone anxious to shovel in the congealing bacon and stone cold tea as rapidly as possible and be done with the job.[1]

And her criticisms did not end there:

> Down the centre [of the ward] stood a long oak cabinet and this was the principal object of the nurses' loving care. Every afternoon, regardless of staff shortages or patients' immediate needs, that cabinet was polished for at least half an hour. When it was mirror bright it was covered with a clean sheet (sometimes there was a patient who would have been glad of that clean sheet), and under the sheet, for extra protection, was a red blanket.

With the realisation that her bed and locker would be her home for the next fifty years or more, Michelle Gilbert decided to study a correspondence course but the nurses didn't take kindly to the books and papers which cluttered the space around her bed:

> On one occasion an irate sister confiscated everything I needed for my studies and locked them away in a cupboard. It was only my doctor's intervention that got them back for me. When after several years I at last managed to get a typewriter, the comment was: 'And where do you think you are going to keep that'?

Another account of infirmary life by a former patient shows that on occasions nursing care was not always as skilled and devoted as some might have imagined. In 1943 (the same year that Michelle Gilbert was admitted to hospital), John Vaizey, then a schoolboy of 14, was struck down by acute osteomyelitis and was admitted initially to an adult male ward of a former Poor Law infirmary. Vaizey's account of his treatment by a number of insensitive nurses makes harrowing reading: significantly, he dedicated his book, *Scenes from Institutional Life*, to Kay and Richard Titmuss who agreed that institutions gave inadequate people what they want – power'[2].

There is no reason to doubt the veracity of these accounts, or the impact they must have had on their readers. Nevertheless, it seems likely that the situations they described were probably the exception rather than the rule. Aranovitch, for example, thought the problems of the institutions lay with their organisation, not the nursing. Leslie Banks, a principal regional medical officer of the Ministry of Health writing in 1945, said that whilst his colleagues at the Ministry were frequently critical of the facilities provided for the chronic sick, their principal redeeming feature was 'the devotion and skill of the nurses'.[3]

Another doctor who was full of praise for her nurses was N.H. Nisbet who took up an appointment at Foresthall Institution shortly after the introduction of the NHS in September 1949. At Foresthall she was the sole qualified doctor for 600 hospital patients and 500 Part III (welfare) inmates. Firstly, she summed up in a paragraph what nursing the chronic sick entailed:

Elderly people, confined to bed for years, are supremely hard to nurse: many become heavy and helpless, apathetic or aggressive, careless or even disgusting in their habits ... it takes time and patience to feed them and to soothe their querulousness; and it takes infinite skill to keep intact their tender skins, subjected to the pressure of long years in bed and the incontinence which so often occurs in such circumstances.[4]

Despite this, the Foresthall nurses possessed patience, interest and a sense of humour, Nisbet said.

They are genuinely attached to their patients and know all their idiosyncrasies. They are mines of information on the ramifications of their family trees, and know the names of their relatives, though seldom or never seen. They shop for their patients and bring them presents of sweets and clothes, and cheer them with supererogatory cups of tea. The scoldings are affectionate, and the hard words merely repartee, or teasing, as one would tease a child ... the words 'a dear wee patient' are often on their lips ... situations which would try the patience of a saint are taken in their stride.[5]

There is no doubt that nurses like those described by Gilbert and Vaizey existed, or that many possessed the qualities earning the praises of Banks and Nisbet. However, whilst it is impossible to determine the possible numbers of each, or where the balance lay, it seems more than likely that the basic problem so far as nurses were concerned was not one of attitudes but the shortage of staff. Hospitals caring for the chronic sick were simply unable to recruit sufficient nurses to achieve a satisfactory standard of care on the wards. At the heart of this was the fundamental problem best summed up, perhaps by Lord Amulree, one of the pioneers of geriatric medicine, who wrote in 1947:

> The absence of bedsores and other signs of pressure in patients, who have lain hopeless in bed frequently for many years, is a remarkable tribute to the skill and devotion of the nursing staff. But the prospect of years to be spent in caring for backs, feeding and dealing with bed-pans, is not one that is likely to appeal to the young woman who wishes to become a nurse.[6]

According to one estimate, in the spring of 1945, 16,000 additional nurses were needed in England and Wales whilst Scotland needed almost 2,000 more. One cause of the problem, according to the Ministry of Labour, was that the public assistance institutions were not providing facilities for training pupil assistant and student nurses. This probably accounts for the situation noted in the report into the recruitment and training of nurses which followed the setting up a working party under

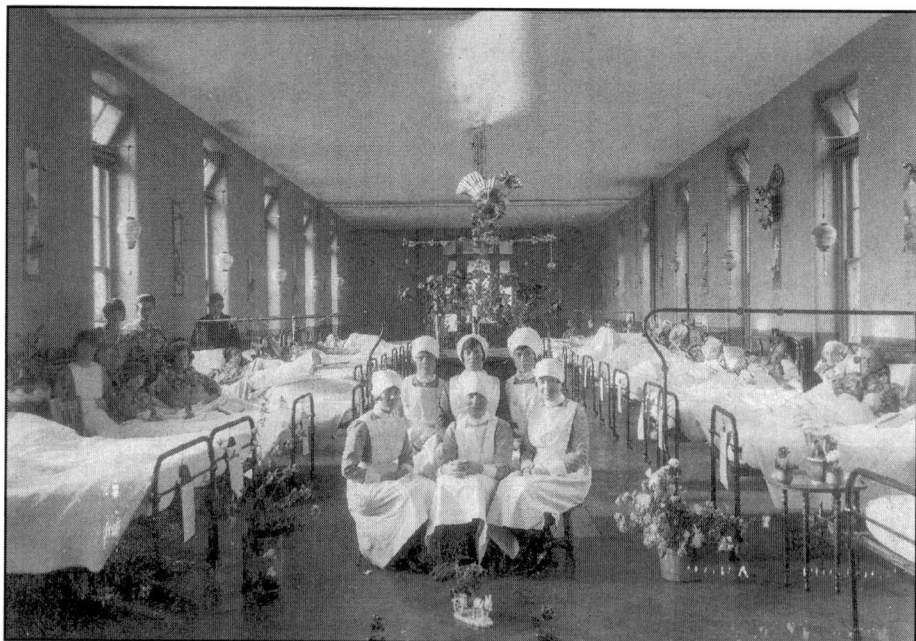

30. *A postcard picturing nurses at Brighton Institution, probably taken at Christmas 1929.*

31. A group of Hastings nurses in 1934 with the medical officer Dr L.H. Booth, superintendent nurse Smith (centre) and deputy, nurse Dixon.

Sir Robert Wood by the Ministry of Health in 1947. According to the Wood Report, voluntary hospitals were rapidly increasing their intake of student nurses (from 7,950 in 1937 to 10,050 in 1945) while the municipal hospitals were virtually standing still (3,800 in 1937, 4,050 in 1945). In 1929 there had been about twice as many poor law nurses as voluntary hospital nurses; by 1945 the position was very different.

Whatever shortcomings might have existed in East Sussex, the lack of nurse training facilities, particularly in the municipal hospitals, was not one of them. Brighton boasted the largest nurse training school in the county while Hastings provided training for assistant nurses. Eastbourne was recognised as a training school in 1933 and one result of this, according to the medical officer, was that it resulted in a saving in salaries (no doubt much appreciated by the borough treasurer). However, perhaps this should have been set against the cost of providing an additional five bedrooms for the nurses two years later – £2,900 out of some £6,900 allocation for structural alterations to St Mary's. According to the application form for nurse training at this time, the commencing salary for probationers on the three year course was £24 10s per annum, rising to £35 when they passed the first examination of the General Nursing Council, then to £40 six months later and £60 on passing the final examination. Nurses were also provided with rations, washing, lodging and uniform. Applicants had to be single or widowed.

Steyning had been approved as a nurse training for state registration as early as 1923, although at that time it was subject to the proviso that the third year's surgical training should be undertaken at Kensington Poor Law Institution, but the remainder of the East Sussex institutions had no training facilities. This meant they were particularly likely to suffer from nurse shortages, which a brief examination of the history of the nursing profession helps to explain.

Although nursing may have had its origins in domestic work, it developed during the 19th century and into the twentieth as a profession for ladies or women with social aspirations. This, coupled with a tradition of selfless devotion to the sick, a rapid turnover of staff and the strong and personal influence of the matron, meant there was a general reluctance on the part of nurses to join trade unions.

In 1930, the medical journal *The Lancet* appointed a commission to inquire into the reasons for the shortages of candidates, trained and untrained, for nursing the sick in general and special hospitals and also to offer suggestions for making the service more attractive. In the same year, Labour MP Fenner Brockway made an abortive attempt to introduce a Bill to regulate working hours and salaries which received a chilly reception from nursing organisations.

However, it was not only low pay and long hours that caused the service to fall in disfavour with young people in search of a career. There had been rapid social changes in other professions and these had been slow to penetrate 'the cloistered institutions of medical care', a point made by the Lancet Commission which was reported in 1932.[7] Growing militancy, especially in London, finally resulted in the setting up of a second inquiry, this time by the government under the chairmanship of the Earl of Athlone, which made far reaching recommendations in its interim report (the final report never being published because of the outbreak of war).[8]

Against this background, it is hardly surprising there were considerable problems in recruiting sufficient nurses to care for the chronic sick. In 1934 the East Sussex PAO wrote to the College of Nursing about the county's difficulties in obtaining the services of fully trained nurses, but

32a. Eastbourne student nurse K.H. Jenner who trained at St Mary's Hospital from 1945–1948.
32b. Nursing chart for Nurse Jenner.

the College replied 'it was impossible to suggest a remedy'.[9] Undoubtedly, one answer was believed to be the provision of more and better nurses homes – Southlands, Battle and Newhaven were among the institutions which adopted this approach. Some hospitals, like Newhaven for example, seemed to rely on the employment of assistant nurses supervised by fully trained staff; others employed a large number of orderlies.

At Newhaven Institution, the medical officer suggested another way of overcoming nursing staff shortages: there was, he said, some of the 'St. John's women (VAD) who would like to work on the wards'. But his suggestion that 'it would help a bit and also teach them' appears to have fallen on deaf ears and within eighteen months he was again urging that they should be allowed to work on the wards.[10] It was not until 1939, shortly before the outbreak of war, that they were allowed to start training.

Shortages of staff became even more acute during and immediately after the Second World War. At Newhaven, in 1942, the medical officer reported that nursing staff shortages made it impossible for a nurse to be constantly on the ward and recommended that someone should always be on duty in each ward, not necessarily a nurse.

33. The nurses' home and gardens at Southlands Hospital.

34. The official opening of the nurses' home at Newhaven Institution in 1938.

35. A group of nurses at the opening of their new home at Newhaven Institution. From left, nurses Ennis, Sherwin and Atkins, an unknown nurse and sister, medical officer Dr Summerhayes, matron Annie Milnes standing between two unknown guests, sister Hillier and nurses Open and Gibbs.

36. *The nurses' home at Cuckfield Hospital, formerly West Hylands Institution. 37. The new nurses' home at Newhaven (pictured in the 1960s). 38. The nurses' home at St Helen's opened in 1938 when it was Hastings Municipal Hospital.*

A year later he was again reporting a shortage of nurses while in 1944 he reported that this situation was 'acute' with three nurses off duty because of sickness while the matron also unwell and possibly having to undergo a major operation.

In 1946, the county's public assistance committee in an attempt to overcome the shortage of nurses decided to recruit staff from Eire. However, being unqualified, they were not allowed to be called nurses and were known as nursing assistants. The dependence of the use of unqualified staff was perhaps best evidenced at Southlands Hospital. There some of the male chronic sick wards were almost completely staffed by male nursing assistants[11]. With large numbers of beds at several institutions left empty because of the shortage of staff and growing waiting lists as a result, the committee appealed to the County Councils Association that the salaries of probationer nurses should be increased to £75 rising to £100 per annum. Clearly this was intended to have an impact on recruitment of probationers since at this time the institutions were able to pay the lowest grade of resident female domestic workers

39. *Newhaven Institution nurses in 1945. Betty Sprague, second right back row, began working in the infirmary as one of the medical officer's VAD nurses. Also pictured from left with her are Mary Bashford, nurse Worrall and Pat Dean. Front: Nurses Watson, Grace Wells, sister Hillier, Mary King and Nurse Ward.*

40. *A group of St Mary's nurses c. 1945.*

41. *St Mary's nurses pictured before the nurses' home including a Red Cross nurse. Nurses from the Red Cross and St. John Ambulance helped to cover staff shortages on the wards in a number of infirmaries from the late 1930s onwards.*

£106 12s per annum (compared to only £55 for probationers) while the lowest grade of male domestic staff were paid £163 16s per annum.

A year later there appeared to be no real improvement in the nursing situation. The East Sussex public assistance officer appealed through the press for people who could give part time nursing service to the county's hospitals and institutions. Later in the same year it was reported that the master of East Grinstead Institution was trying to persuade assistant nurses formerly employed there to return to work. In addition the Ministry of Labour and National Service in co operation with the Matron's Association for Brighton and Hove had inaugurated a nursing recruitment drive for Southlands and other hospitals in the district although it was 'not yet possible to say what results had been achieved'.[12]

The shortage of nurses did not only affect the standard of care on the wards, however. It also led to a shortage of beds which meant that many elderly and other chronic sick people were denied the care they desperately needed. A survey by Kent's medical officer of health in November 1946 revealed there were 822 chronic sick people waiting for admission to hospitals in the county. This led Richard Titmuss, the distinguished social researcher, to conclude that if Kent was typical of the rest of the country some 25,000 people were in the queue for chronic sick beds. *The Lancet*, referring to the same survey (and noting that the number had subsequently risen to 928), pointed out that much of the nursing work was heavy ('20% of the patients are incontinent of both urine and faeces and over half are bedridden'), a problem which could be eased through active treatment which was being hindered by the lack of nursing staff. One solution, according to *The Lancet* might be found in 'a well planned part time nursing scheme'.

This shortage of nurses on the chronic sick wards and the consequent long waiting lists for admission was something that was to plague hospitals in East Sussex for many after 1948 when they became part of the new National Health Service.

6. Casuals at the Gates

Officially it now had another name, but to us, and the sad, ragged tramps, who shuffled towards it past our door, it was still 'the workhouse' — feared, hated and menacing.
— Norman Longmate, 'The Workhouse'.

How much the tramps, or casuals as they were officially known, contributed to the continuing fear of the workhouse during the 1930s is not easy to quantify. It seems certain, however, that they must have done a great deal to bolster that public perception of what by then were public assistance institutions.

The casuals, waiting for admission, queued at the entrances and the authorities, wishing to create a different image, were sometimes forced to consider providing a separate entrance for these unfortunate beings, many of whom aged over thirty were former soldiers or sailors who had served in the First World War.[1] Eastbourne is a case in point: there a new entrance meant that casuals no longer had to enter through the hospital precincts.

The casuals were a particular problem on the south coast where they travelled mainly east to west, or vice versa, journeying from one workhouse to the next: Steyning to Brighton, Brighton to Newhaven, Newhaven to Eastbourne … and so on. They also moved inland from Hastings to Battle, for example, and on from Battle to Ticehurst. The admissions and discharges register for Newhaven in 1939 showed that for the most part the casuals were admitted from or moved on to Brighton and Eastbourne and, less frequently, Cuckfield, East Preston or Hastings.

Originally, relief for the destitute was the responsibility of their parish or their place of settlement. Despite the passing of the 1834 Poor Law Act, vagrants and strangers from outside the area were liable to be refused relief. In 1837, however, the poor law commissioners ruled that no tramp or casual should be refused a night's lodging if he were without money. Later, it appears, the tramps were allowed admission carrying a small sum, variously said to be two or four pence.

As a result, the sight of tramps burying any surplus, even a halfpenny which would have denied them admission, became quite a common one. At Hastings they would place the cash in a tin and bury it at the end to Union Lane, the former Cackle Street, and retrieve it after their discharge

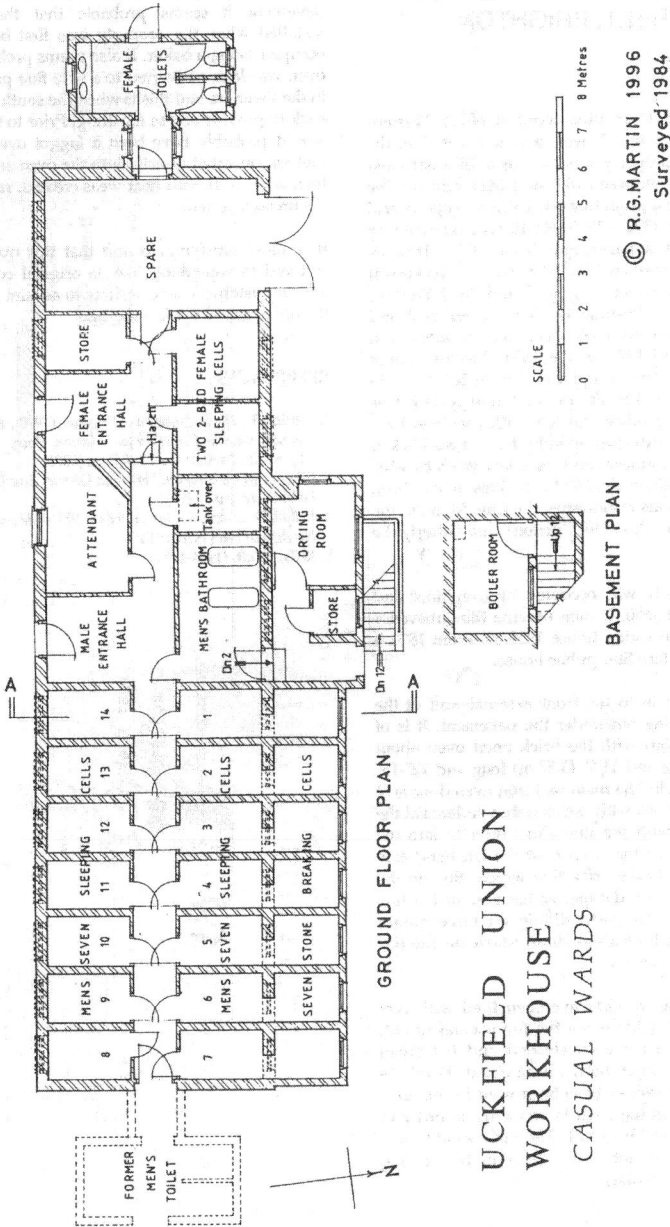

GROUND FLOOR PLAN

UCKFIELD UNION WORKHOUSE
CASUAL WARDS

BASEMENT PLAN

© R.G.MARTIN 1996
Surveyed 1984

SCALE
0 1 2 3 4 5 6 7 8 Metres

FEMALE TOILETS

SPARE

STORE

FEMALE ENTRANCE HALL

TWO 2-BED FEMALE SLEEPING CELLS

ATTENDANT

MEN'S BATHROOM

DRYING ROOM

STORE

MALE ENTRANCE HALL

BOILER ROOM

CELLS 14 13 12 11 10 9 8

MENS SEVEN SLEEPING CELLS 1 2 3 4 5 6 7

MENS SEVEN STONE BREAKING CELLS

FORMER MENS TOILET

42. *A plan of the casual wards published in Sussex Industrial History, Issue 26, 1996. Note the stone breaking cells and the smaller number of cells for women who were provided with a separate entrance. Mr Martin, who surveyed the site in 1984, wrote: 'Looking at this bleak building, one realises what a hard life these itinerant tramps led in the early part of this century, when they came to places like this for a bath a food and a night's rest in exchange for some menial work. It is a salutary thought to consider whether today's' homeless would tolerate such conditions.'*

the following morning.[2] At Newhaven in the 1920s they were observed by children burying items in a bank at the top of Church Hill.[3] At Steyning, a house visitor's report in 1935 referred to 'regular visitors' who deposited their belongings under the sheds and removed them on discharge.[4]

One problem posed by the tramps was that they sometimes carried infectious diseases. In 1928 there was an outbreak of smallpox in the casual wards at Brighton believed to have been carried by travellers who had visited Horsham and East Preston casual wards where there were many infected inmates. In order to control the outbreak, officers dealing with the casuals had to be vaccinated. The casuals, themselves, were not allowed to work in the main building or the infirmary blocks or to have any contact with their inmates. Steyning responded to the East Preston outbreak by closing its own casual wards for a time.

Scabies was another problem. In 1935, the medical officer at Newhaven reported that several of the casuals had scabies: 'how they escaped the other institution, I do not know'. About this time it was the practice at Newhaven, because of the risk of infection, for all blankets to be put in the incinerator once a fortnight. Earlier, in 1925, it was ordered at Brighton that casuals should be bathed in clean, warm water using real carbolic soap because scabies cases were numerous. This inadvertently led to a local scandal when a temporary inexperienced woman was employed to cover the duties of an attendant who was off sick. When a verminous woman

43. *Casual wards at Hastings pictured after St Helen's Hospital had closed.*

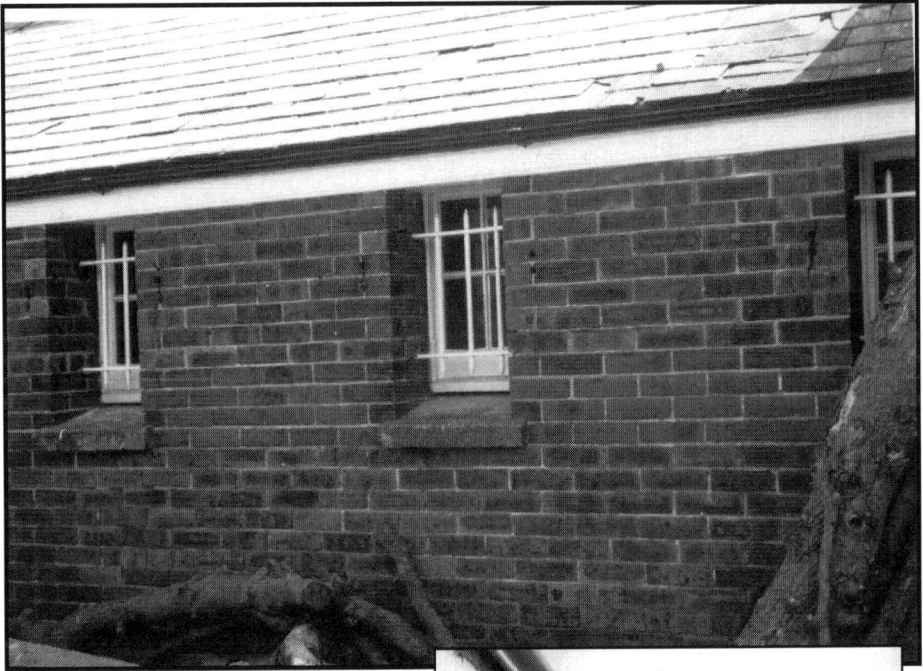

was brought into the female receiving ward, the attendant bathed her, despite the woman's screams, in a bath of neat Lysol, a powerful disinfectant, from which she died.

Having secured admission for the night, the man or woman had to perform a task before being allowed to take their discharge. Stone breaking or oakum picking were no longer allowed in Brighton after 1925 although it appears that stone breaking persisted in B Block as a form of punishment in the cells. From 1932, the men's tasks at Brighton were confined to gardening, washing, scrubbing and cleaning and similar tasks were allotted to the tramps at

44. Barred windows in the casual block at Newhaven. 45. Flint walls topped with broken glass adjacent to Newhaven's casual block. 46. Inside the corridor showing a cell door at Newhaven being used a store in the 1960s.

Eastbourne. At Chailey, oakum picking and crushing flints and bones were being dropped from about 1921 in favour of work in the large vegetable garden and helping with general running of the institution.

On 25 January 1939 the admissions and discharges book for casuals at Newhaven listed the tasks of those admitted on that day which included wood sawing, wood chopping, kitchen, cleaning, sweeping drive, bundling wood, wheeling coke, potatoes, coal yard, garden, scrubbing corridors and working in the laundry. A later entry also listed work in the boilerhouse. Many of these tasks were not particularly popular with the tramps and may well have accounted for their attempts to escape before they could be allocated. A house visitor's report at Southlands in February 1935 called for spikes to be set on the wall above the water meter shed where practically all the slates had been smashed by casuals crawling up and escaping over it. He added: 'One casual escaping in this way was recently killed by a passing motor car'.[7]

At Newhaven the boundary wall adjacent to the casual ward was topped with broken glass, still visible many years after the accommodation was used for other purposes. Possibly members of the public were unaware of the prison-like cells inside, complete with a peephole in the solid door and a folding iron bed affixed to the wall inside or, as at Uckfield or Chailey equipped with permanent hooks for the suspension of hammocks. But the barred windows were certainly quite visible while at Eastbourne, for example, although the former casual wards had long since been used as stores, as late as 1989 some of the low-set windows with bars remained and it was still possible to make out the stone-breaking cells despite the many alterations.

The prison-like appearance of the casual wards certainly seems to have been appropriate. A notice printed in 1931 displayed in the institutions reminded casuals that attempting to abscond or escape before being entitled to discharge themselves were deemed an idle or disorderly person within the meaning of Section 3 of the Vagrancy Act, 1824. This was an offence that could be punished, the penalty upon conviction one month's imprisonment with hard labour. A second attempt at escape risked being deemed a rogue and vagabond under Section 4 of the Act. In this case, the penalty upon conviction was three month's imprisonment with hard labour.

It was mainly men who applied for admission during the 1930s. The daily number at Newhaven ranged from 22 to 54 with just one woman.

47. The casual block at Eastbourne. 48. The tramps' cells at Eastbourne, later used for storage purposes. 49.The casual wards at Cuckfield behind the porters' lodge, and 50. The reception centre at Brighton General Hospital pictured in the 1970s.

At Eastbourne in September 1937, 1,936 men, 46 women and one child were admitted, 58 of whom needed medical treatment including twelve who were transferred to the infirmary. The numbers fell off during and immediately after the war years. At Cuckfield, for example, where in 1937 over 1,000 casuals, including 34 women and one child were admitted over an eight week period, there was a dramatic decline in 1940.

On 5 July 1948 a notice signed by the public assistance officer in East Sussex referring to the National Health Service Act 1946 and the National Assistance Act 1948 stated that it was illegal to offer relief to a casual at an institution. But this does not appear to have been the case at every former workhouse now functioning as an NHS hospital. At Brighton, for example, despite protests supported by the regional hospital board, the casual wards were perpetuated in the form of a reception centre, immediately in front of the main entrance, that remained a reminder of the hospital's origins for many more years to come.

7. The War in East Sussex

We have had an epidemic of deaths, old people, not many of whom would usually have died at home. The Blitz upsets these old people. — Dr Summerhayes, medical officer, Newhaven Institution, October 1940.

he Second World War was quite different to earlier conflicts, not least in the way it affected the civilian population. Twentieth century technological advances especially the development of the aeroplane, meant that aerial attack became a very real threat. The belief that this would result in large numbers of casualties led to the setting up of the Emergency Medical Service (EMS) in order that a sufficient number of hospital beds could be made available for treatment.

The EMS was also expected to cope with military caualties but it was the sheer scale of anticipated air raid casualties which largely set the target number of beds which the Ministry believed would be needed – some 300,000 in all. Many were to be provided in specially constructed hutted accommodation but to achieve the overall target it was necessary to empty 100,000 beds in participating hospitals who, in the event, discharged approximately 140,000 patients at the outbreak of war.

East Sussex provides more detailed evidence of the way the Emergency Medical Service was introduced and its effects on elderly chronic sick patients in the county's institutions, all of which were included in the scheme.

At its meeting in April 1939, the PAC was informed of the improvements necessary to make a number of institutions suitable for use as Class I hospitals in the event of a national emergency. These included surgical, laundry and kitchen facilities at Shoreham Institution and Southlands Hospital and Battle, East Grinstead, Cuckfield and Newhaven institutions. It was pointed out that these improvements should be regarded as 'of the greatest urgency' and that the Civil Defence Bill (then before parliament) provided a grant of a least 70 per cent of the expenditure incurred. The total East Sussex cost was estimated at £4,000 of which the council would have to find not more than £1,200 if the bill became law.[1]

The following month a report was adopted which classified the East Sussex infirmaries as Class IA ('the larger hospitals which have, or can without great difficulty, be given facilities for dealing with medical and surgical casualties').[2] Later, however, it was decided to downgrade Battle and Newhaven for EMS purposes on the grounds of cost:

> The effect of the decision is that instead of dealing with medical and surgical casualties, these two institutions are now earmarked for the reception of medical cases and other cases requiring in patient treatment but not requiring any special facilities.[3]

At its September meeting, the PAC noted that considerable upgrading work had already been carried out. At Cuckfield and East Grinstead existing wards had been converted into operating theatres and anaesthetic rooms; the kitchen had been enlarged at Cuckfield and additional work – the provision of ward kitchens, improved sanitary conveniences and lighting – had been carried out at both institutions so that rooms normally used for House cases, for example, could be occupied by patients. At Southlands further operating rooms had been provided and alterations carried out in some of the wards so that they could be used by chronic sick and convalescent patients.

Minor works were also in hand at Battle and Newhaven to enable them to receive more patients – mainly the provision of ward kitchens, additional duty rooms and improved sanitary facilities. Meanwhile, they and the other Class 2 hospitals, with the exception of Uckfield, were to be surveyed again to see whether any further alterations were desirable.

All casual wards in the county had been closed under emergency arrangements, including Cuckfield, Newhaven and Rye for an indefinite period. At St Mary's in Eastbourne the casual ward became a decontamination centre. The wards at Cuckfield were used to accommodate patients from the House wards which were being used for sick cases; the recent extension to Newhaven's casual ward was earmarked for the admission of additional sick patients for the infirmary. West Hylands Institution at Cuckfield was exceptional so far as East Sussex was concerned as the Ministry decided to provide hutted accommodation on the site for 300 patients. Nine wards were erected and patients from Great Ormond Street and King's College hospitals in London were evacuated to them. At the outbreak of war, many London children were evacuated to the south coast as it was considered safe from possible enemy action. In the early summer of 1940, however, when the air raids on London began in earnest, many of these evacuees, particularly those in the coastal towns, were again evacuated, together with local children, to other parts of the country.

Details of discharges from West Hylands are not available, but it is recorded that the male and female infirmaries, which would have accommodated the chronic sick, were converted for use as a maternity and children's hospital. At the outbreak of war, the institution provided about 250 beds (133 in the House and 114 in the Infirmary on September 2nd) and at the time of the Canadian Army's application to take over the institution the number of inmates was recorded as 262. This figure included 33 aged and infirm men who were transferred to other public assistance institutions and 23 women who were moved to 'Ashfold', at Handcross.

Bare statistics conceal the tremendous upheaval which resulted in the changing function of an EMS hospital. At Newhaven Institution, the master recorded details of the considerable number of patients who were discharged on the outbreak of war to make space for evacuees: 28 into the care of relatives and friends; 41 sick evacuees were received from London hospitals. In February 1940, there were a total of 152 patients in the institution. 17 London patients were transferred to Dartford in May and in July he noted: 'Soldier patients are frequently being admitted. Today we have 13'.[4]

Some indication of the way activity in the institution changed as a result of its inclusion of the EMS scheme can be seen in the medical officer's report written in June 1940. Among the cases dealt with during the month were four confinements, 'all rather difficult – war tension', all

51. One of the Nissen huts erected at West Hylands Institution.

boys born; five Belgian refugees, 1 woman and 2 children, 2 injured and still under treatment; 3 soldiers, one with a fractured leg, one fractured collar bone, one gastric ulcer; 3 survivors of a potato boat; two other refugees, various other accident cases. 'So we have all been busy' he commented.[5]

Subsequent to the promised review of the proposed Class 2 institutions, alterations had been made at Newhaven – an operating theatre was provided, for example – and in one of his reports written in 1942 the medical officer suggested making fuller use of the facilities: 'I would plead that the Infirmary might be used as a General Hospital for Newhaven District for minor surgery etc.'[6]

In its minutes for the September 1939 meeting – held less that four weeks after the outbreak of hostilities – the county PAC recorded the total number of patients transferred to its institutions:

Patients transferred to East Sussex institutions on the outbreak of the Second World War.

Name of Institution	From where transferred	Number
Chailey	London	46
Cuckfield	London	23
East Grinstead	London	19
Newhaven	London	41
Southlands	London	213
Battle	Hastings Municipal Hospital	45
Rye	Hastings Municipal Hospital	41
Uckfield	Southlands Hospital	50
Ticehurst	Cuckfield Institution	14

Source: East Sussex PAC minutes, 26 September 1939, ESCRO/C11/66/7.

Brighton Municipal Hospital records also provide evidence of the effects of the emergency on its patients. The inmates from A block at Elm Grove Home were evacuated and the building was adapted and prepared for Class 1 hospital purposes. A fully equipped operating theatre was supplied and 80 beds made ready for immediate occupation. 219 patients were received in one day (although some were later transferred, for example to the Borough Sanatorium) but by crowding wards to their utmost and utilising bedsteads supplied by the Ministry the numbers in the hospital were increased from 576 to 664.

In September 1940, instructions were received from the Ministry to vacate the hospital and as many patients as possible were returned to their own homes. 154 were transferred to Park Side Hospital in Macclesfield and by the end of the month 168 service cases and 43 air raid casualties had been admitted. St Mary's Hospital at Eastbourne was also evacuated and until the fall of France in 1940 only civilian emergencies were admitted. At Hastings, patients were transferred to the institutions at Battle and Rye.

There were also references to overcrowding at Battle Institution. In 1940 a house visitor reported that the institution was very full and contained a considerable number of heavy cases. Three years later, a visitor commented that the wards were overpopulated, 'no doubt due to staff shortage and wartime reserve beds'.[7] In 1944 another visitor reported: 'It would be an improvement to the nursing conditions when the Hastings patients can be returned – they are heavy cases and the ward they are in is full'.[8]

At Newhaven, the medical officer reported in December 1939 that the female wards were full and that six men from Cuckfield and six from Seaford all chronic cases, had been admitted. When, a few months later, the empty casual wards were utilised as infirm wards, he reported that the wards were 'full, but not overcrowded'.[9]

However, the situation clearly deteriorated for when Dr a'Brook took over as medical officer in November 1942 following the death of Dr Summerhayes, he reported that 'it will be necessary to have an additional trainee nurse if the number of patients remains at it present high level.'[10] In 1944 he reported that the female beds were full to capacity and that the men's wards had a few empty beds 'for the first time since last summer'.[11]

The following month, the ground floor of the infirmary was evacuated to make room for the anticipated influx of casualties from the landings in France (in the event only nine cases were admitted) and the casual wards were again used for female patients. However, these were returned to the main wards when the cases from bomb damaged Ticehurst Institution were transferred to Newhaven.

The records show that between 1940 and the end of 1943 there were 723 EMS admissions, the majority of them servicemen. The numbers fluctuated throughout this period and a considerable number of Royal Army Medical Corps nursing auxiliaries, some from the hospital train based at Newhaven, visited to gain practical experience. Between November 1942 and March 1943 the casual wards were set aside as a sick bay for naval personnel and during this time 221 ratings were admitted for treatment.

In Eastbourne, the chronic sick and infirm were removed from St Mary's to facilitate the hospital's functioning under the EMS scheme although in this instance the decision taken by the Social Welfare Committee in January 1943 to transfer up to 50 cases at 25 shillings each a week to All Saints Hospital may have perhaps been seen as beneficial for it actually resulted in their removal to accommodation under the control of a religious body and not the PAC. St Mary's also had a busy war. In June 1940, following the evacuation from Dunkirk, convoys of wounded were admitted from Newhaven. Shortly after, eight sailors whose ship had been torpedoed on the Channel were admitted. After the summer, air raid casualties were dealt with and space was found for people whose homes had been destroyed. Eastbourne was considered to be the most bombed town on the south coast and it was not uncommon for hospitals to treat fifty casualties at a time. In 1945, St Mary's admitted some of the ten thousand Australian prisoners of war who were repatriated to Eastbourne while they waited for ships to take them home.

52. *St Mary's nurses' home was not completed until shortly after the outbreak of war in 1941. The five storey building was apparently regarded as a good landmark for German aircraft and so, Lord Haw Haw was reputed to have said in a German radio propaganda broadcast, it would not be bombed.[12]*

Thus the immediate effect on the chronic sick was that many were sent home – or from cities where large numbers of air raid casualties were expected – to hospitals in the provinces. Throughout the war fewer hospital beds were available for them. Often they were nursed in overcrowded wards in the unpleasant conditions because of the nature of the buildings, many, especially those on the upper floors, were exceptionally vulnerable in the event of enemy air raids.

There was some criticism of the fact that because of countrywide shortage of beds, evacuation plans for chronic sick patients were soon abandoned. Top floors were regarded as unsafe and left empty with the result that the remaining beds in London institutions became blocked. Moreover, numerous institutions suffered bomb damage, although no statistics regarding this were collected nationally.

East Sussex was certainly not in the same degree of danger as London, but the South Coast had more than its fair share of enemy air action and the county's hospitals and institutions did not escape unscathed. Both

53. The entrance at Newhaven Institution. The gates, which would always have been closed at night, were removed during the war as part of a campaign to obtain scrap iron for munitions. At Hastings, all the railings surrounding the hospital were similarly removed. At Steyning Institution, however, photographic evidence suggests that the railings survived.

Uckfield and Newhaven suffered bomb damage and while at Newhaven the medical officer was fearful of the possible effects on the patients if a bomb came in ('all my old friends of years damaged beyond repair')[13] the damage was only minor, the master noting 'it was fortunate, however, that everyone was under cover, as a fair quantity of splinters fell in the grounds.'[14]

Only one high explosive bomb fell at Brighton Municipal Hospital. This landed on the tennis court and no-one was injured although there was extensive damage to the roofs of B block and the medical superintendent's house. Ticehurst Institution was bombed in 1944 and some of the inmates were transferred to Newhaven. Several bombs fell near St Mary's Hospital in Eastbourne, one causing severe damage to the operating theatre; at Hastings in 1941 a bomb landed on the laundry, partially destroying wards B, C and D.

Although East Sussex was perhaps relatively fortunate in escaping the amount of bomb damage suffered elsewhere, the fear of the possible consequences was always present.

At Battle Institution the upper wards in the infirmary were a cause of concern to a house visitor who wrote: 'I shudder to think of the result should incendiaries be dropped, and consider some better access should be made.'[15] Even at Newhaven, where bedridden cases were nursed on what was regarded as the less dangerous ground floor, the medical officer reporting that there were no confinements because the women had been 'sent away', added 'I am of the opinion that the time has come to send the bedridden cases away, keeping any others who can walk who are not helpless.'[16] In fact the institution's worst wartime damage was the result not of bombing but was caused by a barge loaded with 180 tons of high explosive which drifted ashore during a heavy storm in 1944 and struck a land mine. Almost every building in the town was damaged and it took three members of the staff three weeks to cover up all the institution's broken doors and windows.

Precautions taken against the possibility of air attack included in some instances the provision of brick built shelters. At Brighton Municipal Hospital, the basements of D and E blocks were adapted for this purpose. But there was criticism of the shortcomings of precautions taken in other institutions and even where sandbagging and sometimes bricking up of windows had taken place they could produce unpleasant conditions inside the wards for the patients: at Battle, for example, there were

54. The nurses' home air raid shelter at Newhaven pictured some years after the war when it was used as a store and 55. One of the brick built shelters at Eastbourne, also later used as a store.

several references by visitors to blackout arrangements which produced ventilation problems. At St Mary's too the blackout arrangements, consisting of hardboard frames slotted over the windows, were said to make the wards hot and stuffy.

Gains and losses

There was no doubt the elderly suffered as the result of the war, and the chronic sick were as vulnerable as any. On the credit side, some improvements were made to existing hospitals and the additional accommodation provided, as at Cuckfield, became available for use after it ended. There the Canadians had been given 'carte blanche to alter the buildings as they wish' with the proviso they reinstated if required.[17] They improved the roads and provided additional hutted accommodation raising the accommodation to a total of 800 beds with four operating theatres. However, these gains were more than offset by the postponement of capital expenditure.

When in 1940, following a few weeks' bombing, hospital waiting lists in London and other parts of the country had grown alarmingly, the problem of the chronic sick who were effectively blocking hospital beds was considered to be too serious to be ignored. The fact that many civilian sick were unable to obtain admission to hospital led to a flow of complaints to the Ministry of Health in 1940-41 and 'among the four main groups of patients who competed for hospital care, the aged and chronic sick were the least favoured.'[18] Instructions were given to transfer patients from bombed areas to beds in outer hospitals at an increased rate, although many chronic patients did not benefit because they were not entitled to be transferred to the country.

8. Aftermath: Towards the NHS

The most disturbing feature of these reports is the reference to the provision for the chronic sick. Regrettably common are inadequate barrack like buildings, (cheerless and devoid of conveniences), insufficient medical classification, insufficient trained nursing staff with not enough untrained help, and overcrowding — The Lancet, 1946.

Out of war at least a few good things come, especially in the field of medicine. Florence Nightingale's experiences in the Crimea led to improvements in nursing; the school medical services established in 1906 were a response to a report concerning sickness and mortality of troops in the Boer War; the First World War led to the creation of the Ministry of Health. Lung and brain surgery and blood transfusion were just a few of the developments that were almost non-existent until experience of the techniques was gained with battle casualties. Similarly, it is difficult to imagine the emergence of the welfare state in the latter part of the 1940s without the impetus provided by the Second World War and with it the prospect of improvements in the country's somewhat disorganised hospital system.

The publication in 1942 of the Beveridge Report, which regarded the establishment of a national health service as one of the pre requisites of an effective social security system, and later, in 1944, of the White Paper, might have been expected to draw attention away from matters of detail such as the future care of the chronic sick. In fact, this was not to be the case. Naturally, discussion and debate over the future of Britain's health care services was dominated by the proposal to set up a national service, but the very existence of the debate also helped to draw attention to the growing problem of elderly care.

The Hospital Surveys

Although they were not published until after the war, the Hospital Surveys were among the earliest official acknowledgments of the existence of the problem. The object of the surveys was, firstly, to gather information about hospital facilities which had not previously been collected but which was considered essential to any planning for future services; secondly to assess the adequacy of existing facilities; and, thirdly, to provide 'a body of expert advice on the way in which the existing facilities could best be co-ordinated and if necessary expanded to serve the community in each area'.[1]

In 1942 a distinguished London physician, Dr (later Sir) Archibald Gray, and Dr Andrew Topping, the London County Council's deputy MOH, were invited to survey hospitals in what were to become the four Thames regions and Wessex. There was little indication in the first published report by Gray and Topping of what was to follow so far as the chronic sick were concerned. Their detailed survey tended to stick quite closely to their terms of reference: 'to advise Minister what area would appropriately be served by a hospital system centred on London, and what modifications or extensions of the existing hospital facilities would be necessary or desirable to give effect to that policy'.[2] They were also asked to provide other information including descriptions of the hospital accommodation available, their equipment and medical, surgical and nursing staff, and particulars of the origin of patients treated. Their report for the chronic sick in Sussex included information about the East Sussex public assistance institutions and hospitals:

East District. Hastings Municipal Hospital (298 beds including 34 chronic). 'Mainly old hospital on sloping site with some narrow and awkward wards, poor maternity accommodation ... In addition there are three mixed Institutions at Battle, Rye (now closed), and Ticehurst which are scarcely suitable for the chronic sick...'

South East. St. Mary's Hospital, Eastbourne. (252 beds, including 44 chronic). 'Mainly old Public Assistance Hospital'.

Mid Sussex. Brighton Municipal Hospital (546 beds including 159 chronic, 87 mental). 'Mainly old and in need of considerable reconstruction'. West Hylands P.A.I., Cuckfield. (152 beds including 124 chronic). 'A mixed institution with four sick wards which has been upgraded ... There are also old and unsuitable Institutions at Chailey, Newhaven and Uckfield'. The surveyors also suggested that West Hylands could be linked with a general practitioner hospital at Haywards Heath to form a sub district with about 100 acute, 15–20 maternity, and 50–60 chronic beds for that part of the district. The remaining beds, they suggested, should be used 'for chronic sick from Brighton and other parts of the district after examination and diagnosis at the appropriate District or sub District Hospital'.

South West. The report for this district included a reference to Southlands Hospital, Shoreham (336 beds including 91 chronic): 'A Public

Assistance Hospital with considerable potentialities. Although belonging to East Sussex C.C. it is over the boundary in West Sussex'.

According to the Nuffield Provincial Hospitals Trust, the reports of the ten teams of surveyors were in most respects 'almost monotonously unanimous' with their bitterest comments reserved for the provision for the chronic sick. There is no reason to suppose that in London and the South East conditions for this group were materially different from elsewhere, but the comments of the surveyors in many of the other surveys paint a far more detailed picture. Commenting on the reports for the North Western Area, Sheffield and the East Midlands and the Yorkshire Area, *The Lancet* observed: 'The most disturbing feature of these reports is the reference to the provision for the chronic sick. Regrettably common are inadequate barrack like buildings, (cheerless and devoid of conveniences), insufficient medical classification, insufficient trained nursing staff with not enough untrained help, and overcrowding'.[4] The *British Medical Journal (BMJ)* also drew attention to the 'one unanimous recommendation' of the survey concerning the chronic sick.

'All the surveyors seem to have been impressed by the deplorable lack of accommodation or the poverty of the accommodation for this unfortunate class of people. There are exceptions in progressive towns, but in general the oldest and worst buildings seem to be assigned to these patients... this does seem to be the Cinderella of hospital administration, and the subject will need special attention in the Government's plans'[5]

The Nuffield Trust itself devoted a section of its report to the issue:

There is, perhaps, no side of hospital provision which has given rise to more disquiet of mind in the part of the Surveyors than the provision made for the chronic sick, and the attitude of the public – both professional and social – towards the needs of this section of hospital patients and hospital life. It would not be true to make a wholesale charge which would be applicable in every instance to the hospitals concerned, but it is true to say that in general the care of the chronic sick requires complete and revolutionary change if these people are to be adequately cared for ... in a reasonably humanitarian and social sense ... In most instances, the wards do not provide either the physical or mental amenities to be found in even the most ordinary well conducted domestic dwelling.[6]

The surveyors commented on 'the reproach of the masses of un-diagnosed and untreated cases of chronic type which litter our Public Assistance Institutions and must be removed' (Eastern area), young children and senile dements 'herded together' without proper classification and investigation (North Western Area), and 'bare, over crowded, large wards, cheerless, uncomfortable dayrooms and primitive facilities for nursing' (Sheffield and East Midlands Area).[7]

All in all, the Hospital Surveys provided a sad commentary on the care of the elderly patient in the former workhouses under the stewardship of the county and borough councils. But the situation was not without the promise of hope in another direction ...

The birth of British geriatrics

The NHS White Paper also helped focus attention on the chronic sick for a different reason. Most doctors feared the establishment of a state run salaried service for which many regarded the municipal hospital services as a possible model. For example, a doctor writing in the *British Medical Journal* in a major article on the White Paper said: 'The Public Assistance institution remains, despite its change of name, a dump for destitute chronic patients, controlled by a lay committee and lay officials with grossly inadequate medical staff possessing little authority. This kind of hospital should go.'[8] In another article in the same publication, somewhat scathing references to doctors working for local authorities were linked to the hospitals in which they felt 'no pride or affection', generally more than half full of chronic patients ... who were 'never going to get any better, and are, in fact, life members'.[9]

The medical author of this article maintained he was 'speaking from hard experience'. However, a small number of doctors like Dr Marjory Warren of the West Middlesex Hospital were not content simply to complain about conditions in the poor law infirmaries. They set about doing something to change things:

> At a time when acute hospitals were saying 'We can't do anything for her – send her to the infirmary', Marjory Warren was discovering for herself the principles of curative medicine for the elderly, and she may fairly be called the mother of geriatrics, though others have since added a scientific and sociological framework to the empirical basis she laid.[10]

Marjory Warren's first description of her work was published in the *BMJ* in 1943. At this time, the Ministry of Health was concerned about the lack of treatment of elderly chronic sick patients evacuated to peripheral hospitals under the Emergency Medical Service. There they were looked after by doctors and nurses, often seconded from teaching hospitals, who had little experience of dealing with such patients, who were usually washed, fed, kept clean – but nursed in bed.[12]

According to Howell, himself another pioneer of British geriatrics, who in 1944 was to publish the first original research into the physiology of old age for many years:

> Dr Sturdee, Dr Banks and their assistant, Lord Amulree, now came to visit the West Middlesex Hospital and see what Marjory Warren had achieved. They were extremely impressed. They began to search for any similar work being done elsewhere. They found three other hospitals where the aged chronic sick had been given active treatment with considerable success. These were Orsett Hospital, Essex; St. Helier Hospital, Carshalton; and the Royal Hospital, Chelsea, which housed the famous Chelsea Pensioners.[13]

At Orsett, a young surgeon, Lionel Cosin, had begun operating upon fractured femurs then getting patients out of bed in a short time with excellent results. Aided by a team of able physiotherapists, he used similar mobilisation techniques with medical cases and greatly improved his discharge rates. At St. Helier, the medical superintendent, Dr Eric Brooke, concerned about the length of his waiting list for elderly patients, began visiting them in their own homes accompanied by the first geriatric social worker, Mrs Pillinger. They found that many patients had social problems which could be solved by charitable agencies while others required treatment which could be given in the out patient department.

Howell himself, who was medical officer at the Royal Hospital, had used sulphonamides to bring about a dramatic fall on the death rate of his pensioner patients. Ambulation and early discharge from the sick wards had long been the practice there. Active treatment of rheumatic disorders also improved the turnover and when Dr Sturdee and Lord Amulree visited the Infirmary at the Royal Hospital, they found only one pensioner in bed!

The part played by the Ministry of Health in the development of geriatric medicine should not be underestimated. 'Without the encouragement and support of the medical officers in the Ministry of Health,' Howell was to write later, 'this speciality would not have become recognised nor could the present national network of geriatric units ever have been established'[14]

Dr E.L. Sturdee was a senior medical officer of the Ministry whose responsibilities included medical aspects of the poor law. 'He became informed about the activities of these doctors with eccentric interests in the disabilities of old age through a colleague who had held a temporary appointment pre-war in another department, but was "frozen" as a member of Sturdee's staff throughout the war'.[15] The colleague was

Lord Amulree who was later to return to his former teaching hospital as a physician to develop a geriatric department.

Amulree himself referred to other doctors who were instrumental in furthering the development of the new specialty of geriatrics including Howell's assistants, doctors Mitchell and Piggott and Dr T. Wilson, who later left to work in Cornwall where, with the backing of Dr C. Andrews of Truro, he established a geriatric service for the county based on the Barncoose Hospital at Redruth

> These doctors showed that by means of proper diagnosis and adequate treatment it was possible to remedy a large number of what were then known as the 'chronic sick' who were for the most part aged and in the old Poor Law hospitals, to such an extent that it was possible to discharge a number to their own families or to some form of communal living in a welfare or other home. At the same time it was possible to prevent patients newly admitted from ever becoming 'chronic sick'. The Ministry of Health was not unnaturally interested in these results, which effected a considerable reduction in the number of hospital beds required for the care of such patients. Thus, by the time the National Health Service became operative, in July 1949 [sic], the way was clear for the expansion of these services.[16]

In 1946, Amulree and Sturdee spoke to the Parliamentary Medical Group about the problem of the aged and the long term sick patient. Some members of the Ministry's medical staff had been studying this for some time, they said, 'but have only touched the fringe of it, because the ramifications are so many and because the subject is comparatively new'[17] With regard to the chronic sick, they reminded the parliamentarians that the elderly faded imperceptibly into different grades of acute, chronic, infirm and those requiring little more than skilled nursing oversight and suggested that 'all such grades should be included in a hospital service, though not necessarily on the site of the hospital itself'. Proper classification of patients and accurate diagnosis and treatment were essential, they said. Moreover, 'many of the patients who are kept out of hospital because they seemed likely to stay a long time might, if admitted earlier, receive treatment which would prevent their remaining in hospital ... general practitioners should, therefore, be encouraged to obtain skilled advice and treatment for patients with conditions such as arthritis or hemiplegias as soon as possible so as to avoid contractures'.[18] Finally, added Amulree and Sturdee:

> An attempt should be made with all infirm patients to house together persons who are likely to mix well, but there will always be patients who are likely to upset others and will need special discipline. For long stay patients small units with a 'homely' atmosphere are necessary, and everything should be done to remove the

institutional atmosphere. Not only is the problem of the treatment of the chronic sick not being met, but most people do not realise that there is a problem.[19]

Post-war Reports

Awareness of the problem was to become more widespread at about this time, however, and the address by Amulree and Sturdee was part of the post-war process of drawing attention to it. An increasing number of articles appeared in the medical press and a number of reports were published which gave rise to articles and comment in daily and weekly newspapers read by a wider public.

The first of these was prepared by the Institute of Almoners. It appeared in May, 1946 and was said to have aroused public interest and stirred hospital authorities to give attention to the subject. Following a suggestion by Sir Ernest Rock Carling, the Institute had sent a questionnaire on the care of the chronic sick to almoners at the 350 hospitals throughout the country which provided an almoner service and an analysis of its replies, said the *BMJ*, bore out the view of Amulree and Sturdee that the chronic sick problem was not being met.

The questionnaire was concerned with cases of advanced malignant disease for whom active treatment was no longer possible but who required continuous nursing. The replies showed unequivocally that there was a great shortage of accommodation throughout the country. In Carlisle there were only six female and six male beds available for the chronic sick; at the County Hospital, Pembury, it was 'almost impossible to arrange for the admission of a patient who has a roof over his head and even some destitute cases are kept waiting'; in the South West Region a dying patient had to wait six weeks at home after application had been made for her admission to hospital; in Hull the wards in the municipal hospitals were so overcrowded it was difficult to get a dressing trolley between the beds; the Victoria Hospital at Burnley which, according to the Hospital Surveys, had 60 beds for the chronic sick was using only about 20 for that purpose; in Leicester, the public assistance institutions contained a number of senile patients netted into cot beds who were 'not only depressing for the ordinary patients to look at, but are very noisy and disturbing, especially at night';[and closer to home] at Brighton, a holidaymaker admitted to the voluntary hospital with cerebral thrombosis who was considered chronically sick, could not be transferred to the municipal hospital because the medical officer said the waiting list for Brighton admissions was 'already far too long'.[21]

And so the catalogue continued. The *BMJ* commented on the references to 'old workhouses', accommodation in 'a grim, depressing, and ill cared for place', and 'out of date buildings quite unsuitable for the nursing of patients who need special care'.[22] Vast improvements were needed – less institutional wards (divided by screens), comfortable day rooms, more light and cheerful wards with good decoration, and smaller wards where possible. Better equipment, more homely conditions, room for personal possessions, no unnecessary rules, more small attentions and personal small comforts.

The almoners also called for better classification, special wards for long stay patients with bright and cheerful surroundings, opportunities to go out into the grounds, cinema shows and concert parties, occupational therapy, segregation of senile or difficult cases and, above all, a higher standard of nursing. The report concluded:

> In general an urgent need is felt for a more humane, enlightened, and individual outlook towards the chronic sick, particularly those who suffer from malignant disease, and the acknowledgement that such patients are just as deserving of the best kind of care as those for whom there is hope of recovery.[23]

Two months later, in July, the representative body of the BMA adopted a resolution instructing its council to set up a committee to investigate the 'inadequate provision ... at present made for the treatment and care of the elderly and/or infirm'.[24] This committee included several of the names referred to earlier: Lord Amulree, Dr Brooke, Sir Ernest Rock Carling, Lionel Cosin and Marjory Warren. Dr A. Greig Anderson was appointed chairman. Six months before the BMA committee published its report in June 1947, however, another influential report appeared. Entitled Old People, this was the report of the survey committee set up by the Nuffield Foundation during the war. Chaired by Seebohm Rowntree, the committee's remit was to consider the problems of ageing and the care of old people.[25]

The survey covered the entire field of elderly care: incomes, housing and living conditions, homes and institutions, recreation and employment. In a chapter on homes and institutions, the report noted that on 1 May 1946, 62,957 aged persons (1.16 per cent of the total population of pensionable age), including the long term sick, were being cared for in public assistance institutions and in homes run by local government bodies in England and Wales. The committee referred to the basic poor law principle that provision must be made for the shelter and care of any destitute persons, 'perhaps the best feature of Poor Law administration'.[26] However, so far as the elderly sick and infirm were concerned, they found this provision was no longer available in many districts of England and Wales, a situation which they blamed on three factors: many local authorities used hospital accommodation for 'the general body of citizens'; the transfer of many poor law establishments to the Emergency Medical Service and the war damage sustained by others; and thirdly, the shortage of nursing and other staff.

> The result has been to inflict a serious hardship on old people; cases have come to the notice of members of the Committee of aged persons dying in circumstances of great squalor and loneliness because local authorities, although asked, have been unable to fulfil their legal obligations to receive them into an Institution.[27]

The survey confirmed that little had changed since 1930 and that it was still a frequent practice for institutions to contain a 'motley assembly of the destitute: the great majority are aged, but there are also children, epileptics, and feeble minded young, the blind and the sick'. It was highly critical of many of the institutions, 'built in the early decades of the nineteenth century' with their outwardly pleasing architectural exteriors and spacious and imposing entrances which were nevertheless internally structurally inadequate when judged by modern standards:

> They usually have two or three storeys reached by steep, narrow, stone stair cases. Narrow wards – lit by windows that are too few and too high up – lead one from another, and they contain far too many beds, sometimes as many as a hundred, separated from each other by less than two feet.

When the BMA's report appeared later in the year, it paid tribute to 'the admirable report on Old People'.[28] The committee quoted from an article by one of its members which had appeared in *The Times* that focused attention on the more fortunate among the elderly, those fit enough to lead normal lives.

> There is as yet no commensurate awareness of the plight of the infirm, the decrepit, the incapacitated, the sufferers from long lasting ill health or recrudescent disease, and the permanently incurable. For most of these, concealed from the public eye in institutions, no services are yet provided which in any way meet their needs or their deserts.[29]

The article, by Sir Ernest Rock Carling, prominently featured in *The Times*, placed before the public a detailed statement on the deficiencies of current policy for the welfare of the elderly in which he also argued that even the most enlightened public assistance authorities had assumed that a lower grade of building, inferior medical and nursing skill, a lower scale of nourishment, and few amenities would suffice for the chronic sick.

The report suggested that the elderly and infirm – people suffering from the disabilities of age but not from extreme frailty or chronic disease – should be admitted to suitable homes under the guidance of the geriatric department. The supervision of these homes by the geriatric department was believed to be crucial so that a two way traffic between home and hospital could be established. This could prevent people from being unnecessarily labeled as chronic sick – and perhaps even overcome the reluctance of the elderly to go into hospital as they would have no reason to fear that this would necessarily mean leaving home for ever.

Quoting the regional hospital survey reports that 'the care of the chronic sick requires complete and revolutionary change', the authors of the BMA report dealt briefly with the needs of the elderly acute sick and added: 'But it is for the long term sick and those suffering from incurable disease that greatly improved arrangements are most urgently required'.[30]

The report anticipated that an ageing population would inevitably mean a rapid increase in the number of aged sick and that the situation would be accentuated by the success of chemotherapy in the treatment of respiratory disease, 'hitherto one of the prime causes of death in elderly folk'. In the past, many elderly patients had found their way into institutions and hospitals for the chronic sick where in some cases 'with but few facilities for rehabilitation and in an atmosphere of defeatism, they have been treated with little more than recumbency'. The results of this treatment were all too well known to those with experience of such conditions:

When confined to bed for long periods these patients soon drift into the 'infirmary decubitus' with its avoidable contractures and deformities. In such positions they become fixed and immobile and often unable to feed themselves. The muscles of the back and abdomen become atonic from disuse atrophy, so that even sitting up in bed is difficult and often impossible. Subsequently for many the only movement of the body is during the frequent nursing changes necessitated by incontinence and for the prevention of bed sores. Under such conditions the patient soon sinks into apathy and, having lost hope of recovery, grows fretful, irritable, and morose. This atmosphere of hopelessness is shared by staff and patients alike, for the latter are equally aware that life now offers them no more than slow deterioration under regular nursing attention.[31]

The end of an era

The National Health Service Act was passed in 1946 but it was not until the 5th July 1948 that the new service came into being which was to mark the end of the long association between hospital care for the elderly and the poor law.

The years leading up to the introduction of the NHS saw the publication of an increasing number of articles in medical journals about care of the elderly which included a series in *The Lancet* entitled 'Modern Care of Old People'. Introducing the series, the journal commented that protests about the neglect of old people were common and shocking, but bad as things were, some hospitals, counties, voluntary bodies and individuals were making a good job of the old, and the aim was to describe a few of the best examples.

The medical journals also reported what appeared to be an increasing number of meetings and conferences on the subject of elderly care, many of them addressed by the authors of the articles appearing elsewhere in their pages.

During this period, the doctors at the Ministry of Health began to bring together all those interested in the active care and treatment of old people. Drs Howell, Warren and Brooke and surgeon Lionel Cosin were encouraged to visit each others hospitals and discuss problems of mutual interest. Visits to workhouses and similar institutions were arranged. It soon became obvious that some kind of club or society was desirable. In September 1947, Howell convened a meeting attended by Lord Amulree, Dr Sturdee, Dr Warren, Dr Brooke, Mr. Cosin and two members of Howell's staff, Dr Thomas Wilson and Dr Alfred Mitchell. At this meeting it was decided to form a society for those interested in the problems of old age and the chronic sick and The Medical Society for the Care of the Aged, later to become the British Geriatrics Society, was formed.

Nurses too appeared to show greater awareness of the needs of the elderly. The Hastings branch of the Royal College of Nursing, for example, held a conference on the subject in the summer of 1945. Nursing journals included an increasing number or articles on the subject by medical writers including Marjory Warren, who argued that ward sisters should be given chronic sick wards 'only as senior posts'.

Despite the acknowledged need for change, however, it was to prove slow coming. Developments following the introduction of the 1929 Local Government Act had been hampered by the process of establishing the new bodies which were to control the hospitals and infirmaries, then by the economic and financial situation resulting from the depression and, finally, by the outbreak of hostilities in 1939. Similarly, after 1945, developments were also to be affected by an impending economic situation, so priorities had to be determined and the priority for capital expenditure in the immediate post war years was not hospitals but housing. A resolution from the BMA, for example, on the inadequacy of care for the chronic sick brought forth a reply from the Ministry of Health that the need for house building was necessarily restricting the labour and materials for institutions.

The importance of housing in the immediate post war period, especially to the new Labour government, should not be under estimated. Because of the cessation of house building during the war and the damage to the housing stock caused by air raids, housing became the most important social issue to the electors in 1945 general election. Labour candidates stressed the importance of the issue and reminded the electors that Lloyd George's promise of 'Homes for Heroes' following the First World War had never been fulfilled. Moreover, Bevan, the Minister of Health, was also responsible for housing. This meant he was likely to be judged by his contribution to the building of new permanent housing.

Whilst in the light of all the circumstances it is difficult to criticise that particular policy, it was nevertheless to have far reaching effects on future hospital provision for the elderly chronic sick.

Part II

1930-1948:
The Hospital Management Committees

9. The Years of Make Do and Mend

Capital expenditure, one of the principal keys to bringing about change for the elderly chronic sick, was clearly inadequate during the 1950s. It compared unfavourably with, for example, education and housing which had increased by 100 per cent and 43 per cent respectively, while investment in hospitals had fallen by 2.3 per cent in 1954 — Charles Webster, 'The Health Services Since the War', Vol. 1.

On the Appointed Day, 5 July 1948 a number of East Sussex institutions were transferred to the South East Metropolitan Regional Hospital Board and commenced their transition to chronic sick NHS hospitals or, in the case of the larger institutions already functioning as poor law hospitals, began the process of establishing themselves as NHS hospitals eventually destined to contain geriatric units.

Day to day responsibility for hospital administration passed from the local authorities to hospital management committees (HMCs). In East Sussex, control of chronic sick provision passed to four HMCs: Brighton, Eastbourne, Hastings and Mid Sussex. Management committees were also established for the county's mental hospitals: St Francis and Lady Chichester being responsible for the former Brighton County Borough mental hospital, and Hellingly HMC for the former East Sussex mental hospital situated near Hailsham.

Brighton & Lewes HMC was responsible for Brighton Municipal Hospital and Newhaven Institution, now renamed Brighton General Hospital and Newhaven Downs Hospital. Eastbourne HMC took responsibility for St Mary's Hospital. Hastings HMC's responsibilities included St Helen's Hospital (formerly Hastings Municipal Hospital) and Stone House Institution, now renamed Battle Hospital. Mid Sussex HMC included Cuckfield Hospital (formerly West Hylands and renamed in 1949) and Pouchlands Hospital (formerly Chailey Institution).

Southlands Hospital, which had been such an influence on the development of East Sussex public assistance institutions, was transferred to the control of Worthing HMC in West Sussex and, despite cross boundary flows of patients in certain specialties, was no longer to play more than a marginal role in the creation of geriatric hospital services in East Sussex.

How these hospitals developed over the early years under the control of the local management committees, however, has to be seen in the context of the national situation, and that was influenced by the economic situation following the end of the Second World War and events that followed it. In addition, of course, there was the very real problem of the nature of their inheritance from the local authorities. Added to this was the fact that the purse strings were now under the control of the newly constituted regional hospital boards (RHBs): in the case of East Sussex this was the South East Metropolitan RHB.

A leading article in *The Times* in 1946[1] suggested that the way the new regional boards dealt with the chronic sick would be a test of their success. In the same leader, it was acknowledged that 'buildings and other not easily attainable facilities are ultimately required' and in the event the problems of replacing their inherited stock of obsolete and unsuitable buildings proved to be almost insuperable in the first decade following the establishment of the National Health Service. Whilst *The Times* had argued that 'the most urgent need is for an imaginative use of what exists', the clear fact remained, as the surveyors' reports had shown, that considerable capital expenditure was required if real progress was to be achieved. In point of fact, post war stringencies and the claims on national resources of other much needed developments – accentuated by the devaluation of the pound in 1949, the Korean War (from 1953) and the 1955 credit squeeze –confounded these hopes. As a result, the first decade of the new service was rightly dubbed an era of make do and mend.

Spending contracted until the middle of the 1950s, so aggravating the deficiencies inherited in 1948. There was a trickle of additional money in the middle 1950s, principally to improve conditions in the mental health field (the 'mental millions'), to replace a worn out and inefficient plant, and to make a start on a centrally financed programme of major building projects. But the sums available were still inadequate.

The economic evidence placed before the Guillebaud Committee, set up in 1953 to inquire into the cost of the National Health Service, provided confirmation that capital expenditure had been relatively small:

> About £12 million has been spent each year. As prices of building work and other capital assets have risen substantially over the period, the real rate of capital expenditure has progressively declined ... It was generally agreed that the hospitals taken over in 1948 were too small, too numerous, and too old. In fact, approximately 45% of all hospitals were originally erected before 1891. A high level of hospital building was expected to be achieved under the National Health

Service. These hopes have not been fulfilled. The rate of fixed capital expenditure on hospitals has averaged about one third of the pre war rate in real terms. At this rate it would take over 200 years to replace our stock of hospitals.[2]

Thus capital expenditure, one of the principal keys to bringing about change for the elderly chronic sick, was clearly inadequate during the 1950s. It compared unfavourably with, for example, education and housing which had increased by 100 per cent and 43 per cent respectively, while investment in hospitals had fallen by 2.3 per cent in 1954.[3]

Capital expenditure on hospitals was largely absorbed in unglamorous but essential works such as replacing boilers, rewiring and upgrading kitchens and laundry services, and many of the emergency schemes were uneconomical. The Guillebaud Committee estimated that £1 million spent on modernisation involved an extra £400,000 in running costs, £1 million on new building only £150,000 extra.[4] In addition, the mental health services, which suffered from severe overcrowding and lengthening waiting lists, took an increasing share of the allocation – nearly 30 per cent of total hospital capital expenditure was devoted to mental hospitals in 1954–5 compared to 17 per cent in 1950–1; in May 1954. Health Minister Iain Macleod laid the foundation stone of only the second new hospital to be started since 1948, a mental deficiency hospital at Southport, and, in the same year, set up a Royal Commission whose report published in 1957 was to do much to enlighten mental health care in Britain.

The problems in the mental health field cannot be denied, nor should they be underestimated. But there were bed shortages for the chronic sick, too. In the summer of 1950 a deputation from the National Old People's Welfare Committee presented a memorandum to the Minister on the subject. In a Parliamentary answer in 1951, the government acknowledged the 'serious shortage ... which could be finally cured only by the provision of additional beds'. Meanwhile a field survey of general practice in 1951–2 found 'long waiting for admission to hospital for the aged and infirm sick, and for old people, is almost a universal problem' with 80 per cent of practitioners complaining of difficulties.[5] Speaking at the BMA's 1953 annual meeting, a general practitioner said:

The 1946 Act, with its obliteration of the Poor Law hospital, however progressive it may have been, virtually cost, in my area, the use of 1,000 chronic sick beds, and the general practitioner who prior to 1948 could easily lodge his chronic sick is now faced with a grave problem; for in spite of the excellent treatment afforded in a few geriatric unit (sic), they cannot be accommodated in hospital.[6]

But the problem was not simply one of a shortage of beds, as a Parliamentary Answer in 1951 indicated. This stated that 7,712 people were on the waiting list for admission to chronic sick beds on the 31st December 1949. On the same date 7,575 beds were empty in chronic sick hospitals, but more than half the beds were unstaffed.[7]

Despite all the efforts made to conquer the problem since the 1930s, nurses continued to be in short supply. Speaking at the annual meeting of the general council of the King Edward's Hospital Fund for London in 1949, the president, the Duke of Gloucester, described the nursing shortage as one of the three main problems encountered by the National Health Service to which the Fund had responded by opening a residential staff college to train staff nurses to become ward sisters. One of the pioneers of geriatric medicine, Dr Brooke, told another conference on the care of elderly patients attended by over 200 local authority representatives and others that 'the problem in a nutshell was "too many patients in search of too few staffed hospital beds".[8]

In 1956, the nursing shortage was the subject of an adjournment debate in the Commons during which the parliamentary secretary to the Ministry of Health, Miss Pat Hornsby Smith stated that the number of full time nurses in hospitals had increased from 117,000 in 1948 to 143,000 and that part time staff had increased during the same period from 20,000 to 32,000. The government was doing its utmost to stimulate recruitment, she said, especially in mental nursing where she acknowledged the rate of entry of students was still inadequate. However, despite these increased numbers, the problems remained, especially in the chronic sick hospitals and wards. Wastage rates were high and the situation was not helped by the introduction of an 88 hour working fortnight two years later, which, although it brought about an overdue reduction in working hours, meant less nursing cover for patients.

One possible solution to the shortage of nurses was the recruitment of more part time staff and the Ministries of Health and Labour had launched a campaign with this end in mind in 1947. Miss Hornsby Smith's figures reveal the extent of the success of this campaign which, while it was claimed to have saved some hospitals from closing, and whilst it was believed to be of benefit to the part timers themselves and to their patients who would enjoy increased contact with the outside world, cannot be said to have been as successful as had been hoped. Part time staff were, in any event, not always welcomed by other staff working on the wards who resented having to cover for their alleged more frequent absences from work and their reluctance to work unsocial hours, such as at weekends.

The chronic sick survey, 1954–55

The difficulties of recruiting nurses to work with the chronic sick were referred to in the summary report by Dr C.A. Boucher of a survey of services available to the chronic sick and elderly carried out during 1954 −1955.

In December 1954, the Chancellor of the Exchequer had presented the report of the Phillips Committee to Parliament. This had been set up to review the economic and financial problems in providing for the aged and had concluded, so far as hospital treatment was concerned, that 'it would be premature to embark on long term building plans for the accommodation of increasing numbers of chronic sick and other old patients in hospitals until there had been more experience of recent developments'.[9] The Ministry's survey which was based on visits to every hospital region, came to a similar conclusion, and in the process provided a fairly detailed account of the prevailing position regarding the care and treatment of the elderly chronic sick. It began in May 1954 with a pilot study of eleven districts (which included Hastings County Borough) and the national survey was completed, with the exception of two regions, by June 1955.

One of the factors prompting the survey was that an early result of the National Health Service was an increased demand for beds for the elderly chronic sick. This was particularly apparent in London and the south of England, for example, where an unusual demand for accommodation was being experienced in the autumn of 1948, well before the usual seasonal increase. Despite an increased number of beds and more active treatment, this demand persisted and the size of the waiting list failed to alter appreciably during the following five years.

The findings relating to the state of hospital buildings were not surprising bearing in mind the antiquity of the inherited stock and the low rate of capital investment since 1948. Thus reports referred to 'three storey buildings with difficult and narrow staircases, no lifts, and sometimes with damp'.

Although money had sometimes been spent on these buildings, particularly in redecoration, such amenities as baths, washing facilities, sluices and day room accommodation were often inadequate. Heating was sometimes poor and there were reports of draughts, the lighting both natural and artificial was insufficient for the comfort of the patients.[10]

Some accommodation was provided in huts erected during the 1914–18 war and some in EMS huts erected during the Second World War. Nevertheless, two EMS huts in Northallerton provided 'very suitable accommodation' in contrast to the female ward at another hospital which was sited on the first floor of an old building with no lift, approached by an outside cast iron staircase, with wooden floors and partitions and a boilerhouse and paint store underneath. There was an alternative means of egress for the mainly bedfast patients – by another narrow outside staircase. The chronic sick in rural areas were usually to be found in former public assistance institutions 'with all their disadvantages'.[11]

On the other hand, the survey teams did find several examples of successful adaptations of old buildings including Preston Hospital in North Shields and Middlesborough General Hospital where two chronic sick wards had 'undergone extensive renovation and redecoration; the walls had been plastered and the floors re laid; wash basins had been provided, also sluices with heated bedpan racks and washers, and the ward kitchens had been re-equipped; ceiling and bedside lights were excellent'.

A number of solutions to the chronic sick problem were suggested during the 1950s including, even, emigration and euthanasia![12] There were frequent appeals for Halfway Homes to accommodate those patients who, usually because of frailty, were not acceptable to welfare authorities but who, nevertheless, did not require hospital services. Boucher commented on the value of out patient clinics and the development of day hospitals and discussed the contribution that could be made by the development of geriatrics as a separate specialty.

Referring to the shortage of nursing staff, Boucher noted that national statistics for the survey period gave a figure of 3.3 beds per nurse, varying from 4.5 in East Anglia to 2.2 in Liverpool, but numbers were often below establishments and 350 chronic sick beds were closed for lack of staff. At Pouchlands Hospital in East Sussex 'the number of patients who could be accepted from the hospital waiting list was subject daily to the number of nursing staff available. The position was so serious in some areas that the absence of even one nurse for sickness or any other reason could disorganise work in the wards'.[13]

The difficulty of recruiting nurses to the chronic sick wards reflected partly the poor working conditions, the slow turnover of patients and the frustration arising from beds blocked by cured cases. The work was often tiring and unpleasant and the majority of nurses preferred to work in the acute wards. Teaching facilities were not always well developed, and some nurses felt that duty in the chronic sick wards implied a loss of status. Doreen Norton (The Age of Old Age, London, Scutari Press, 1990) was to write later that the chronic sick wards were also used as punishment wards: 'In a sense they were a repository for nurses who had displeased in some way – such as abandoning their training and working their notice or breaking a hospital rule – or those who were considered physically unfit or clinically unsafe to work elsewhere. Thus old people's wards were colloquially known as 'punishment wards'.

Boucher pointed out that nursing in the chronic sick wards was heavy and often irksome. There was often overcrowding and badly designed and equipped accommodation. In spite of this, he said a very great deal of skilled and devoted service was being given by nurses to the chronic sick patient but much of the success depended on the attitude and enthusiasm of the ward sister:

> In one hospital there were two separate ward blocks for the chronic sick: in one block all the patients were kept constantly in bed, many of them being doubly incontinent, senile, confused and apathetic; in the other, with a younger and more imaginative sister, many of the patients were up for a few hours daily, very few were incontinent, and all were interested in their surroundings and in visits of their relatives and friends.[14]

In the penultimate chapter of his report, Boucher noted there was frequent reference to the absence of co-ordination of the services and the lack of co-operation between them. In part this was the result of division of responsibility for elderly care between hospitals and the local authorities brought about by post-war legislation. The demise of the relieving officer who, under poor law, could secure the admission of an old person to hospital, was seen by many as contributing to the problems of the chronic sick: 'Patients gained entry to hospital beds only if consultants accepted them, and few consultants, where the aged were concerned, felt so inclined'.[15] Not surprisingly, there were calls for the establishment of combined health and welfare departments or for the return of an official comparable to the old relieving officer with his powers to ensure hospital admission and, to ensure that sufficient beds were available to achieve this, for the construction of temporary, prefabricated buildings.

However, the Minister of Health, Iain Macleod, who was later to acknowledge that the care of the aged was 'unquestionably the most difficult social problem of the age in all civilised countries', was not impressed with these suggestions. 'Short term solutions might remain longer than was intended, and it would be the final irony of the Welfare State if all they could find to solve this immensely difficult problem was to bring back the relieving officer and rebuild, in whatever form, the workhouse'.[16]

In his response to the 1954–55 Chronic Sick Survey[17] the Minister of Health acknowledged that the development of services for the aged was one of the most urgent tasks confronting the National Health Service but pointed out that other demands on financial resources and absolute shortages of certain types of staff might make it impossible quickly to reach a high level of achievement.

It was against this background that the local hospital management committees formed in 1948 faced the challenge of transforming their former workhouses into hospitals providing a long-overdue adequate service for the elderly chronic sick.

10. Brighton's Two Kinds of Care

When the new hospital secretary arrived at Brighton General Hospital from a Sheffield teaching hospital in 1951 and saw the geriatric wards he 'nearly ran away. They were just like big cow sheds filled with people' — Evening Argus (Brighton), 4 May 1971.

The newly formed Brighton and Lewes hospital management committee inherited thirteen hospitals including two former workhouses, now renamed Brighton General Hospital and Newhaven Downs Hospital. Brighton General with more than 600 beds contained a mix of patients, acute and chronic sick and the differing standards between the two were marked. The acute wards were praised in a report issued in 1952 as needing only minor improvements. On the two long stay blocks, the male wards still had an old fashioned heating system and the floors needed renewing. The women's block, on three floors, had large wards with beds arranged in four rows. A catering survey carried out during the same year added further details of the chronic sick wards. In J Block all crockery on the top floor was still washed in a bath which was also used for bathing patients.

Newhaven Downs with 160 beds also possessed something of a split personality, in this case between the infirmary and the House block. As a so-called joint user establishment its infirmary block was to serve as a long-stay chronic sick annexe for Brighton General. The House catered for the ambulant Part III (of the National Assistance Act) residents, who were the responsibility of East Sussex Council. Not surprisingly, it was not easy to throw off its workhouse image and despite renaming the old institution the break with poor law was not particularly noticeable.

Two years later [August, 1950] I began work as a junior clerk at Newhaven Downs Hospital which still bore the scars of its history as a workhouse and poor law and public assistance institution. Classed as a 'joint user establishment' its 160 beds were split between chronic sick patients who were the responsibility of the new Regional Hospital Board and sixty or more former public assistance inmates who as 'welfare' cases were the responsibility of East Sussex County Council. My first and remaining impressions were of dingy dark green and chocolate brown paint, 25 watt lamps, spartan conditions – only a few open fires to keep patients warm – rows of prison like cot beds in some of the wards, pinafored old ladies on their hands and knees scrubbing stone corridors and stairs, weatherbeaten old countrymen working in the gardens; there was a mixture of caring staff and some who perpetrated minor cruelties; and, of course, the matron and her husband, the administrator, still known by his workhouse title, Master – a formidable couple for whom the patients welfare really was paramount.[1]

At Brighton General Hospital poor law associations lingered primarily to the left of the site which housed the chronic sick blocks, especially the much neglected J Block. This presumably was the block to which the new hospital secretary referred to when arriving from a Sheffield teaching hospital to take up his new post as having wards like cowsheds filled with people. At this time, J Block was warmed only by coal fires, contained wooden floors and had no curtains at the windows.[2]

A scheme of improvements for J Block had been deferred by the regional board in 1951. When they were told that the regional board had deferred a scheme 'which had long been desired', the hospital's house committee adjourned its meeting so that members could tour the block. On their return, they noted that 'all the alterations were very necessary' and instructed the administrative officer to send a report to the management committee recommending that the cost of the work, £10,500, should be met from endowment funds.[3] It was not until late in 1954, however, that the capital scheme was finally completed and the patients returned to their upgraded accommodation in February 1955.

Despite continual pressure from the hospital house committee, no improvements were made to F Block throughout the 1950s. As a result of representations by the committee supported by the medical staff, a lift was installed in 1957 when the house committee reminded the HMC of the need to upgrade the block. Their report referred to a complete absence of central heating, the extremely poor state of the wooden flooring, makeshift electric wiring and deficient sanitary arrangements. Following another reminder to the HMC in April, the house committee was eventually 'dismayed' to learn, in January 1958, that the upgrading had not been included in the capital programme and a year later once again reminded the HMC of the 'bad conditions' still existing there.[4]

The geriatric unit at Brighton General Hospital was established quite early – in March 1951 – when Dr Firth outlined to his medical colleagues the steps he was taking to reduce waiting lists including making domiciliary visits. Patients would not be expected to remain in the treatment block longer than eight weeks, he reported. Elderly patients in the acute wards not requiring further treatment but unable to be sent home could be referred to the geriatric unit 'which would co operate to make suitable arrangements for their dispersal'.[5]

In September 1954, the HMC received reports about shortages of finance and nurses. The finance committee chairman told members that the regional board had said no addition could be made to the current maintenance allocation and that cuts of over £11,000 would have to be made.

To help stimulate nursing recruitment, members were asked if they would join members of staff in speaking at meetings and participating in brains trusts at local organisations such as women's institutes, townswomen's guilds and youth clubs. The following month the committee received a report from its planning sub committee on immediate

56. Dr Stanley Firth, Brighton's first geriatric consultant. Dr Firth was born in 1902 in Manchester Wythenshawe workhouse where his parents were Matron and Workhouse Superintendent. His first appointments after qualifying were at Manchester and Hastings. He was appointed as medical superintendent at Brighton in 1931 and was responsible later for two more former workhouses at Newhaven and Cuckfield.

future developments in the group which acknowledged the shortcomings at Brighton General Hospital.

> The generally unsatisfactory nature of a considerable portion of Brighton General Hospital is well known to the Committee (e.g. out of date wards, sanitary and sterilising rooms, lack of lifts in certain blocks, no connecting bridges between ward blocks etc).[6]

The appendix to the report showed that there was a shortage of chronic and geriatric beds in the group: 335 beds compared with the regional board estimated requirement of 400, and in a reference to the 58 beds occupied by Part III residents the report enquired whether this accommodation, when freed by the county, could be used to provide extra chronic sick beds.

57. *F Block at Brighton General though in desperate need of upgrading, no improvements were made to the block throughout the 1950s.*

The report listed some of the problems that were being encountered: changing techniques and demands for services, for example fewer children and more old people. It commented on the difficulty of effective long term planning 'chiefly on the grounds of finance, capital and maintenance'.[7] The planning sub committee's suggested priorities were a new orthopaedic/traumatic/casualty unit followed by improvements to the radiotherapy department. There was no reference to the elderly although it was noted that at Brighton General 'reconditioning of J Block for the chronic sick is in train'. However, in a report from the group secretary on bed statistics, there were details relating to the chronic sick. The number of beds allocated totalled 335; Average occupancy was 327; Patients treated during the year numbered 871. There were 109 patients on the waiting list in December 1953, 99 in the following May. It was estimated that 50 additional beds were needed to eliminate the waiting list.[8]

In 1956, bed availability was threatened by staff shortages. The matron, administrative officer and geriatric consultant were asked by the Brighton General house committee to suggest what steps could be taken to avoid the possible closure of female chronic sick beds. Their suggestions included the provision of equipment to ease the work of the nurses, the employment of more ward orderlies and part time state registered nurses and the possible transfer of staff from other blocks. The recruitment of nursing auxiliaries was also being made more difficult because they were required to be paid monthly rather than weekly. A suggestion that this should be changed was turned down by the nursing and midwifery sub committee who pointed out that new employees could on request receive weekly salary advances for the first two or three months if they wished. It was noted that an 'unofficial easing of admissions' had made it unnecessary to approach the board with a request to close L Block 'for the time being' and that the possibility of paying travelling expenses to potential recruits from overseas was being investigated.[9]

Within a month, however, six beds had been closed on F Block and on learning that payment of travelling expenses of recruits from Germany was permissible, it was decided to ask the regional board to pursue this possible source of nursing auxiliary recruitment. The board later reported, however, that the Central Planning Office in Germany had no suitable candidates and that the likelihood of help from that direction was remote.

There was little support in Brighton at this time for the establishment of a geriatric day hospital. The matter was raised in September 1957 by a member of the house committee, Mr G. Belcher. His note, 'Day Centres for Infirm Elderly People' was circulated to fellow members but met with a lukewarm reception. The committee 'was generally favourable' to the 'constructive suggestions' contained in the paper but considered it more important to give priority to the upgrading of F Block to enable the hospital to deal adequately with in-patients before attempting to treat infirm elderly people as out-patients. Following this upgrading, more beds for long stay patients were considered to be the priority.[10] The next month, however, the committee was discussing the question again as a result of the receipt of Boucher's report and the subsequent Ministry circular and Dr Firth said he would be preparing a report in due course.

Newhaven Downs

Meanwhile at the long-stay annexe, Newhaven Downs, the principal problems appeared to arise from the inadequate heating system. According to the hospital management committee this needed to be renewed 'whilst the provision of better ward sanitary and sterilising facilities are also required'.[11]

In some respects, Newhaven was more fortunate than its parent hospital, Brighton General. Newhaven, like many former workhouses in small towns, even though to some extent they were closed worlds, did have links with the local community. These were to be exploited after 1948 when those concerned set about changing attitudes locally and bringing conditions in hospitals more into line with the times. The question of heating provides a good example.

The inadequate heating of the wards had exercised the minds of those responsible throughout the 1930s. Now, in the early years of the NHS, the main wards were still warmed only by two open fires set in vast rounded chimney breasts in the centre – useful, as in many hospitals over the years, as a centrepiece for Christmas decorations but quite inadequate for their intended purpose. Conditions in the sanitary annexes especially were positively Arctic-like in winter. It took the persistence of two local men in particular to bring about much needed change: local councillor Joseph Pargeter, who was chairman of the hospital's house committee and a member of the regional hospital board which ultimately held the purse strings, and Harry Randall a member of parliament for a north-east constituency but who lived in Newhaven.

Mr Pargeter pressed the case at the regional board at a time when although the plans had been approved, it appeared they might be

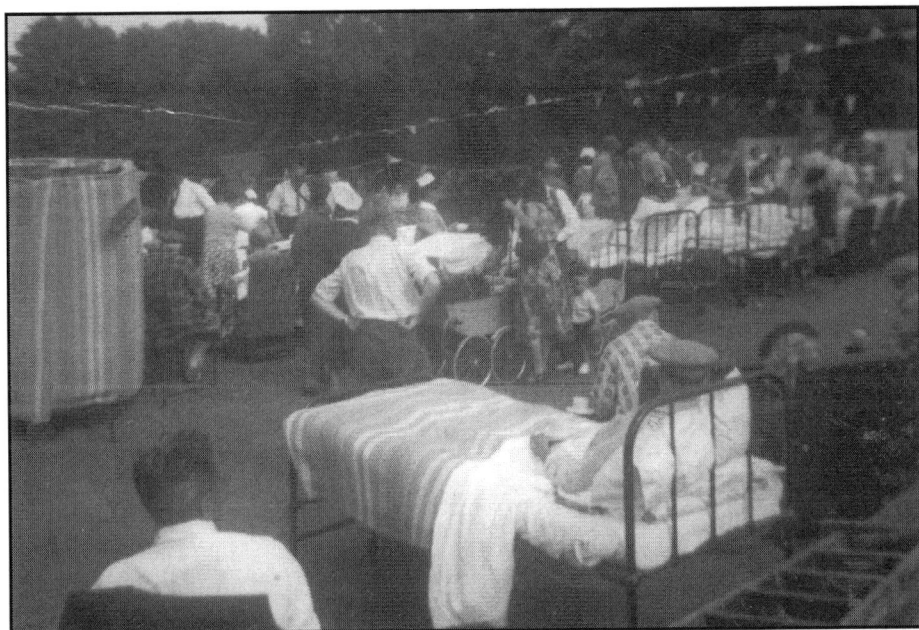

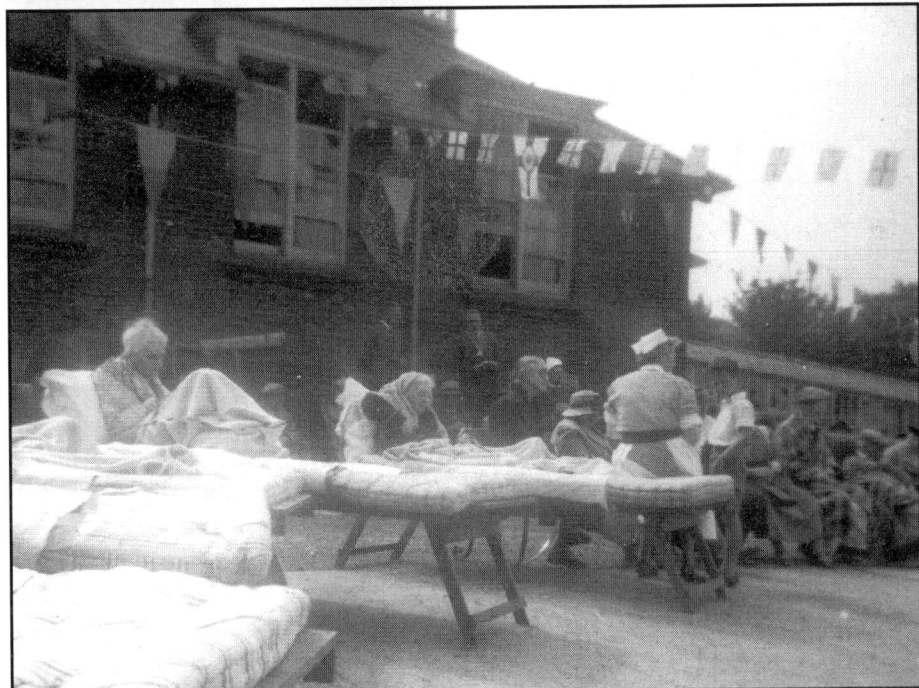

58. Patients at Newhaven enjoying the fresh air for the first time since their admission at a garden party at Newhaven Downs Hospital in the 1950s. 59. Because their beds could not be manhandled down the stairs, folding beds supplied to the institution in case of wartime emergencies were used for women patients from the first floor. For some, it was the first time they had been outside their ward for years.

frustrated because of difficulties in obtaining a supply of radiators locally. Mr Randall took the opportunity of a health debate in the House of Commons to draw the attention of the minister to the issue. Within months, work on the installation began.

However, this still left the House block which was warmed by a few open coal fires. The hospital's house committee expressed concern, but it was not until an inspector from the Ministry of Health saw the conditions for himself, that the hospital management committee provided funds to provide supplementary electric heating.

The lack of a lift was another outstanding problem that took longer to resolve. New arrivals had to be manhandled up two flights of stairs to the first floor and discharges (and bodies) carried down again. It was not until 1965 that a bed lift was finally provided.

In the meantime, staff could only make the best of the situation. They organised a series of annual garden parties that provided an incentive to carry some quite heavy patients down stairs and out into the grounds from the wards in which effectively some had been trapped for years. The garden parties were also seen as a way of bringing local people into the hospital in order to help dispel its workhouse image – still remembered as 'The Spike' where parents threatened to send their children as a punishment if they misbehaved.[12]

In spite of these efforts, change in the physical conditions overall was very slow in coming. Visitors coming into the hospital for the first time who had not been acquainted with the pre-war workhouses still found the experience something of a culture shock. In fact, several years later, the chairman of the health authority recalled visiting the building for the first time. 'It was,' he said, 'the biggest shock I had since joining the authority when I went round that sad place on a cold winter morning'.[13]

11. Overcoming the problems at Hastings

A great feeling of hopelessness about the possibility of obtaining admission for patients exists among doctors and many agree that often they do not even make application because of this. They also state that a great fear exists among the patients themselves because they dread a long period of comparative helplessness with no prospect of suitable care and help — Hastings Old People's Welfare Committee, April 1959.

At Hastings there were early indications that the group, despite its problems, or perhaps because of them, was to develop into one of the leaders in the development of geriatric care. As early as April 1949, recommendations were submitted to the regional board that all 'so-called incurables' should be periodically reviewed and transferred back to the main hospital where necessary in order to achieve a regular turnover of beds, and that for the purpose 'of stimulating active treatment and rehabilitation', a consultant physician should be appointed.[1]

Hastings HMC's records show that the South East Metropolitan regional board was giving serious consideration to the problems of dealing with the chronic sick. A file, Hospital Plan 1948–50, contains a letter received from the board in August 1949 regarding a plan suggested by its Medical Advisory Committee to provide a comprehensive service. This said it was hoped to build up 'a definite geriatric service within the region divided into sectors with a consultant organiser responsible for each sector'.[2]

A little over six months later a letter was received from Brigadier Glyn Hughes, the board's senior administrative medical officer, enclosing a copy of the final plan for Hastings which had been approved by the regional board. This stated that it was intended to establish an efficient geriatric service in each HMC area and that to cope with 'this urgent problem' the main essential was to form a correct staffing structure. Apart from the day- to-day care of the chronic sick, the board believed it was imperative to find a medical practitioner to 'take in hand the problems of the area by carrying out periodical domiciliary surveys of all cases on the waiting list, investigating all new applications, and generally arranging priorities and the method of admission'. The letter continued:

> Each HMC area must have accommodation, preferably in general hospitals where ancillary services are available, for a small number of cases of both sexes to be diagnosed, observed and assessed, a block of beds should be set aside where physiotherapy etc is available for cases undergoing active rehabilitation and finally there should be a long stay annexe.[3]

Additionally, the board hoped, where possible, to co-ordinate the work of adjoining groups by the appointment of a specialist in geriatrics.

The first task undertaken by Hastings was to look into the possibility of converting the former Battle Institution into a chronic sick hospital with 109 beds. In November 1949, the group secretary wrote to Brigadier Glyn Hughes: 'I believe you have some strong views on this question and verbally mentioned that we should increase the beds in this direction as soon and as far as possible'. However there were staffing difficulties and a lack of accommodation so the house committee had suggested that wards not required for the scheme should be turned into cubicles for domestic staff. Brigadier Glyn Hughes was asked for an instruction on the board's long term policy which the house committee would endeavour to put into operation as soon as possible.[4]

Another problem was the need to remove Part III residents accommodated at Battle. The group secretary telephoned the county's assistant welfare officer about this and was told that East Sussex took the view it was a 'two-way' problem. The county council planned to open five hostels during the following year but these would only be able to house the ambulant aged. The county's view was that the type of case in Battle would require a more institutional type of accommodation, for example Uckfield or East Grinstead, which at that time contained about 100 hospital cases. Thus, even at this early stage, a one-for-one exchange between hospital and Part III accommodation was suggested by the local authority, a response that was made time and again over the years, and not only in Hastings, whenever the question of blocked hospital beds arose.

At this time Battle contained 88 beds, 33 of which were for Part III cases. It was proposed to increase this total by 12 male and 10 female beds and the regional architect was asked to prepare sketch plans based on the scheme recently completed at St Pancras Hospital in London. In the view of the sub committee established to consider the scheme, it was not simply a question of providing extra beds: they wanted to provide 'a really high standard of accommodation' similar to St Pancras and the one planned for Lewisham Hospital.[3]

The Battle conversion proposal provides another good example of the difficulties faced in dealing with the chronic sick problem at this time: many of the old institutions established a century of so before for an entirely different purpose, were not really suited to their new role. At Battle, the regional architect reported, there were a number of difficulties. Floors were on different levels and would require the installation of ramps, covered ways or realignment of the floors. The existing stairways were too narrow and the 'winding type' would have to be demolished. The existing wards were mostly of the size favoured by the board but their lack of width was a disadvantage and the sanitary services were very poor. Because the Ministry was not in favour of providing lifts in buildings with only two floors, bed cases might be placed on one floor. Since it was agreed the stairways should not be used for the conveyance of chronic sick cases, exterior stairways might have to be provided. Faced with these problems, the sub committee, realising that conversion would take three or four years to complete, decided that an interim scheme, including additional accommodation for nursing and domestic staff in cubicles or huts and some reconstruction of certain stairways, should be submitted as a matter of urgency.

In April 1950, the HMC received a letter from Hastings and District Old People's Welfare Committee. The OPWC had become 'increasingly concerned about the difficulty in securing hospital treatment for elderly sick people' and enclosed an analysis of replies received from local general practitioners who had been sent a questionnaire on the subject. There was general agreement among the doctors that 'great difficulty exists in obtaining beds for the elderly sick needing hospital treatment in this area'. Most cases, they said, were placed on a waiting list and admitted for treatment 'after an indefinite period' although 78 cases had failed to be admitted during the preceding twelve months. The letter continued:

> A great feeling of hopelessness about the possibility of obtaining admission for patients exists among doctors and many agree that often they do not even make application because of this. They also state that a great fear exists among the patients themselves because they dread a long period of comparative helplessness with no prospect of suitable care and help.[4]

The OPWC also referred to the doctors' wish to see new units established for elderly ambulant patients who needed medical attention but did not need to occupy hospital beds or the services of fully trained nurses. Daily visits to their homes by district nurses and home helps did not meet the needs of these cases, the doctors believed. They then asked the HMC to give immediate consideration to make urgent representations for more hospital accommodation for elderly sick patients and contractual arrangements with private nursing homes for the admission of urgent cases. The Hastings district was officially recognised as over-populated with old people, the letter continued, and an allocation of beds based on the population as a whole was not the correct proportion for the area.

Following advice from the general medical committee, the HMC decided to seek immediate regional board approval for the establishment of a consultant appointment (which was granted the following month) and also to explore other possible hospitals that might meet the situation.

Meanwhile, a survey had been commissioned on group needs for occupational therapy and the subsequent report showed that Battle Hospital accommodated at that time approximately 110 elderly patients, about 26 of whom were permanently in bed. Quite a number worked in the gardens or undertook maintenance work; some of the women mended socks or repaired linen. One man was engaged in rug making. Despite numerous difficulties, the staff tried to encourage all the patients to do something, the report stated. At St Helens, there were about 470 patients, including some 100 Part III and mental defectives. 'The patients are mainly medical cases,' the report noted, 'and many of them are elderly whose length of stay ... is likely to be fairly long'.[7]

The second annual report by Hastings HMC provides a graphic illustration of the effect of the 'make do and mend' years at local level. During the year, the report stated, it became clear that the development of a comprehensive health service must be slowed down to accord with the amount of money which the nation could afford. This meant not merely slowing down any new development and improvements in the Hastings area, but further postponement of repairs and renewals of buildings, plant and equipment which still accrued from years of enforced neglect during the war and in the years prior to July 1948, when the NHS was established. The report also noted that the proposed reopening of two chronic sick wards at Battle Hospital had been postponed because of lack of staff and finance (the HMC's budget having been cut by almost £30,000 was restricted to £558,300 and this had to cover salary awards to senior nursing staff costing an additional £5,400), while the report from St Helen's Hospital house committee noted that 'recruitment of trained nursing staff has been difficult'.[8]

In 1951, the Hastings & District Old People's Welfare Committee again wrote to the hospital management committee stating that difficulties regarding hospital accommodation for old people suffering from serious or chronic illness were causing great strain upon the resources, equipment and staff of their hostels and flats for old people. The committee asked the HMC to make representations to the regional hospital board pressing them to make contractual arrangements with nursing homes in the area for such cases and the HMC agreed to do this.

A month later the secretary of the HMC reported that he understood the board had written to the OPWC stating that every effort would be made to admit occupants of their flats and hostels with as little delay as possible. The amount of accommodation was being increased as much as possible as resources permitted but 'owing to existing conditions of financial stringency' the board was unable to make indiscriminate use of private nursing home accommodation.[9]

The house committee of St Helen's Hospital was the next to express concern and informed the HMC that it was 'greatly perturbed' about the growing waiting list for female chronic sick patients. Extra staff were requested to open another ward and it was suggested that some patients could be transferred to Battle.

In January 1952 the regional board discussed a scheme to relieve the pressure on hospital beds by boarding out selected patients with 'suitable landladies'. The Women's Royal Voluntary Service was asked to find the landladies, a total of twelve for the region, three of whom had been allotted to the Hastings group. However, the group medical committee recommended that no action should be taken on the suggestion and towards the end of the year the board wrote to the HMC intimating that results had not justified the labour and expense involved and the scheme was being discontinued.

The fourth annual report of Hastings HMC for the year ending 31 December 1952, noted that 'many of the hospitals in the group are now obsolescent...' and referred to the board's restricted capital allocation, £448,000 in 1952/3 and only £399,200 in 1953/4 – which had to be shared between 28 groups in the region. The report by St Helen's house committee noted that Dr Booth had been appointed geriatrician, Part III residents had been removed to local authority homes for the aged and the ward converted to a chronic sick ward for women.

In 1954 Hastings was selected as one of the hospital groups to take part in the pilot study for the Ministry survey of facilities for the chronic sick, the results of which were later to be published as the Boucher Report. Waiting list figures for the year fell from 978 to 759 but the number of chronic sick rose – from 6 to 10, a remarkably low figure in view of the problems experienced in previous years. In 1955 the total rose again to 23, despite a great improvement in the nurse staffing at Battle Hospital which had made it possible to transfer five patients there from St. Helens. In 1956 there was a waiting list of 20 at the end of the September quarter but nursing staff shortages caused problems and admissions were restricted from June until November.

The reliability of waiting lists as an indicator of need was referred to in Boucher's report and certainly it was suggested in Hastings on more than one occasion the figures understated demand because of the reluctance of GPs to refer patients in the belief that there was an acute shortage of beds. At a meeting of the geriatric sub committee in 1958, when a total of 29 patients were reported to be waiting (21 of them for less than a month) the view was again expressed that GPs were not referring patients because they felt it would be useless to do so and that domiciliary arrangements had to be made for patients who should really be nursed in hospital. Certainly there was a shortage of beds, especially for women, during the winter months and, in addition, a considerable number were unavailable, mainly because of nursing staff shortages.

According to Boucher, waiting list figures could be inflated or deflated. It is relatively easy, through an examination of the lists, to determine whether the lists have been inflated by, for example, patients who no longer require admission, or have died. Demonstrating claims that lists reflect somewhat less than the real need is more difficult, nevertheless situations such as those revealed by the Hastings statistics tend to make credible the claims that GPs would refer for admission only cases of extreme urgency based on the belief that there was little hope of admission because of pressure on beds which were already in short supply.

In 1959 Hastings appointed a new geriatric consultant, Dr Irvine, who immediately started to apply the methods of active geriatrics he had learned from Dr Olbrich in Sunderland. Up to the time of Dr Irvine's arrival, the highest number of patients admitted to the group's 210 beds in any one year was 571. In the first two months of 1959, without a single extra bed and with the number of nurses depleted through influenza,

60. Dr R. E. Irvine in his office at St Helen's Hospital in 1973. (Photo: Eric Ford), and 61. The day hospital at St Helen's, the first of its kind in East Sussex. Day hospitals were initially developed for psychiatric services and later modified to become a key service for the emerging specialty of geriatric medicine.

the unit admitted 188 patients, only 25 of whom came off the waiting list after an average wait of four days, the remainder, 153 in all, were admitted as emergencies. Hastings told the regional board that it would like to embark on certain additional expenditure as quickly as possible and pending a full report requested authority to engage additional porters and orderlies for physiotherapy and occupational therapy and to purchase 18 modern geriatric beds at a total cost of approximately £2,800. Dr Irvine also requested the assistance of an additional registrar or junior hospital medical officer because he expected the unit to handle 1,100 patients before the end of the year and to run a geriatric outpatient clinic which was an essential factor in maintaining a high turnover of patients. By June, when the group secretary wrote to Dr Fairley, the senior administrative medical officer (SAMO), confirming the management committee's approval of the request for the appointment of a registrar, the results of the first three months work were available:

> Admissions to the Geriatric Unit at St Helen's totalled 349 during the first quarter of this year, which gives an estimated number in a full year of 1,400. There is now no waiting list, and average stay in the unit is one month approximately. 905 of the admissions are accepted immediately as geriatric emergencies.[10]

The letter also referred to the out patient clinic which was said to feature largely in the success of Dr Irvine's methods and which demanded two mornings a week of his time.

At a meeting of the Geriatric Sub Committee in December, Dr Irvine gave a full report on the geriatric service. Its aims, he said, were to provide a hospital bed immediately to any old person who needed one and by careful investigation, good medical treatment and through rehabilitation to restore him to the community as soon as possible; also, to provide relief for relatives and for other hospital departments. The department had a duty, he said, to provide long stay accommodation for those patients who had little hope of cure or rehabilitation and who for medical or social reasons needed care of a kind which could not be obtained outside hospital. Some 10% fell into this group and about half the geriatric beds were occupied with long stay patients at the time of the report.

For Dr Irvine, unlike his counterparts in Eastbourne and Brighton, the establishment of a day hospital was 'the most important major development needed'. He also favoured the development of a functional assessment unit (comparable to one at Kings College Hospital) at St Helens in which physiotherapists and occupational therapists worked together to help the handicapped regain personal independence. He was critical of the access to wards 9 and 10 which put a strain on the porters and referred to the 'unrest which occurred at the end of May'. He suggested the provision of a ramp to improve access and ultimately a lift. At Alexandra House the accent on rehabilitation instead of custodial care had raised certain difficulties – for example, additional lavatories were urgently needed. At Battle, valuable beds were standing empty for lack of nurses. The hospital was inconveniently situated a mile out of town and 'lack of popular interest in geriatric nursing make it seem unlikely that sufficient staff will ever be recruited locally'. The only answer, he believed, was to second assistant nurses in training at St Helens for a period of geriatric training at Battle. Structurally, the most valuable asset at Battle was its lovely garden and more should be done to see that every patient who could do so had a chance to enjoy it. Two lifts were also needed for access to the top floors.

According to Dr Irvine, one of the main reasons Hastings was able to admit so many patients immediately and did not have a waiting list was because patient turnover was so high (three times the national average). Because of the large amount of work, the unit needed a larger number of staff.

> As far as I am aware, there are only two other geriatric units in the country whose activity is comparable with our own. One is Sunderland, the other is Oxford.[11]

Using these two units as a basis for comparison, he was able to show that there was a case for a significant increase in medical staffing. The proposals he had outlined were, he said ...

> ... designed to give Hastings a geriatric service worthy of her status as the town with the highest population of old people in England. Hastings is dealing today with a population whose age structure is very similar to what is expected to exist throughout England by the end of the century. Geriatrics here, has in a sense, to be 50 years ahead of its time.[12]

Hastings was certainly a leader in the field of geriatric care. In 1960 a comprehensive plan for the development of geriatric service at St Helens Hospital was formulated, new patient visiting patterns were established and new equipment was developed (for example, The St Helens patients locker). Early in 1964, the matron was able to compile an impressive list of articles that had been published in the *Postgraduate Medical Journal*, *The Lancet*, *Health Horizon*, *Nursing Times* and *Medical World News*. More than

100 visitors had been recorded during the previous two years including such well known names as Dr Exton Smith, Miss Doreen Norton and Miss Campbell of the Ministry of Health who came to see for themselves the system of progressive patient care. This was in addition to visitors to Dr Irvine from all over the world, including Rotterdam, Rome and Australia.

And yet for all the success of Dr Irvine and his team in applying 'the methods of active geriatrics', Hastings was not without its problems. Possibly there is an early indication here that the pursuit of active treatment was to produce a situation like the earlier acute/chronic sick divide, many of the erstwhile chronics in the light of new-found knowledge and techniques now becoming acute, capable of responding to treatment. But this still left a residuum, the true chronics, those for whom hospitals could offer little by way of cure, at best only a more tolerable decline towards death. It would hardly be surprising if, by focusing attention of the many patients who could be helped to lead a fuller existence, the spotlight was turned away from those for whom custodial care was the only thing which could be offered. And the numbers of such patients, as the years passed, could only grow: not simply because the proportion of older people was growing, but because, as part of the price of success of the geriatricians, greater numbers of people were being enabled to survive still longer, from old age into 'old old age', to 75 years and above.

Whatever the reason, there were signs in Hastings – a hospital group which was one of the leaders in the provision of geriatric care – that there were unmet needs and problems. Early in 1965, the group secretary wrote to the medical officer of health regarding a report made by the latter on the provision of geriatric beds locally. The letter showed that on the basis of the increased proportion of old people since the 1951 census, the group should have 300 geriatric beds. The original proposal had been for 243-280 beds and this had been reduced in the Ministry's Ten Year Plan to 220. According to the 1961 census, the total population over 65 served by Hastings HMC had risen to 33,185.

Two months later, the board's senior administrative medical officer (SAMO) wrote to the secretary of the hospital management committee saying he had discussed the position of long stay geriatric beds in Hastings with representatives of the county borough council – the mayor, the chairman of the health services committee and the medical officer of health. Their discussion had 'touched on the inter-relationship of Part III accommodation and hospital accommodation'. The council's representatives had said that there were 20 people in Part III who needed long stay hospital beds.

The SAMO raised the question of where an extra 20 beds should go. Battle was excluded because of staffing problems. Bexhill (which contained the greatest concentration of elderly people in the county) suggested itself, but 'not if we are to provide an early solution'. As a stop gap he suggested using Ward 10 at Mount Pleasant Hospital when mental defective patients were moved out, although 'I realise the accommodation is not very good.'[13]

The group secretary was clearly not impressed with the suggestion. Moving the mental defectives was part of the group's long term policy of evacuating these patients from old and unsuitable buildings. Attempting to accommodate geriatric patients on the first and second floors of Ward 10 'would be regarded as a most retrograde step'. Access to the wards was very poor, there were narrow stone staircases which were difficult to negotiate and a lift would be essential. Adequate sluice rooms and bathrooms would also be needed. There were differences in floor levels throughout the wards. In view of the high cost of conversion, the group secretary suggested that the provision of a prefabricated ward would be preferable.[14]

The argument about the best solution to the problem of making extra long stay beds available continued throughout the remainder of the year. There might be other claims with a higher priority, wrote the SAMO, but 'I think it would be very difficult to resist putting additional geriatric beds as your possible first priority'.[15] Dr Irvine believed it was desirable to have some beds at Bexhill and suggested using the women's convalescent hospital there or the interim use of Alexandra House.

Consideration was also given to Battle (although this was remote from the town, the bus service was not good, and there were lift and staffing problems), Darvell Hall (a TB and chest hospital at Robertsbridge) and Eversfield Chest Hospital (at St Leonard's). The latter was probably the best solution the group secretary told the regional board. 30 beds could be made available there, although a lift would be needed in the male block in support of which the matron wrote 'should anyone slip whilst carrying a patient up and down those stairs ... compensation would be considerable'.[16] The board agreed to pursue the Eversfield suggestion further, perhaps, in view of the financial question, proceeding in two stages. In August, the group secretary told the board the proposal to provide beds at Eversfield Chest Hospital had been approved by the management committee and was its fourth priority in the capital programme.

Three months later the board indicated it had approved improvements to the female block at Eversfield to provide 15 beds for long stay geriatric patients, ten of whom would be transferred from Mount Pleasant Hospital. The estimated cost was £4,528 and the scheme would replace approved improvements at St Helen's Hospital costing £5,000. Even then, twenty years after the end of the Second World War, constraints on capital expenditure were still severe: only the least costly part of the scheme was to go ahead, and in response to the HMC's requests for new beds and commodes for the new unit, the deputy secretary wrote: Why are 15 new beds needed? Why all of the Hi Lo type [which possessed distinct advantages for both patients and nurses]? Why a commode for every patient? If these were considered to be essential, please put up a case for them 'For the present, please limit your purchases of these items to 5 beds and 5 commodes'.[17]

12. Eastbourne: A Desperate Search for Nurses

There was only one reply to an advertisement in Switzerland. Other advertisements were placed in France and Belgium. Dr Brown suggested recruiting auxiliaries from Jamaica but an enquiry by the matron to the principal nursing officer there was not fruitful — December 1959-February 1960.

Like neighbouring Hastings, Eastbourne contained an elderly population well above the national average. Whilst the two hospital groups suffered from similar problems, however, the approach in Eastbourne was rather different. Throughout the period 1948–1974, geriatric care was the responsibility of the physician superintendent of the former municipal hospital. Unlike Hastings and Brighton, there was no appointment of a geriatric specialist from another part of the country to take responsibility for elderly care.

From the very outset, Eastbourne was plagued by nursing staff shortages. These were especially acute in the former municipal hospital, St Mary's, despite an early decision to free the nurses there from 'the restrictions with regard to absence from the hospital during off duty times' subject to signing in when returning to the hospital after 11 p.m.

In August 1948, when the nursing staff shortage was 'accentuating the acute shortage of beds which is now very serious' at St Mary's, the hospital management committee was told that the region's senior medical officer and his deputy had visited the group and engaged an architect to report on the possible provision of more accommodation for nurses.[1]

In September a suggestion that a hotel should be leased to provide extra nursing accommodation was forwarded to the region. At the end of the year, the group medical committee made a suggestion based on the experience of Portsmouth, which was to bring more positive results: advertisements were placed for 'active women' to work as nursing attendants with 'hours to suit the individual'.[2] Over 100 applications were received with the result that St Mary's was able to reopen one ward and a waiting list of applicants established in the hope that it would be possible to open more beds later.

In the summer of 1949 there was confirmation that Eastbourne felt it was suffering from an insufficiency of chronic sick beds. According to the minutes of the ad hoc medical planning committee there was a 'shortage of acute beds caused by so many being occupied by the chronic sick'. 40 chronic sick patients were reported to be in acute beds and the number of chronic sick beds (60) was considered to be 'totally inadequate' with 30 urgent cases awaiting admission to St Mary's. 'Eastbourne is a difficult area with a high proportion of old people,' commented the committee, 'eventually 150 beds are required'. The committee suggested that 100 beds were required immediately, 60 at St Mary's, 40 in two pavilions at the isolation hospital, Downside.[3]

In April 1950 the allocation sub committee noted that 132 chronic sick patients were being treated, 32 more than the 100 beds allocated in the regional plan. The patients were all a mixture of chronic sick and moribund patients, and there was no room for 'pure geriatric cases'. Nor was there room for those chronic sick who might respond to treatment. The following month it was reported that the excess number of chronic sick patients being treated had risen to 41. It was proposed that a local practitioner should be appointed to relieve Dr Brown, St Mary's physician superintendent, by visiting the patients at Downside Hospital weekly and that he should also visit waiting list cases in their homes.[4]

In December 1951, there was a fall in demand for male patients. However, because there was a long waiting list for female beds the general medical committee approved a suggestion that a 28 bedded male ward should receive female patients At the same time, a 15 bedded female ward would become a male ward; moreover, the surplus male staff were to be allowed to nurse female patients.

A year later the committee considered the additional staff that would be necessary to give any rehabilitation. A house officer post had been placed on the priority list and additional nursing staff had been approved 'when funds were available'. An almoner was not considered a high priority while physiotherapy needs might be met by rearranging existing staff. The occupational therapist would devote more time to the chronic patients, less to the acute.[5]

In 1953, there were difficulties with junior medical staffing. No satisfactory replies were received to several advertisements for a geriatric house physician and it was recommended that the post should be upgraded to SHO (senior house officer). At the HMC's fourth annual meeting (at which the guest speaker was Dr Boucher), the chairman mentioned that 20% of hospital beds in Eastbourne contained chronic sick patients and 'stressed the magnitude of the problem of the elderly sick'. Two years later, he again referred to the continuing difficulties of providing sufficient beds for old people and to a 'similar lack' suffered by the local authority.[6]

Eastbourne's waiting list figures, as in Hastings, were considered to be misleading. The physician responsible for geriatric patients agreed with a statement made by the chairman of the general medical committee that general practitioners 'are fully aware that the possibility of admission is remote and therefore refrain from adding to the list unless the case is extremely urgent'.[7]

In 1957 five infectious diseases beds were made available for the chronic sick on the understanding they would revert back to infectious diseases beds if required but it was not until consideration was given to the Boucher report later in the year that there is evidence of pressure for more radical measures to deal with the chronic sick problem. Dr Brown told his colleagues that practically all the circular's recommendations had been implemented in Eastbourne but that the number of beds available fell below the national average. The matter was debated at length by the Eastbourne and District Joint Health Consultative Committee and a letter was sent to the Minister stating that the number of beds was 'totally insufficient' to meet the demand imposed by high numbers of elderly residents and requesting the provision of a long stay annexe for senile confused patients.[8]

The HMC responded by admitting six geriatric patients to fever beds at Downside Hospital as a temporary measure. A letter to the regional board stressed the hardship being caused by the shortage of geriatric beds and urged the acquisition of All Saints (a convalescent hospital that had been run by an order of nuns). The regional board chairman agreed later to discuss this personally with the Minister of Health and it eventually bore fruit. In April 1959 an ad hoc committee was established to plan the development of the hospital which the HMC planned to open with a minimum of 20 geriatric beds 'as soon as practicable'.[9]

At the initial meeting of the committee it was decided to plan for 48 convalescent beds on the ground floor with 108 female geriatric beds on the first floor. It was estimated that a total of 89 staff would be required: one medical, 48 nursing and 40 others. In July the committee wrote to the regional board regarding the decisions it had taken. The maximum number of beds being planned for had been adjusted to 129 – 54 convalescent and 75 chronic sick. All patients were to be female, an adjustment in the numbers for male chronic sick being made at Downside. The cost of adaptations was limited to £5,000 excluding furnishings which the RHB hoped could be kept down to a further £5,000. The committee decided that for the time being the first floor ward should not be opened as it was not possible to include the initial cost of adaptation and furnishing. It was also agreed that the opportunity should be taken of acquiring the items required cheaply from other hospitals no longer requiring them. In fact, furniture came from Stepney, Mid Sussex and Dartford.

In October one of the recurring problems of geriatric care became evident: the matron reported that she had recruited sufficient staff to open the first floor ward with the exception of staff nurses. To date, she said, she had been unable to recruit any. Dr Brown suggested opening a staff nursery to encourage married nurses with young children to apply. He also suggested recruiting staff from the continent. The committee doubted whether the cost and difficulty of establishing a nursery was justified but agreed with the recruitment suggestion and also decided to approach the local newspaper to publicise their difficulty. However, there was only one reply to an advertisement in Switzerland. Other advertisements were placed in France and Belgium. Dr Brown suggested recruiting auxiliaries from Jamaica but an enquiry by the matron to the principal nursing officer there was not fruitful.

The recruitment problem was serious enough to warrant the attention of the hospital management committee. The closure of St. Luke's Home had reduced the number of beds available for the admission of geriatric patients from the waiting list and the situation was made even worse by the HMC's inability to open all the authorised beds at All Saints. A letter from Dr Jack, hon. secretary of the Eastbourne local medical committee, urged the HMC to expedite the provision of more geriatric beds by taking every possible step to recruit nursing staff. Nevertheless, the minutes of the meeting noted 'suggestions that large scale recruitment abroad should be attempted were not considered to be a satisfactory solution' to the problem.[10]

In April 1960 the geriatric consultant again wrote to the HMC 'urging the necessity of recruiting more staff from abroad' but at the same meeting which considered his letter the HMC's view was endorsed by the regional nursing officer who, following a visit to All Saints Hospital, wrote stating that she could not agree with the suggestion that nursing auxiliaries should be recruited direct from the colonies. Nor did she consider it advisable to send the matron to the continent or Eire for recruiting purposes. In her view, the best policy was to obtain approval for the establishment of an assistant nurse training school in the Eastbourne group as soon as practicable.[11]

Addressing the HMC's annual meeting at the end of the year, the mayor, a former chairman of St Mary's Hospital committee, 'noted with pleasure the many improvements that had been brought about in the hospital' and welcomed the increase in old people's beds which had been provided by the acquisition of All Saints. She also assured the committee that the corporation would do its best to increase accommodation for old people not in need of hospital treatment.[12] The following year, however, the chairman told the annual general meeting that he expected the shortage of nurses to be a problem in 1962 and referred to the possible establishment of an enrolled nurse training school. Within a month of this meeting, the HMC was noting that 20 beds were closed at All Saints, eleven because of the 'current shortage of nurses', the remaining nine had never been staffed. Later in the year, because of the financial situation, the regional board ordered a standstill in nursing recruitment. Only ward sisters and higher grades could be replaced and the board placed an embargo on advertisements for pupil and student nurses. When the HMC was told of this situation at its meeting in December, the minutes noted 'nursing staff in geriatric units are constantly changing and failure to replace those leaving will place an added burden on those in post'.[13] Those attending the HMC's annual general meeting held two days later were told that 66 per cent of the committee's £¾ million budget was spent on salaries and wages. The Ministry and the regional board were said to be anxious because the NHS budget as a whole showed signs of being overspent and, as a result, it might be necessary, in order to balance the local budget, 'to effect economies in the coming months'.[14]

The shortage of money, however, had already placed constraints on the development of All Saints Hospital. A year earlier the HMC had told the hospital's house committee there were insufficient funds to provide dayrooms for two wards, Devonshire and Meads. Now the HMC was asked to reconsider 'as a matter of importance, the need for ... dayroom accommodation for all long stay patients'.[15] Later in the year, the house visitors also complained about 'unheated, cold toilet compartments' at the hospital.[16] In April 1963 they noted that some beds in Seaside ward were still not provided with box spring mattresses while in 1964 there were complaints by relatives about the poor quality of bed clothing which led to a request to the HMC for more money for linen in the next financial year.

In spite of these problems, the house visitors noted that there was a 'happy, cheerful atmosphere' at the hospital and that many long stay patients expressed their appreciation of the care they were given,[17] views which were expressed quite frequently in visitors' reports at this time.

But it was the shortage of staff which dominated committee reports during the 1960s. In 1965, the geriatric consultant, Dr Brown, asserted that 'the public did not appreciate the extremely serious situation' and the chairman of the HMC was asked to make an appeal in the local press. Three years later, another local newspaper appeal resulted in 52 enquiries as a result of which it was hoped to fully staff Downside Hospital. However, the situation at All Saints remained very difficult and it was agreed by the HMC that the chairman, vice chairman and group secretary should meet the press and give details of the situation.

Eventually the situation was relieved to some extent at nursing auxiliary level through the recruitment of a number of 'continental girls who seemed, like their colleagues, to be pleasant and intelligent young ladies',[18] the matron told All Saints house committee – although she was later to give the committee examples of some of the problems 'when staffing depended so much on young nursing auxiliaries from Scandinavian and other European countries.'[19] The five Scandinavians started work in Eastbourne on July 1st and by August the matron was at last able to report that all beds at All Saints were fully staffed.

13. Mid Sussex: A New General Hospital and an Old Workhouse

The rash of glass walled primary and secondary schools built since the Second World War [contrasted] with the 'poor law institution turned hospital' making do 'with tasteless internal redecoration and inadequate augmentation of its primitive lavatory accommodation'
— *Former dean of Manchester University Medical School (1973).*

The situation in the Mid-Sussex hospital group was quite different from the other three. Unlike Brighton, Eastbourne and Hastings, Mid Sussex had no large county borough as a centre of population and being inland was less attractive as a retirement area. The total population served by Mid Sussex HMC was smaller, the proportion of residents of pensionable age was less, and the proportion of available beds to elderly residents was much higher.

Despite its relatively favourable situation, Mid Sussex did not escape the problems encountered by other East Sussex HMCs. Management committee minutes dated 7th December 1948, showed that there were 36 chronic sick beds allocated at West Hylands but the Cuckfield Rural District Council did not believe this figure to be sufficient to meet local needs. In a letter to the HMC the council complained that local medical practitioners were experiencing considerable difficulties in securing the admission of aged sick persons and sought an assurance that the situation would be improved as quickly as possible.

In April 1950, the imbalance of male and female beds was highlighted by a family doctor. He told a meeting at Burgess Hill Women's Institute that it was impossible to obtain accommodation for female patients whilst men could be admitted within 48 hours. The chairman of the HMC considered it deplorable that 'such an emotional appeal should be made to the Women's Institute unsupported by the facts, and given wide publicity in the press'. It was decided to prepare a draft letter for publication in the local newspapers. According to this, there were 25 female beds at Cuckfield Hospital and 51 female beds and 37 male beds at Pouchlands.

The letter also gave the number of beds in Mid-Sussex for aged people who were not sick but who were able to take care of themselves – 60 female beds at Cuckfield and 14 female and 11 male at Pouchlands. This showed, the letter continued, that the HMC appreciated the greater demand for female beds and had attempted to meet it.

Not surprisingly, the letter referred to the fact that considerably more chronic sick beds were available in the area than normal. It attempted to explain why the demand for women's beds was greater. Most men married women younger than themselves and when they fell ill tended to be nursed at home by their wives. Elderly women, on the other hand, were more often spinsters or widows who could not look after themselves. This explained 'the reasons for the greater demand and the more consistent long term occupation of female beds'.

The letter concluded by asserting 'the problem of the aged sick is being tackled in the Mid Sussex area with considerable vigour and understanding' and added that the HMC had taken active steps to institute rehabilitation for the chronic sick by way of physiotherapy and occupational therapy in its hospitals.

The letter concluded by asserting 'the problem of the aged sick is being tackled in this Mid Sussex area with considerable vigour and understanding' and that the HMC had taken active steps to institute rehabilitation for the chronic sick by way of physiotherapy and occupational therapy in its hospitals.

A proposal made in 1952 to change a large chronic sick ward at Pouchlands Hospital from male to female patients provides an illustration of the problems involved. The hospital secretary opposed the move, saying it would lead to redundancy among the male nurses. Moreover, extra female nurses would be needed and at the time it was impossible to obtain sufficient staff for the existing female wards.

In 1950, the responsibility for chronic sick services in Mid Sussex was still being undertaken by local general practitioners. At a meeting of the medical committee in June, however, there was a discussion about the establishment of a geriatric service and the chairman announced that a consultant appointment would be made in the near future. In fact, the group was to share the services of the Brighton consultant, Dr Firth, who was also given the task of co-ordinating the geriatric service in the whole of the county in accordance with the regional plan.

Dr Firth's appointment was in fact a benefit to the elderly chronic sick of Brighton and Lewes for he was able to use surplus beds in Mid Sussex to make up for the shortfall in the Brighton group. Nevertheless, in Mid Sussex, as elsewhere, the familiar complaint of general practitioners being unable to find beds for their elderly patients was experienced, just as it was in Hastings, Eastbourne and Brighton. The question of unused male beds continued to be raised while the problems through shortage of staff (for example at Pouchlands) were also being encountered.

Progress at Cuckfield

West Hylands was the first East Sussex institution to undergo major changes following 1948. Thanks to the developments undertaken by the Canadian military authorities it was well placed to develop under the name Cuckfield Hospital as the main general hospital for the district. The wartime huts that were lying empty or being used for storage were redecorated, equipped and put into use as wards. The administrative offices were set up in the main building and the remaining elderly ambulant infirm together with some mentally sub-normal patients were transferred, some to the wards, others elsewhere. Approval to establish a nurse training school was given in 1952 and the first ten nurses graduated two years later.

By 1953 the various specialties had been developed at the hospital. Much of the acute medicine and surgery previously carried out at Haywards

62. *The main building at Cuckfield Hospital that housed the administrative offices. Part of the first floor was converted into accommodation for resident medical staff and the other part became a preliminary training school for nurses.*

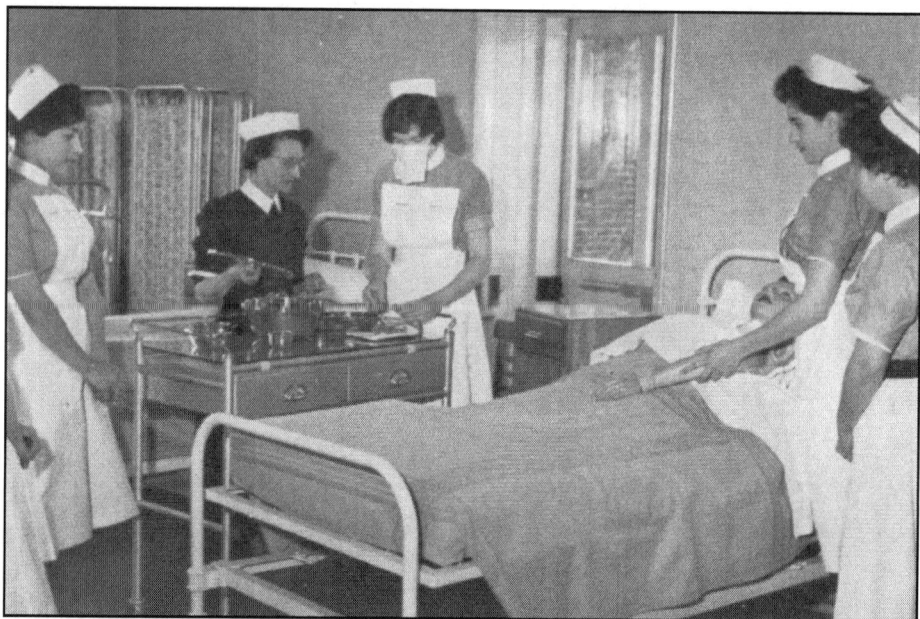

63. Nurses in the classroom in the new assistant nurse training school at Cuckfield that opened in 1952. The first ten nurses graduated in 1954.

64. VIPs at the opening of the children's ward at Cuckfield in 1953 that was originally planned for Haywards Heath Hospital. From the right, consultant surgeon Mr J.R.H. Turton, Mrs Joslin, wife of the group secretary Mr Bill Joslin, Mrs Turton who opened the ward with Miss Joslin, Matron, Miss Richmond, and Mr Joslin.

Heath Hospital had been transferred to Cuckfield. The hospital was divided into two parts: Administration was in front with the maternity and surgical wards in the old infirmary behind. Medical, orthopaedic, gynaecological, geriatric and paediatric beds were situated in the hutted wards. The number of staffed beds had increased to 163 for general use with an additional 60 beds for long-stay patients. The huts that had been heated with centrally placed coal or coke burning stoves were provided with central heating and later dayrooms were added, some provided by the hospital's League of Friends.

Extra accommodation was made available for nurses and two bungalows were built near the medical wards for married medical staff. A new out-patient department was opened and the following year, in 1954, the Minister of Health, Iain Macleod, formally opened the new operating theatres. Cuckfield Hospital then became Cuckfield General Hospital.

The last refuge?

Pouchlands Hospital provides an example of what was a very real problem so far as many patients were concerned – the poor law origins of many of the county's chronic sick hospitals. Progress at Chailey was somewhat slower than in neighbouring Cuckfield, possibly reflecting the fact that conditions there were so poor. Evidence of this emerged in the retirement reflections of the medical officer who was first appointed in 1948.

65. New dayrooms between two of the hutted wards.

According to Dr Caldwell, the subnormal wards were like a prison. 'There were railings round the exercise yards. The wards were locked and the Superintendent Nurse carried the keys on a chain.' There was no plaster on the walls. The stone stairs leading to the chapel were worn by the feet of countless paupers. On its brick walls was painted the message: 'O Lord, we thank you for all our blessings.'

The geriatric wards appear to have been no better. There were no dayrooms, only balconies. There was very little lavatory accommodation, and the patients were not allowed out of bed.' The doctor also recalled the sight of 'little white heads in beautifully made beds ... 'there were white sheets, white pillows, white-haired heads resting on them. But underneath the covers was a sea of fifth.'

> I never imagined that things like this existed. It was Dickensian. This was a Poor Law Institution and nothing you or I or anyone else said made any difference.[3]

Four years later, in 1952, the house committee made proposals to the HMC to upgrade the status of the hospital 'which is still regarded in the locality as a workhouse'. When the HMC advocated a policy of open days at its hospitals, however, the house committee declared itself not to be in favour of the idea.[4] Why this should be is not clear. Certainly it contrasts strangely with the attitude at its former workhouse neighbour at Newhaven which had a policy of throwing open its doors to the public primarily by means of an annual garden party which in the event of inclement weather actually took place on the wards. According to the organiser:

> Public relations and local interest may also benefit as a result of a garden party or fete, for it provides members of the general public with an opportunity to see the hospital and, what is probably more important, to sense the atmosphere and spirit existing within it ... Public goodwill is of particular value to the hospital which in former days functioned as a public assistance institution. Whatever may be our feelings with regard to the old regime, there can be no doubt that present impressions of our chronic sick hospitals, for example, are too often coloured by past associations.[5]

Perhaps the house committee's reluctance stemmed from the fact that conditions at Pouchlands had failed to improve significantly since it became an NHS hospital. According to the retirement reflections of another member of staff, painter George Murphy, who recalled the time he first went to work at Pouchlands 25 years before – 1953, the year of the coronation:

66. *The chapel at Pouchlands Hospital before it was converted in 1960 into a staff dining hall. 67. A recent picture of part of the former workhouse. In the 1950s and beyond it housed what were then known as mentally subnormal patients. The bell-tower on the roof of the main building was known locally as the spike. In earlier times the bell was rung at intervals through the day to summon inmates to their meals and to wake them in the mornings.*

It was a workhouse. The walls were unplastered and when we had our weekly dances the flaking paint descended from the walls. Next morning I had to go in and sweep it all up.

Even in 1953, the floors were bare wooden boards. There were only two paid domestic staff in the whole hospital. The floors were scrubbed and polished by patient labour. Other patients spent long hours every day, slicing bread by hand and peeling potatoes.[6]

The fact that so many chronic sick patients were still accommodated in former poor law institutions was given prominence by the publication of Peter Townsend's survey of residential institutions in 1962.[7] Although primarily a condemnation of the concept of residential care for the elderly, Townsend's research confirmed that, despite the efforts of the Ministry of Health and enlightened hospital boards and management committees, many elderly chronic sick were still being cared for in sub-standard conditions in buildings with workhouse associations by staff many of whom were imbued with attitudes coloured by the old regime. Hospitals for the elderly in the early 1960s were still in a state of transition from the old order.

What is more, the pace of change in hospital provision was lagging behind new provision for the elderly in residential homes by the local authorities. In East Sussex the greater part of hospital provision was in the former workhouses – in its entirety in Mid Sussex and Brighton and to a large extent in Hastings. Even Eastbourne, despite its acquisition of All Saints and its use of the former isolation hospital, Downside, still relied to a large extent on St Mary's Hospital. According to Townsend's figures, however, only 47% of elderly people in residential care provided by East Sussex County Council were being accommodated in former public assistance institutions. In the county boroughs the figures were even more impressive: Hastings 16%, Brighton 9%, Eastbourne 0%.

The reasons for this disparity are no doubt varied but one of the underlying causes has almost certainly to do with cost. This was especially the case in 1972 during the 'make do and mend' years. At that time the capital cost of providing a bed in an old people's home was £4,000. To provide a bed in a district general hospital cost more than £10,000.[8]

14. Press, Pressure Groups and Hospital Scandals

What in God's name are we doing, to inflict this on old men and women, once dear to those among us? – C.H. Rolph, New Statesman, 1966.

Despite readers letters and articles in newspapers such as *The Times* and the *Manchester Guardian*, and continuing fears of the elderly, just how much did the country at large know about the former workhouses now providing hospital care for the aged and infirm?

Writing in the *British Hospital and Social Services Journal* in 1967, the comparison made by Dr T.N. Rudd, a Southampton geriatrician, of the lack of knowledge about the way old people were cared for in hospital with the 'ignorance expressed by many Germans as to events in wartime concentration camps',[1] was quite apposite.

Just as the advancing Allies armies opened the gates of the concentration camps at the end of the Second World War to reveal for the first time the horrors within, so the effect of the publication of Barbara Robb's book *Sans Everything* in 1967[2] was to throw open the doors of the country's hospital wards for the elderly to reveal to the public gaze a state of affairs which many found difficult to believe.

Prior to 1967, there was little to indicate that the care received by elderly hospital patients gave any real cause for concern. Although there were deficiencies in many of the buildings in which patients were treated, medical care, as a result of the development of the new speciality of geriatrics, was improving. But little was known about the daily life of patients on the wards and information about the standards of nursing care was virtually non-existent.

One exception, although it did not have the impact of *Sans Everything*, was the publication in 1964 of a Penguin Special, *What's Wrong With Hospitals?* This was inspired by hospital patients' experiences where, in author Gerda Cohen's view, despite receiving 'the very best of medical attention', they had 'no rights, no dignity, no status'.[3]

Cohen took as her starting point the 1945 Hospital Surveys with their references to bare, overcrowded, large wards, primitive nursing facilities and 'the reproach of the masses of undiagnosed and untreated cases of

143

the chronic type which litter our P.A institutions.'[4] In her view, it would have been odd had no reforms brightened the years since 1945, and she instanced the development of geriatric medicine and the policy of active rehabilitation which invigorated the work in some chronic hospitals. However, despite the improvements she still found them 'at best an inferior workshop for reconditioning, at worst a long dreary halt before the grave'.[5]

Sans Everything

The publication of *Sans Everything* arose from visits in 1965 by Mrs Barbara Robb to an elderly friend, Miss Wills, in Friern Hospital. Mrs Robb, who had trained as a psychotherapist during the war, was accompanied by eleven of her associates, including Lord Strabolgi. Concerned about the way Miss Wills was being treated, they eventually managed to secure her transfer to a convent home.

Six months later, Lord Strabolgi made a speech in the House of Lords about conditions existing in certain old people's wards at the hospital. Then, according to Mrs Robb:

> The press took up the story, and Lord Strabolgi and I received a great many letters from members of the public, notifying us of hospital wards all over the country where they had seen conditions strikingly similar to those he had described in his speech ... Approaches we made to the Ministry of Health were anything but reassuring. So on October 10, 1965 we formed AEGIS (Aid for the Elderly in Government Institutions), with Lord Strabolgi as our president, and on November 10 that year a letter was published in *The Times* protesting about the cruelties endured by many people in hospital and inviting the public to send us instances of these.[6]

Admittedly much of the discussion at this stage concerned mental hospitals, but as many old people with psychiatric problems ended up in these institutions. Moreoever, it later transpired that what happened to the patients in mental hospitals was also witnessed in general hospitals.

Lord Strabolgi argued that many old people who were not psychiatric cases were being admitted to mental hospitals simply because there was a great shortage of old peoples homes or because many homes were unable to take those who were incontinent or enfeebled. Many of these hospitals were good, Strabolgi continued, but some were a 'disgrace to a civilised country'.

He then referred to the practice of 'stripping':

This means that on entry, all personal belongings were removed, including spectacles, deaf aids and dentures. There are no personal lockers. The food is appalling. In some cases the last meal is served at half past three in the afternoon … Without their spectacles they cannot read or sew. There is rapid deterioration through boredom.[7]

Also to the possibility of cruel treatment:

The nursing staff do their best but they are overworked which leads, I think, to lack of attention and even, in some cases, although it is not the fault of the staff, indirectly to cruelty.[8]

When asked whether he was aware of 'the practice in some hospitals of depriving elderly or mentally disordered patients of their spectacles, dentures and hearing aids', Kenneth Robinson, the Minister of Health replied:

I deplore this practice … which I am aware is still followed in the minority of hospitals … I intend to issue guidance to hospitals and local health and welfare authorities in due course.[9]

Mrs. Robb and her associates were clearly not satisfied with this assurance and the formation of AEGIS and the letter to *The Times* set in motion the process that was to result in the publication of *Sans Everything* in June 1967.

The first print run sold out and the book was reprinted before publication largely as a result, presumably, from publicity arising from a pre-publication mental health week feature in the *Sunday Times*. This devoted over a page to two case reports taken from the book which were accompanied by comments by journalist Hugo Young. The *Sunday Times* called its feature 'The Old in Hospital – a Public Scandal.' The extracts were headlined. 'You can't be a nurse, dear; you don't hit or shout at us'. And 'We've had no bread delivered to the ward for four or five days.'

Also prominently featured were two quotes: 'I've seen six or seven people bathed in the same water until it was coal black', attributed to a male nurse in a northern mental hospital, and 'Dentures often disappeared soon after a patient was admitted, hairbrushes and combs were used by the nurses to do the hair in a whole ward'.[10]

The book itself consisted in the main of two sections. The first included evidence of the way elderly patients were treated by six nurses writing pseudonymously, evidence by two social workers, and Diary of a Nobody; which was Mrs. Robb's account of her visits to 'Miss Wills', the elderly friend whose treatment was the initial cause of her concern.

The first chapter, 'Cruelty in the Old People's Ward', was in fact reproduced from the journal *Mental Health* and confirmed that the problems were not confined to mental hospitals. The author, C.H. Rolph, had written an article for the *New Statesman* in 1966 about the plight of the aged in geriatric wards which resulted in 'a steady flow of letters'.[11] One of these was from an auxiliary nurse working in a geriatric hospital in the Midlands who, with the help of a colleague, had made a list of things from which their confused patients suffered from the most. Rolph asked her to send it to him.

> Selecting my words with responsible concern, I say that it is a catalogue of cruelty, callousness, filth and depersonalisation such as I have not read since I was reviewing the reports of the Nuremburg trials – and such as I thought never to read again ... What in God's name are we all doing, to inflict this on old men and women once dear to those among us?[12]

Reaction to the book was mixed and far from muted. A delegate to the Confederation of Health Service Employees (COHSE) conference at Eastbourne said it should have been called "Knock Everything"; another, from one of the hospitals concerned said it would be untrue to give a picture of absolutely no cruelty: 'There is sadism in every profession'.[13]

A charge nurse from the West Middlesex Hospital told the Royal College of Nursing (RCN) conference that the book had been extremely damaging and had harmed the work of nurses in geriatric hospitals. However, the chairman of the college's psychiatric committee, a hospital matron, said that not one member of the committee denied the validity of 'the ghastly material' contained in the book: 'some felt very guilty that lay people had highlighted the problem'.[14]

Reviewing the book in the *British Medical Journal* Dr E. Woodford-Williams commented:

> The danger is the lack of facts may enable it to be too easily dismissed, for those who have worked with the aged know that there is some truth in the accusations. Most voluntary and hospital workers will know of geriatric institutions where the doctors bring nothing of modern medicine to the care of their patients and where the nurses are more concerned about their authority and their concept of discipline than about understanding and kindness.[15]

A number of hospital authorities responded to the book by inviting newspapers to send reporters to visit their hospitals and to talk freely to staff and patients. At Newhaven Downs Hospital, in response to a suggestion by senior nursing staff, an open day was held so that local people could see for themselves 'that long-stay geriatric hospitals are rarely the kind of places that the more sensational reports would lead people to believe'.[16]

One of the problems of *Sans Everything* and some of the press reports that followed was that they were inclined to focus on the more extreme acts of cruelty perpetrated on patients. Without this, of course, it is possible they would not have attracted the same degree of attention. On the other hand, highlighting the worst acts probably also tended at first to mask the wider and probably more general problems of the standards of care.

There was little evidence in the Thirties to contradict Crowther's view that boredom, not violence, was the hallmark of life in the former workhouses. It was not until the accounts of former patients published in 1943 that a different picture began to emerge. *Sans Everything* demonstrated that by the 1960s, some 20 years after the establishment of the NHS, quite considerable problems really did exist.

But were the complaints of ill-treatment merely isolated instances or were they symptomatic of a more widespread disease? *The Times* reviewer of *Sans Everything* who observed that there were 'not enough to be regarded as a representative sample, but too many to be regarded as isolated aberrations'[17] was probably quite near the mark. Even as inquiries

68. *Students from Brighton's School of Nursing visited the hospital to act as programme sellers at the open day at Newhaven Downs that had been suggested by senior nursing staff.*

were proceeding into the *Sans Everything* complaints, two others, which received far less publicity, were reporting.

In South-East England, for example, Dartford Group HMC stated that an inquiry had shown there was no cruelty to old people in its hospitals. However, the committee did find that 'reprisals' were taken against patients for worrying nurses or attendants. These included leaving them on bedpans for too long or refusing to give them one.[18] Meanwhile, in Scotland, an independent committee of inquiry issued its report on allegations of cruelty at Randolph Wemyss Memorial Hospital in Fife. In one incident a male orderly dealing with an elderly man who was proving 'somewhat unco-operative' twisted one of the patients arms backwards and up behind his back until he screamed out in pain. A second incident concerned a pupil nurse. She placed a sticking plaster over an elderly woman's mouth to keep her quiet while she was being bathed. A third concerned a patient propped up in bed who slipped and spilled his porridge. A male orderly lifted the patient up and pushed him backwards 'where he was made to lie back in a most uncomfortable and nasty mess'. In a fourth incident, a male member of staff struck a patient's wrist with the side of his hand when the patient would not let go of a handrail.[19] Unlike the *Sans Everything* incidents, all these complaints were found proved by the inquiry.

What is not known, however, is how many other inquiries were held that were not made public. In East Sussex, for example, members of the Mid-Sussex hospital management committee were convinced that all was not well at Pouchlands Hospital, the group's long-stay geriatric unit.

When the HMC received the press statement from the Ministry regarding the *Sans Everything* allegations in July 1967, it immediately set up two working parties to look into the position at Cuckfield Hospital and Pouchlands. After some delay, their reports were presented at a special meeting, closed to the press and public, when a working party member Mr Wray, reported:

> Although there was a great deal of evidence of dedicated service by members of the staff at Pouchlands Hospital, they had come to the conclusion that there was evidence of some inhumanity in the treatment of patients. This, he indicated, could never be beyond a shadow of doubt, unless a full judicial inquiry was conducted.[20]

Mr Wray hoped that no disciplinary action would be taken or contemplated against any members of staff. The hospital should be permitted to continue without disturbance of any kind, thus allowing the normal retirement of the present matron to take place and enable the new matron to take over smoothly. The meeting agreed to set up three committees to look at various aspects of the report which, on the advice of the chairman, members then handed over to the secretary 'for safe keeping'.[21]

What happened next is not clear. The minutes of a meeting held four months later indicate that the original report was 'no longer in possession of the committee'[22] and that the regional board had subsequently carried out its own inquiry. One member of the HMC had resigned and one, who had participated in the original Pouchlands inquiry, was not re-appointed. The RHB invited Miss Marchant, matron of Cuckfield Hospital, to look into nursing matters at Pouchlands. The HMC decided to rescind the motion setting up the three committees and agreed to await Miss Marchant's report before taking further action.

Mr Wray, who had presented the original report, was clearly not happy with the situation. He could not accept there was no cause for anxiety at the hospital. He felt that the regional board expected improvements as a result of a new medical arrangement, its proposals to introduce staff training, and the appointment of Miss Marchant supported his view. At the next meeting of the HMC, Mrs Lister Williams, a state registered nurse who was the third member of the group originally reporting on Pouchlands, asked to place on record that she endorsed Mr Wray's views.

In the event, Miss Marchant was largely supportive of the nursing staff. The group secretary wrote to the regional board saying there was still a chronic shortage of nursing staff at Pouchlands that 'must reflect on the care given to patients, but quoted from Miss Marchant's report:

> ... because of the unsparing labours of nursing staff all patients receive basic nursing care, at least as far as their physical needs are concerned. The nursing staff, however, feel far from satisfied with the care the patients are receiving.[23]

The group secretary pointed out that there were only 52 staff in post compared with an approved establishment of 60 and a proposed increase to 69.8. 15 beds were unstaffed and out of use. The HMC had therefore recommended an extension of staff transport in order 'to tap the manpower resources in Burgess Hill, Wivelsfield Green and Plumpton'. Extra revenue was requested to cover the cost of a minibus and drivers, as well as for extra staff and additional resident staff accommodation.

Miss Marchant's report, which was enclosed with the group secretary's letter, showed there were vacancies for trained staff and auxiliaries. More than half the staff were part-time. Many worked 'school hours' and very few were on duty at weekends. Although attempts were made to persuade new recruits to work unsociable hours, it was felt 'better to have good care given to patients for part of the day and minimal care for the rest of the 24 hours than barely adequate care round the clock'.[24]

According to the report, nine members of staff came from overseas. Although they worked hard and were kind, their different cultural backgrounds were a barrier to communication with the elderly patients. There was also a shortage of domestic staff that meant nurses had to wash up, clean lockers and sweep floors. There were also recruitment problems because the hospital was isolated. It was not easy for staff to have a full social life and most objected to sharing double rooms in the staff accommodation.

For many nurses, Miss Marchant continued, working in a long-stay hospital represented a career dead-end and 'although it is unlikely that the stigma of the workhouse remains, by many Pouchlands Hospital is still regarded as a refuge for those for whom there is no future'.[25]

Ward accommodation was housed on two floors which were served by a lift. Partitions were being erected between groups of four beds together with a call system, radio and bed-head lights. Although this would fill a great need, in other parts of the hospital there were no bed curtains and no individual lights. Beds appeared too close together and many were under windows which if opened, must cause discomfort to the occupants. Some of the equipment was old fashioned and wooden cupboards for patients' clothing was required.

The principal criticism of the patients' day was that 'in order that patients may be washed and breakfasted by 8.am it is necessary that the washing of patients begins at 3.30 am ... the most disturbing feature of this early wakening is that, there being no individual bed lights the ward lights are put on.' Nurses were aware that the practice was undesirable but the staff/patient ratio made it impossible to find enough staff to feed and attend to those patients who needed help at breakfast time.

In conclusion, Miss Marchant expressed 'admiration for the devotion and diligence' of the nursing staff but commented:

The lot of the geriatric patient [compared to the mentally subnormal patients also cared for at the hospital][26] is less happy and the quality of life poor indeed ...

one of the patients' greatest needs is for more privacy and somewhere for personal belongings ... at present there is scarcely room for screens and trolleys between beds, and patients, although not exactly exposed to the gaze of their fellows, are still not able to have the privacy and dignity that is the right of everyone ...

Just four months later, Pouchlands Hospital was again the subject of a special meeting of the management committee called to discuss allegations ill-treatment of a patient shortly before her death. Although the coroner found no evidence of negligence or deliberate ill-treatment the HMC decided to set up a committee of inquiry and the wards sister's contract of employment was terminated.[27]

15. The Unpopular Patient

The attitude a nurse has towards her (or his) patients is one of the most important factors influencing the standard of care those patients receive —David Boorer, Introduction to King's Fund report on Attitudes Meetings at the Hospital Centre, 1970.

he publication of *Sans Everything* was widely criticised for its tone and contents and the Minister maintained that its allegations were unfounded. And yet, in spite of this, the book proved to be a springboard for a great deal of subsequent action which affected the way the chronic sick were care for in long-stay hospitals.

One of the principal reasons for the continuing unhappy state of affairs was the inadequacy of the hospital complaints system. In 1971 the then Secretary of State (Sir Keith Joseph) announced the names of 98 bodies who had been invited to submit evidence to the Davies Committee which had been set up to consider the complaints procedure. The first name on the list was Aid for the Elderly in Government Institutions.

AEGIS was not the first body to campaign for the appointment of an ombudsman. 'Justice' – established informally in 1956 by lawyers from the three main political parties concerned to ensure fair trials for people accused of treason in Hungary and South Africa – was the pressure group 'which played the crucial part in getting a Parliamentary Commissioner established in Britain'.[1] The Society for Individual Freedom, founded in 1942 by a group of Conservative backbenchers, also played an important role.

Originally, however, the NHS was excluded from the purview of the proposed commissioner. What AEGIS did was to add a powerful voice to those bodies like the Patients' Association, which lobbied party spokesmen in the House of Lords in February 1967, and the Consumer Council, who wanted to get hospital matters put within the scope of the ombudsman, pressure to which the Minister eventually bowed.

Arguably even more important was the establishment of a Hospital Advisory Service, which had been suggested by AEGIS and was given a great impetus by the publication of *Sans Everything* and especially by the later report into conditions at Ely Hospital. Setting up the HAS, Secretary of State Richard Crossman later told the *Sunday Times*, was the proudest moment of all his many achievements.[2]

The first report of the HAS was published in 1970, the year in which the government announced it would be spending an extra £110 million on health and personal social services and that £40 million of this was to be spent on improving hospital and local authority services for old people and the mentally ill, bringing the total increase in expenditure on the improvement of these services over the next four years to nearly £300 million.

In spite of the Minister's somewhat disparaging reception of *Sans Everything*, he did take action in addition to setting up the hospital inquires. Chairmen of regional hospital boards were asked to invite chairmen of HMCs to talk to senior staff to satisfy themselves that there was no inhumanity to patients, particularly the elderly. Whilst there were obvious limitations to the effectiveness of this, it did at least focus attention on conditions in these hospitals. Eastbourne HMC provides an example of the way this worked in practice.

At its meeting in July 1967, the committee had discussed the Ministry's press notices regarding *Sans Everything*. Two matrons told the committee that 'kindly and proper treatment' was provided to elderly patients in their hospitals and the consultant responsible added that in over 20 years experience 'he found nothing which would suggest any kind of ill treatment or neglect of patients'.

Nevertheless, the HMC decided that the matrons, medical staff and chief officers should make 'searching enquiries into the possibility that such practices might exist and to investigate and report any possible cases which might come to light'.[3] Then, in August, the chairman told the committee of the Minister's request as a result of which he had personally interviewed all the group's hospital secretaries and matrons. But, he said, 'he was satisfied that although some old cases had been cited, there was nothing alarming in this Group and nothing approaching the kind of thing referred to my Mrs Robb'.[4]

Sans Everything was also responsible for a unique series of meetings at the King's Fund Hospital Centre in London. This brought together nurses of all ranks and disciplines to discuss their attitudes towards patients. The meetings began in October 1968 and ran until early 1971. Two reports were published which highlighted 'examples of thoughtlessness which have led to patients being treated in cruel ways whether the intention to be cruel is there or not.' The meetings discussed the reasons for the existence of the problem:

There are the obvious reasons, of course, and these were trotted out almost ad nauseum [sic] staffing shortages, poor pay, poor conditions, overcrowding. 'They' – the HMC, RHB, Department of Health, poor communications - all were blamed. All, of course, bear some responsibility for problems in our wards today. But all these things are external to the real problem of attitudes. Not all nurses in overcrowded and understaffed wards behave callously or thoughtlessly. Not all nurses in adequately staffed and equipped hospitals behave well. Other factors must be involved.[5]

A major factor, it emerged was the relationship between staff:

We all know the 'kick the cat' syndrome. What is not always so easy to accept is the fact that in hospital the patient frequently deputises for the cat. The poor junior nurse may have been the victim of a chain of aggression that may have started in the matron's office. The kick, having been passed down the line and having gathered momentum on the way, leaves her with no one else to kick the patient.[6]

Given this climate in some areas of the nursing profession, it is perhaps not surprising that the period following the publication of *Sans Everything* saw the expansion of research into nursing practice. Especially significant was *The Unpopular Patient*, which described a project by Felicity Stockwell.[7]

However, this work was not completed and published until 1972 by which time the allegations of cruelty reported in *Sans Everything*, in Ely and the later Farleigh Hospital reports were now history, the author acknowledged, and the book was received with hostility by the nursing profession.

Stockwell's research showed how good nursing care for some patients could exist side by side with unfeeling and thoughtless treatment of others. The work demonstrated how nurses enjoyed caring for patients who were able to communicate readily with them, knew their names, were able to laugh and joke with them or were co-operative in being helped to get well. But they did not enjoy caring for others, especially those who grumbled and complained, implied that they were suffering more than the nurses believed, or suffered from conditions the nurses felt could be better cared for in other wards or specialised hospitals. In a geriatric ward, the nurses least enjoyed caring for two women 'diagnosed since admission as having endogenous depression, both of whom were volitionally retarded, looked miserable and did not appear to be making any progress' and another with senile dementia who was very noisy and physically aggressive when the nurses attended her.[8]

Discriminatory behaviour was observed regarding these patients, particularly in relation to food.

> A patient might ask for a second piece of cake as the tea trolley returned passed his bed and one might be given some, another refused and yet another given some but with a sarcastic remark … An unpopular patient who had been starved all day for tests to be carried out was given a plate of macaroni cheese for supper, which he did not fancy. He asked if there was any alternative and was told 'No', but his neighbour asked another nurse for some ham and salad which was also one of the diet meals, instead of his macaroni, and when given some he exchanged his plate with that of the other patient.[9]

Stockwell also noted that a few positive rewards were given to some patients. For example, nurses clubbed together to buy a present for a girl who was having her birthday in hospital and a sister in one ward went to a great deal of trouble to arrange for a man to visit his crippled wife at home before he was transferred to a convalescent home.

> Possibly the largest area of rewarding behaviours on the part of the nurses was the way in which they accepted favours from the patients. For example, laughing at jokes made by popular patients, accepting compliments and such things as sweets, fruit and newspapers from them, while refusing such offers from unpopular patients unless they were given as a farewell present on their departure.[10]

Sans Everything appears to have inspired a great deal of post-graduate research which has possibly received less publicity that Stockwell's work but which both confirms and elaborates her findings, especially in regard to elderly chronic patients. Dorothy Baker's Ph.D. thesis, for example, acknowledged that her study arose 'out of difficulties experienced by the nursing profession in making contributions to the care of elderly people in hospital' and referred to journal reports, manifestations of low morale (citing Boorer) and the White Paper on the allegations of cruelty contained in *Sans Everything*.

The fieldwork was carried out between 1971 and 1973 in number of medical and geriatric wards of a general hospital built in the nineteenth century as a poor law institution. The thesis described two contrasting styles of nursing care for elderly patients and in the process gave more examples of the way in which unpopular patients were sometimes treated.[11] A study by Fairhurst researched between 1975 and 1977 also gave examples of the way discrimination occurs, especially with regard to food,[12] while in another, by Fielding, a student nurse asked for her reaction to working in a geriatric ward referred to 'the general impression of a geriatric patient, i.e. "death", "grumpy", "incontinent". "Not much job satisfaction".[13]

Elderly chronic sick patients have never been popular with doctors who preferred to treat the more interesting acutely ill patients. Research in the 1960s and 1970s confirmed that the elderly were among the least popular patients with nurses too.[14] Stockwell showed how nurses could treat unpopular patients quite differently from those they liked and such treatment, as the King's Fund conferences indicated, too easily led to thoughtlessness or cruel treatment. It is unlikely that nurses felt any differently in the 1930s and 1940s; indeed, Gilbert's evidence, for example, suggests that this was so. Possibly, Crowther's view of institutional care was a shade optimistic and by no means all hospital nurses would have behaved as Nisbet believed her Foresthall nurses did (although Stockwell demonstrated that it was possible for the two extremes of treatment to exist side by side).

The question that is almost impossible to answer on the evidence is the extent of such ill-treatment and whether or not this was greater in the post-war period – although circumstances after 1948 were possibly conducive to such an increase; paradoxically, there were no Ministry of Health inspections of long-stay wards, as there had been while they were controlled by the public assistance committees, and the N.H.S complaints system was demonstrably inadequate.

Only one thing is certain: the vulnerability of elderly patients in hospitals. *Sans Everything* and subsequent events revealed all too clearly the truth of the assertion by X.Y.Z in the *Manchester Guardian* letter written over twenty years earlier: 'They are too hopelessly dependent on the officials about them, too much in danger of being victimised if they complain ... if they are ever to be treated as human beings and not as automata, it is outsiders who must fight for them and obtain for them this precious right or our common humanity.'[15]

16. Ancient Monuments and General Dickensia

And all the hinder parts, that few could spie, were ruinous and old but painted cunningly
— Edmund Spenser's 'The Faerie Queene'

During the 1960s a steadily increasing number of books were published, some for the general public, several for professionals. One of the first and most important of these appeared in 1962. *An Investigation of Geriatric Nursing Problems in Hospital*[1] was the result of a fortunate combination of factors. The authors were two nurses, Doreen Norton and Rhoda McLaren and a consultant geriatric physician, Dr A.N. Exton Smith.

The idea for the investigation was conceived some years before and was prompted by Norton's 'unhappy experience of causing a disabled elderly patient to suffer pain when trying to dress her in a hospital nightgown' when she was a student nurse. The opportunity to carry the idea forward was provided by the establishment in 1959 of a geriatric nursing research unit in the Whittington Hospital in London through the generosity of the National Corporation for the Care of Old People and the co-operation of Archway Group HMC.

Thanks to the Nuffield Trust, Norton was able to follow up the work carried out in Whittington Hospital with a survey of 330 hospitals responsible for nursing old people and the results were published in a second book, *Hospitals of the Long Stay Patient in 1967*.[2] This revealed that complaints of old fashioned facilities and cramped wards were common. Often, larger hospitals were worse than smaller ones:

> Hospitals with over 200 beds had more overcrowding, less day space, fewer lavatories, worse sanitary and laundry facilities than smaller ones ... size and deficiencies do not need to be synonymous, but where resources are scarce, the long stay part of a larger mixed hospital is always liable to come off second best.[3]

Described by *The Lancet* as 'an excellent, though depressing picture of the present situation in geriatric nursing hospitals',[4] Norton's survey also confirmed that many units were housed in hospitals built for other purposes, often in remote places badly served by public transport. Patients were, as a result, cut off from activity and visits by relatives. Attempts had been made to upgrade many hospitals, but day space had sometimes been provided at the expense of overcrowding in the ward itself. Furnishings left much to be desired and patients' clothing needed a good deal more thought.

The publication of three reports by regional hospital boards – Birmingham (1961), Manchester (1967) and South East Metropolitan 1970) – all served to underline Norton's findings, especially with regard to equipment and the physical surroundings in which the elderly chronic sick were cared for.

Sheldon's Birmingham Report

With the publication of Dr Sheldon's report on geriatric services in the Birmingham region[5] the public were left in little doubt of the legacy of the workhouse system to Britain's hospital services for the elderly. It brought forth a rash of sensational headlines, even in more sober newspapers such as *The Times* ('Hospital Slum Challenge')[6] and the *Guardian* ('Primitive Hospitals That Should Be Blown Up').[7]

Sheldon's survey was undertaken as a basis for planning future geriatric services in the region. Because he assumed it was intended to be confidential and not available to the public, Sheldon indicated in his preface that the report contained phraseology that had 'not been emasculated to such a level of neutrality as might be thought more apt for general publication'. However, a decision by one newspaper to publish extracts 'created some difficulties' and, after making some additions and correcting some figures, the board decided to print 250 copies of the report to circulate to local authorities, health authorities and the press.

Working on a recommended basis of 1.2 chronic sick beds per thousand of population, Sheldon calculated that the region's 6,289 beds were 764 in excess of requirements. However, he pointed out, there were certain qualifying factors to be taken into account. The regional figures concealed a number of local variations including four hospital groups where the number of beds available was below the optimum level. Some of the accommodation was 'deplorable', there was considerable overcrowding, which affected nurse recruitment and the functional use of the beds. Modernisation, on the other hand, would lead to an inevitable reduction in bed numbers. Bringing about an improvement in technical facilities had, for example, entailed the reduction of beds in one ward from 14 to 8.

It was Sheldon's descriptions of the hospital buildings, however, that gave rise to the newspaper headlines. Sheldon introduced this section of his report with a quotation from Edmund Spenser's *The Faerie Queene*: 'And all the hinder parts, that few could spie, were ruinous and old but painted cunningly'. He used the quotation 'without hesitation' because there were five hospitals in the region which needed demolition, in total or in part. These buildings, he said, were in fact:

> hospital slums which were inherited in 1948. By and large they do no more than provide storage space for the patients under conditions of considerable difficulty, and often unpleasantness, for the nursing staff. It was quite an experience to see bed pans being stored for the night in the bath; to be told of female nurses having to queue up for the same lavatory as the male patients; to find the same room being used for the washing of bed pans and domestic crockery; and to see nurses having to fill a pint pot with water in order to wash excreta from a bed pan down an ordinary lavatory.[8]

The absence of lifts in many hospitals also concerned Sheldon. Often the upper floors could only be reached by narrow angular staircases. Patients who could not manage them had to be carried up and down with the result that many remained upstairs until they died. There were also problems with the delivery of food, coal and linen and 'an ever present anxiety where there are a number of helpless old people on an upper floor is that of the fire risk'.

Sheldon paid tribute to the hospital management committees for their efforts in renovating and transforming many of hospitals. The fact that so much remained to be done was, he said, 'a measure of the heavy liabilities which the hospital service assumed when it was forced to inherit these outmoded buildings'. But he was critical of the allocation of the capital expenditure. 'Whereas the beds for the chronic sick present one seventh of the total beddage (6,000 out of 44,000) they have received only one sixteenth of its capital expenditure during this period'.[9]

In his conclusion, Sheldon made it clear he was not in the business of searching for scapegoats 'to carry the burden of potential blame'. Any failure to achieve success was attributable, he believed, to the sheer scale of the problem. The report was described by the board's assistant secretary as 'the most damning yet publicised by a regional hospital board'.

> Every word is true and we have known it for a very long time. We accept this report as a challenge and if we can get the money I promise the public we shall tackle and resolve the problem.[10]

The region estimated that about £5 million was necessary to achieve this. It set up a team which designed a unit that could be put up quickly and economically at a cost of between £45,000 and £50,000. The single storey buildings were intended to be 'intimate homes for the elderly, with the family spirit encouraged and special assistance for the infirm'. The board included a request for 80 of these units in its 10 year programme.

Birmingham was by no means the only region to suffer acute problems in providing for the chronic sick. Roberts, in a 1959 series of *Guardian* articles gave examples of conditions in the Home Counties. In an otherwise good geriatric unit, 38 old men lived on the top floor of a three storey block approached by two flights of sixteen steps each 'both steep and one of them of stone', which posed a fire risk, made it difficult for elderly relatives to visit or 'to get a corpse down with dignity and decency'. She told of former EMS huts with concrete walls and an asbestos roof, 'the windows, small and badly placed offer the alternatives of a fug or lacerating draughts'. There were no cubicle curtains, no room for easy chairs, one bath for each ward shared with patients with skin conditions.[11]

The catalogue, Roberts added, could continue almost indefinitely.

> The point about these examples is not that they are glaring exceptions but that every region has its quota of them. Recently the South Western Region publicised its problems. It has 270 hospitals – made necessary because of a scattered population – 43 of which are old Poor Law Institutions with all that implies. At 50 of them the board needs to spend on urgent improvements twice as much as it can afford on its present capital allocation. As yet the Ministry has not responded to its importuning.[12]

And even this was not the full extent of the problem; nor was it easily to be solved, as the further reports from other regions, Manchester in 1967 and especially the South East Metropolitan in 1970, were to confirm.

The South East Metropolitan Report

The South East Metropolitan report[13] is particularly noteworthy for two reasons: firstly because it contains a wealth of information about the former East Sussex workhouses and secondly, because the vivid language used earned for it a wide serious and popular press coverage with headlines such as Hospitals for the aged like '19th century human warehouses' *(Guardian)* and Shock Report: 'Old People's Hospitals like Dickens' Story' *(The Sunday Express)*[14], neither of which was really surprising in the light of the authors' conclusion: 'The general picture is depressing ... no one will envy the South East Metropolitan Hospital Board's inheritance of ancient monuments and general Dickensia'.[15]

Geriatric hospitals in East Sussex were among those surveyed by the board's working party. In the period immediately preceding publication of the report each hospital group had been pressing ahead with the development of its hospitals for the elderly in its own way and generally subject to the severe constraints of shortages of staff and lack of financial resources.

In 1968 the mayor of Eastbourne had taken the opportunity offered by a visit of the BMA for its annual conference to voice the opinion that the hospital crisis in the town was so serious that there was a danger of complete breakdown:

> Behind the prosperous and smiling face of our seafront shop window there exists one of the most acute combined social and medical problems in the world today. I refer to the geriatric burden which has overwhelmed the local hospital resources and placed under a tremendous strain the GPs and the local health authority.[16]

In fact, only a few weeks earlier the regional board had agreed in principle to the provision of an additional 90 beds at All Saints Hospital and had approved the expenditure of £39,000 on the first phase which included a 30 bedded ward. The decision followed a period of intense activity during 1967. In September, the HMC received a letter from the medical officer of health stating that the Ministry of Health was unable to allocate money for old people's homes the council had planned to build in 1969 and that work on these was unlikely to commence until the financial year 1971/72. At the October meeting of the HMC, the chairman told members he had written to the regional board stating that the overriding need in the group's capital programme was the provision of geriatric beds and asked the board to look into the possibility of finding beds in neighbouring groups which might be used by Eastbourne patients as an immediate measure.

The following week, the Permanent Secretary to the Ministry, Sir Arnold France, visited the Princess Alice and All Saints hospitals and the medical staff in particular took the opportunity of giving him full details of the 'serious geriatric situation'[17] with the result that the RHB gave an undertaking 'to take quick action'.[18] In December, the board replied to the HMC's suggestion of using beds in other hospital groups saying there was little prospect of finding beds in Newhaven or Brighton, two of the places suggested, and suggesting an approach to the other, the mental hospital at Hellingly. However, this did not bear fruit as the medical superintendent said his hospital was overcrowded and that if any beds did become available they would be required for psycho-geriatric patients.

The prospect of extra beds did not necessarily mean an end to Eastbourne's difficulties, however. As in other hospital groups throughout the country, the shortage of nursing staff was a continuing problem. One possible solution to this was to pay nurses in geriatric wards more money – a remedy which had some support in Eastbourne as the health service trade union COHSE discovered when it held its annual conference there in 1968. Once again the mayor took the opportunity to refer to the town's geriatric problem:

> Here in Eastbourne we have our own domestic problem of an acute staff shortage in geriatric hospitals. It has been suggested this is because nursing geriatrics can sometimes be unpleasant and even humiliating.[19]

There was applause from the delegates when he went on to refer to the local executive committee of the health service who had the previous week endorsed a decision to ask Kenneth Robinson, the Minister of Health, to consider paying extra remuneration as a means of alleviating the shortage.

However, when the 'geriatric lead' of an additional £100 was introduced in the following year it proved to be a mixed blessing. Eastbourne reported that it had resulted in the recruitment of additional nurses on the geriatric wards; in Hastings it had created difficulties in transferring staff between wards because the allowance was only payable to staff working 'permanently and exclusively' on geriatric and chronic sick wards.[20]

The publication of *Sans Everything* was followed by reports of a number of hospital scandals. A consequence of one of these, the Ely Report in 1969,[21] was a proposal by the Department of Health and Social Security to establish minimum standards of care in long stay units. A questionnaire was sent to group secretaries seeking information on the basis of which it was proposed to issue a circular on the subject. The questionnaire for geriatric and chronic sick patients requested information on bed spacing, day space and patients' lockers. The information supplied by Hastings, appeared to confirm Norton's assertion that conditions were generally better in smaller units (such as Battle) than in the larger ones (St. Helen's, for example).

The following month the question of patients' day clothing arose. The matter had been discussed at a King's Fund conference on incontinence earlier in the year. Consultants asked the regional board's senior administrative medical officer (SAMO) for advice on the provision of clothing to patients, irrespective of the anticipated length of stay, for both incontinent and continent ambulant patients. The RHB then sought the advice of the Department and was told that the advice already given (by the Ministry of Health in 1949) remained unchanged but the response added:

> It would, we think, be within the spirit of the advice given issued in 1949 to regard an ambulant geriatric patient as in need of day clothing by reason of his incontinence, even though he may have his own personal clothing which may be suitable. We consider that outer garments and non disposable underwear should always be issued to patients on a personal basis and returned to them when laundered or dry cleaned. The practice of issuing from a pool of clothing is considered to be out of line with modern thinking.[22]

The problem, as so often was the case, was that HMCs had to find the cash for this clothing from their existing budgets 'since no specific sums can be provided to meet increased issues.'[23] When the Hastings geriatrician submitted estimates of the expenditure likely to be involved, the group secretary could only reply that the HMC had always provided a certain amount of clothing to patients unable to purchase their own from their own resources. However, he promised to 'look sympathetically at any extension'.[24]

In Brighton, progress was hampered by the lack of capital resources. In the middle of the 1970 election campaign Richard Crossman, as Secretary of State for Social Services, was reported to have told doctors that he could not meet their pay award in full because the country was, again, 'in a period of extreme economic peril'.[25] Not surprisingly, perhaps, a request from the Brighton HMC to provide two new wards, dayroom accommodation and a gymnasium as the first stage in the modernisation of the geriatric unit at Brighton General Hospital together with full central heating in F Block and a passenger lift in J Block was only partially successful. Eventually it resulted in the promise of a £35,000 scheme to upgrade the geriatric unit in F Block but with the proviso that work would not be undertaken until the 1971/72 programme. In the interim, an allocation of £1,500 was made to provide cubicle curtaining and occupational therapy.

Like Eastbourne three years before, Brighton also complained of serious bed shortages. In the autumn of 1970 the medical executive committee told the HMC that 'unless improvements can be made urgently to the geriatric service, there was now a serious risk of breakdown in all the acute services because the beds needed ... would be blocked by patients who should come under the care of the geriatric department'.[26] Copies of the resolution were also sent to the regional board and also to the Brighton and East Sussex local authorities so that they might consider the matter 'in relation to the arrangements in their areas for the reception into the community of patients fit for discharge from hospital'.[27] Two months later the HMC received a response from Brighton County Borough Council which had reviewed the provision for old people in the borough. The council had asked all local health authorities on the south coast to support them in their approaches to the Association of Municipal Corporations, local MPs and the government for a larger proportion of the national revenue to be allocated to the needs of the elderly.

One of the first public intimations of the forthcoming regional report on geriatric facilities appeared in an editorial in the Christmas issue of *Brighton Hospitals Bulletin*.[28] In addition to the local debate about inadequate facilities, several factors appear to have prompted the article including a television programme in which facilities for elderly hospital patients in Brighton had 'received an unusual amount of attention' and a tour by one of the local MPs.

The editor argued that geriatric patients – all accommodated in former poor law institutions – were the 'poor relations of the hospital world' who were almost always at the end of the queue:

> I once heard a management committee member remark: 'If I'm asked to choose between supplying a new lift for an acute hospital and one for a geriatric hospital, the acute hospital would get my vote every time.'[29]

Referring to 'a recent survey by the regional board' that facilities locally were as good as any elsewhere in the country, the editor argued that this was simply not true: the neighbouring group, Mid Sussex, had done far more 'to improve outmoded facilities'. The article continued with an appeal for improved attitudes towards elderly patients, arguing that nurses were overprotective and that nursing techniques took precedence over 'conversation, entertainment and occupation'. These words would appear to have been inspired in part at least by the publication of a book by a local consultant psychiatrist, Dr Tony Whitehead. This had attracted a considerable amount of attention in the medical press and was widely available as a popular paperback.[30]

Reaction from the many members of the nursing staff was almost predictable: 'You're talking through your hat,' was the response from five anonymous nurses but others admitted 'much of what you write is unfortunately true'. A nursing auxiliary argued that 'getting an elderly lady who cannot stand or sit upright without help into an old fashioned corset takes time and patience'. An assistant matron urged that the voice of the trained nurse should not go unheeded in the upgrading and reorganisation of the wards adding: 'Perhaps with time and a great deal of hard work and with no criticising and blaming of each other we can give the elderly the dignity and comfort they so well deserve'.[31]

17. Sussex Hospitals under the Microscope

Even today the term 'workhouse' is still used by the older generation, sometimes jocularly ('we're not in the workhouse yet') and all too often with dread. For the old buildings still remain, their exteriors a grim reminder that the architects of 'less legibility' were the designers of prisons too... the buildings still stand and with them their memories — South East Metropolitan Regional Hospital Board Report, 1970.

Almost six months were to pass before the general public became aware of the true nature of the RHB report, which it was believed should be made public if it was to be of any real value to both the board and the geriatric service. However, perhaps having learned a lesson from an earlier leaking of the Birmingham report, it was decided to hold a press conference on April 26 and so 'blunt some of the adverse comment'[1]. However, the conference was deferred until May 10 and in the meantime the board's public relations department prepared a lengthy press release. Endeavouring to secure some perspective, this stated that 'the survey shows that facilities and amenities for old people in the region are mostly satisfactory or reasonably satisfactory'.[2]

In spite of these careful preparations, sensational reports appeared in the national press ahead of the embargoed date, May 10. A non press copy of the report was leaked to Robert Chapman of the *Sunday Express* who accordingly ran the story on Sunday May 2. Other national and local newspapers immediately followed. The Sussex

69. The report in the Sunday Express, although printed on an inside page, led to a rash of headlines in other national and local newspapers.

evening paper led with 'Plight of the Old in Sussex: Shock Report'.[3] This was followed up with a full page feature on Brighton General Hospital, 'The Hospital that Progress Forgot', and the next day gave considerable coverage to a report of a press conference given by the regional hospital board.[4]

The *Brighton Hospitals Bulletin*, appearing later in the month, responded to the defensive attitude displayed by many members of staff by dropping the customary full page cover photograph in favour of a full report of news and comment. An editorial argued that, despite any inaccuracies, the report 'is the best weapon we have in the fight to secure the conditions humanity demands for the elderly sick. It provides us with the best opportunity of setting things right we have ever had'.[5]

The language used in the report – and the colourful newspaper headlines that followed – were remarkably similar to the earlier report on the Birmingham region. This was by no means coincidental. The working party had been set up early in 1970 to advise the RHB on the future pattern of geriatric services by the senior administrative medical officer, who had also been associated with the Sheldon report. Moreover, a member of the working party, Dr Clark, the Brighton geriatrician, had earlier worked in the Birmingham region. There he had been associated with the development of a special unit that had been devised as an answer to the problem of providing inexpensive accommodation to meet the region's shortfall. Other members were Professor Brocklehurst, Dr Budd, the chairman, a geriatrician in the Dartford group, and Dr Irvine of Hastings.

70. *Dr Tony Clark, the Brighton geriatrician who had previously worked in the Birmingham region.*

The report gave details of a comprehensive survey which covered all grades of staff –

Brighton Hospitals

BULLETIN

No. 49   May, 1971

New deal for the elderly?

Staff reactions to the report on services for the elderly published earlier this month appear to be mixed. Some are concerned about criticisms they do not think are valid; others see the report as a sign of better things to come for the geriatric services.

The staff themselves emerge from the report with credit. In the preface the authors pay tribute to their colleagues in geriatric medicine throughout the region. "We have been most impressed with the support and loyalty they are receiving from their administrators and nursing staff of all grades. Our dominant impression is of good work done by devoted people".

But the report considers there are often too few nurses who frequently work under conditions more suited to the 1870s than the 1970s.

"We hope by the 1980s the human qualities, which shine through the squalid buildings in which so much of geriatrics is done, will be matched by the provision of reasonable conditions in terms of buildings, equipment and staff".

MORE TO BE SPENT

The report has emerged as a result of a survey conducted for the regional board. Its object was to provide a basis for the future development of geriatric services in the region.

Not only has the board accepted the report of the working party. It also decided to make their findings public – a courageous decision and a unique one. Most recent critical reports – like **Sans Everything** – have been the result of public pressure. This one reflects the board's own initiative.

Expenditure of £1.8 million has been announced for capital developments for geriatric services in the next two years. This approaches the total amount spent – £2 million – in the last 23 years since the introduction of the health service. During that period the board's allocation for all capital works was £34 million.

One of the immediate effects of this increased expendi-

ture will be seen at Brighton General Hospital. "C" Block is to be converted to provide more beds for acute geriatrics. A new day hospital will be built associated with this block. This will provide a composite day unit of fifty or sixty places and an assessment centre with beds. Plans are well advanced for this £170,000 scheme and building work should commence later in the year.

LEGACY FROM THE PAST

Commenting on local shortcomings in geriatric provision, the group secretary, Mr. Robert Alderton says, "It does not appear to have been appreciated that these hospitals were transferred after six years of war. Little was done between 1946 and 1948 because it was known they would be transferred to new authorities".

"The lack of maintenance during the war years," adds Mr. Alderton, "resulted in a tremendous backlog of upgrading. Money has never been available in sufficient quantities to deal with these arrears".

Mr. Alderton says it is easy to criticise existing levels of service and provision of facilities. But since 1948, when Brighton General Hospital was transferred from the Corporation, a very large sum of money has been invested in the geriatric unit in an attempt to bring the blocks up to a reasonable modern standard.

The current state of affairs would not have arisen if the board had been capable of providing the large sums of money required to improve facilities and obtain additional staff.

ANGRY NURSES

Mr. Alderton comments that nurses at Brighton General are angry about a staged photograph included in the report. This showed the method of removal of bodies as being carried out by nurses. Porters and drivers at the hospital have written to the local press about the photograph.

71a and b. Faced with local reaction to the report, claiming it was flawed by inaccuracies, the Brighton hospital house journal publicised and defended the document, dropping its usual cover photo in favour of a text article. An editorial supporting the report was commended to members by the chairman at a subsequent meeting of the hospital management committee.

That report – what it really means

Many people are understandably upset – some are even annoyed – by the publication of the report on services for the elderly.

It is only natural to spring to the defence of your hospital if it appears it is being criticised. But such a reaction is mistaken on this occasion.

As both the group secretary and the chairman of the regional board have pointed out, the management committee inherited antiquated, inadequate geriatric hospitals when the health service took over responsibility for them from the local authorities in 1948.

In the group there are not a few people who recall the conditions of twenty-odd years ago – dark brown and green paint, rusty lockers, no cubicle curtains, centre-ward coal fires, sladoes with sub-zero temperatures, even fewer lifts than we have today. Whatever their shortcomings, Brighton General and Newhaven Downs Hospitals present a rather different face to the world today. Gone are Mr. Werralla cowsheds!

But as the working party's report shows there is still a great deal to be done. That this is so does not reflect on the staff at these hospitals. As the report says, they have worked heroically in the circumstances.

They have put forward proposals in plenty for improvements. But the money simply has not been there. A great deal has been accomplished since 1948 – but the improvements have been wrung out of a reluctant

society.

Despite all our advances, our geriatric wards have, quite simply, failed to keep pace with present-day standards. Compare these units with Churchill Square and the modern stand at the race course adjacent to Brighton General Hospital. No public outcry was needed to create these symbols of an affluent society. That is the measure of what has gone wrong.

"No society deserves to be called civilised when it treats infirm old people as second class citizens," says the Evening Argus.

The remarkable thing is that, on this occasion, the protest has come not from relatives and friends of those who suffer – but from those professionally responsible for their care. It is society that should hang its head in shame, not hospital management.

We should forget the quibbles about the report. Of course it isn't correct in every detail.

But it is the best weapon we have in the fight to secure the conditions humanity demands for the elderly sick. It provides us with the best opportunity of setting things right as we have ever had.

What a tragedy it would be if we were to let that opportunity slip through our fingers.

THE EDITOR

Hospitals out of Dickens

OLD people's hospitals in South-East England are like something out of Dickens, says an official report to be published this month.

One hospital still in use, All Saints, Chatham, Kent, has the ball said to have been used by Dickens as the setting in which Oliver Twist asked for more.

Another, St. Mary's, Eastbourne, Sussex, was built as a barracks in the Napoleonic wars.

A third, Benstead House, Faversham, Kent, is an old workhouse.

PLIGHT OF THE OLD IN SUSSEX: SHOCK REPORT

Hospitals for aged 'like 19th century human warehouses'

By NICHOLAS de JONGH

Fifteen of the 43 hospitals with geriatric services in the South East region are "perfect examples of human warehouses" and are in conditions more appropriate to the 1870s than the 1970s, says a report published today by the South-east Metropolitan Hospitals Board.

The report is a major indictment of geriatric services, with an implicit criticism of the Department of Health for a shortage of nurses and patients which the report says are quite unacceptable.

SHOCK REPORT: 'OLD PEOPLE'S HOSPITALS LIKE DICKENS STORY'

A DEEPLY disturbing report on the plight of old people in some of Britain's hospitals is to be made public this month. It tells of "Dickensian conditions" in which many old folk end their lives.

by ROBERT CHAPMAN

Shock hospital report probes 'desperate' plight of old folk

THE South-East has the worst hospital-building record in the country, and many of its Dickensian wards could still be in use in 100 years unless massive doses of cash are administered.

'Watchdogs were not snubbed' says chairman

72. Some of the newspaper headlines that followed the publication of the leaked report.

doctors, nurses, therapists, social workers, administrative and clerical and voluntary workers – as well as ward facilities, patient amenities, catering and equipment. But it was the physical conditions in which patients were treated, the old and unsuitable buildings, which captured the newspaper headlines.

> Even today the term 'workhouse' is still used by the older generation, sometimes jocularly ('we're not in the workhouse yet') and all too often with dread. For the old buildings still remain, their exteriors a grim reminder that the architects of 'less legibility' were the designers of prisons too... the buildings still stand and with them their memories. There are still courtyards where the inmates once exercised under the watchful eye of the master ... there are still rough passage walls, scarcely covered by modern Portaflek, and stone stairways. The wards are low and often access is by way of a few steps, ceilings are low and adjacent wards rarely on the same level. [6]

An appendix on the history of the buildings noted that in its original state at All Saints, Chatham was the hall said to have been used by Charles Dickens as the setting for Oliver Twist. 15 of the 43 hospitals surveyed were over 100 old years and 'long ago reached the limit of their usefulness and demand replacement at the earliest possible moment'. New buildings, on the other hand were rare – a new hospital at Greenwich, day hospitals at Hastings and Orpington, and new purpose designed wards at All Saints, Eastbourne achieved at the relatively small cost of £1,000 a bed.

The authors referred to the instruction that their recommendations should be 'within the limit of finance and existing resources' but found this an impossible task. Although millions of pounds were needed to provide the essentials of a geriatric service, they hoped the board would present their recommendations to the Department of Health with the object of obtaining some of the £130 million promised by the government to help improve geriatric and psychiatric hospitals over the next few years. Their findings regarding the East Sussex made unpleasant reading.

Eastbourne

St Mary's Hospital. Originally built as barracks in the Napoleonic wars. The existing main kitchen was originally the stables and the tethering posts for horses could still be seen in position. The wards were unsatisfactory in provision of facilities and layout. The hospital was due to be replaced by the new district hospital but the admission wards should be replaced as soon as possible. A shortage of assessment beds put pressure on medical and surgical beds.

Downside. A well adapted former fever hospital apart from difficulties presented by a sloping site. Bright and airy wards, good bed spacing, adequate day space.

All Saints Hospital. Essentially a rehabilitation unit. Despite occasionally forbidding corridors, it provided satisfactory ward accommodation. Two new wards (together with the flexible new Mereworth ward at Linton Hospital, Maidstone) 'should be the pattern for replacing the existing poor fabric throughout the region'.

Hastings

Mal distribution of long stay beds was the main problem: 53 female beds in St Leonards, none in Hastings, too many in Battle, none in Bexhill or Rye, although in Bexhill, the most pressing need, the RHB already had the matter in hand. By most contemporary standards, the geriatric unit was well staffed with 'fully stretched' doctors, nurses and rehabilitation staff.

73. *The former barracks at St Mary's Hospital. The kitchen in the former stables still contained tethering posts for the horses.*

St Helen's Hospital. The main defect was the lack of day rooms. Sanitary annexes had been added to all four ward blocks on the north side. The oldest and worst ward in the geriatric unit had recently been upgraded and was moderately satisfactory. In the older part of the hospital, the main problem was inadequate sanitary provision.

Alexandra House. A long stay unit, homely and popular with patients and relatives, but overcrowded and inconvenient for nursing staff. It should be closed as soon as it could be replaced.

Eversfield Chest Hospital. A chest hospital founded in 1890 with 27 long stay geriatric and 60 chest beds. Splendidly situated on a cliff overlooking the sea, with space for building if necessary. Both blocks had newly been provided with lifts.

Battle Hospital. 'An old country workhouse more than 120 years old, is too inconvenient to be converted to modern use,' could be replaced on the same site by a modern purpose built unit of 30-40 beds with a small

74a. The report's attractive picture of the exterior of Battle Hospital, and inset, 74b. Some of the old equipment at Battle still in use.

day unit added. The previous good new sanitary annexes had been built at a cost of some £8,000 for the male side; similar expenditure on the female side would be justified, even if the foreseeable life of the hospital in its present form was only 10 years or so.

Brighton & Lewes

Brighton General Hospital. Owing to overcrowding and a critical nursing shortage in June 1969, bed numbers (293 allocated beds) were reduced by 60. As a result, there was a six month wait for admission to a female long stay bed. There was no day hospital.

Replacement of F Block, built in 1865 and condemned by Brighton Corporation in 1938, was urgently necessary. There were too many patients in wards that are not centrally heated, damp was coming through the roof and walls, there was a shortage of toilets. Ward A4 had been modernised to a good standard and opened in July 1970 as a 36 bed long stay unit for men. Excessive strains on staff over the previous two years in J Block, which had 69 beds on three floors under one sister, had led to difficulty in recruitment and beds were closed. There was no lift, no bed pan washers, no cubicle curtains and 'we can only offer our humble admiration to the staff who have battled with such intolerable conditions for so long'.

L Block: Provision of a lift is essential: the transport of patients to an from an upper floor on stretchers by way of the stairs was 'dangerous, inefficient and inhumane. Ward HF3 is on the top floor of a ward block. The first two floors had been extensively altered and improved to provide a psychiatric admission unit; the upper floor with 24 beds for female geriatric patients remained unchanged.

Summarising the situation at Brighton General Hospital, the report concluded there was an overall impression of arrested development following partial improvements made eight years earlier. 'There appears to have been a lack of progress due to inadequate finance and maintenance over the past ten years ... these wards must be either radically improved or replaced'.

At **Newhaven Downs Hospital** there was some overcrowding in the 74 long stay bed unit; a reduction of six beds on two floors would give better access for nursing staff and relatives. Dayroom space and toilet facilities were inadequate. 16 male patients had only one w.c. There was a shortage of tables and chairs and no money to buy more. The nurse staffing position had periods of crisis in the summer months.

Mid Sussex

Cuckfield Hospital. 'The overall impression was one of progressive upgrading of this hospital, good equipment and a high standard of morale of staff at all levels'.

Pouchlands Hospital. This old workhouse had undergone substantial improvement in recent years. There was a shortage of trained nursing staff and the hospital had to depend on married nursing auxiliaries more than usual, but the morale of the staff was high.

A framework for future development

In a foreword to the report, written four months after its original (internal) publication, the chairman of the board said the RHB accepted it as a framework for the development of services for the elderly but noted that similar reviews of mental handicap and mental illness services were also being undertaken and that the 'priorities in these three areas of concern' would have to be considered together. He blamed lack of capital for the board's inability to replace or upgrade the many outdated and inadequate hospitals. However, the flow to the region 'has now improved and the Board can embark on a more ambitious programme of development' and was planning to spend at least £1.8 million over the next two years. In the past, between 1948 and March 1971, the total

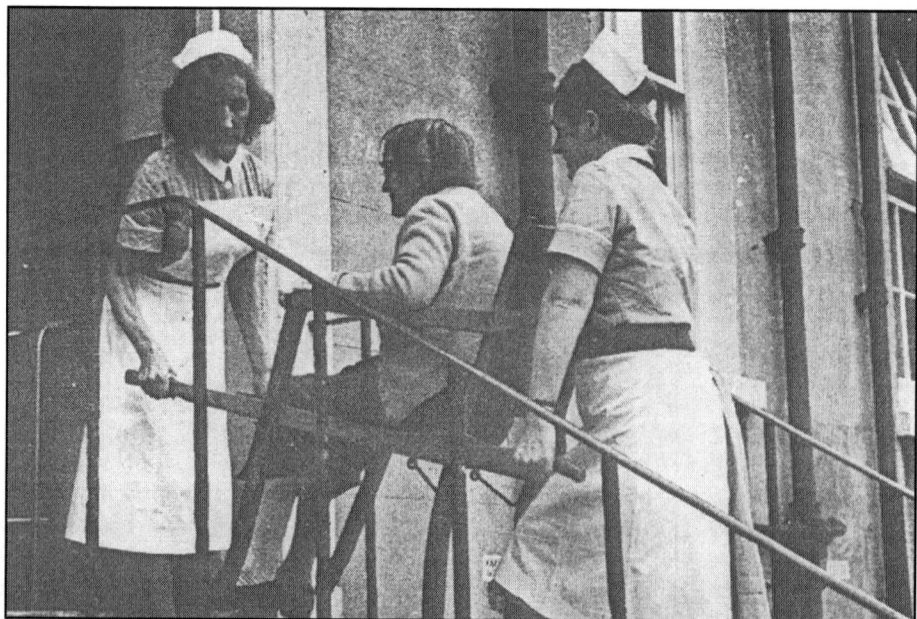

75. *One of the pictures taken at Brighton General contained in the report.*

allocated to the board was only £34 million of which about £2 million had been spent on new or improved geriatric accommodation.

The chairman, Alderman Briggs, who had been associated with Brighton General Hospital for many years, later told a local newspaper he had been fighting for money to bring about improvements for over twenty years. He believed conditions would improve with the proposed adaptation of the former maternity unit in C block. The group secretary told the same newspaper that this work would probably start later in the year and since the report had been made six months earlier, much was being planned to improve the geriatric wards.[7]

More details of conditions at Brighton General emerged in another newspaper report. Lack of central heating meant patients often had to be kept in bed in order to keep warm and there were only four toilets and two baths between 48 patients in the female wards. Patients who died were taken out on a stretcher down a rear fire escape and a serious shortage of space meant furniture was stacked in doorways and on landings. Essential items of equipment ordered eight years earlier had

76. *The use of nurses in this picture was criticised, especially by the hospital's porters, who said nurses were never used to carry bodies down the fire escapes. Other critics said this mistake threw doubts on the accuracy of the report.*

not been supplied. The ratio of patients to staff, almost seven to one, was three times the recommended figure. On the other hand, there had been improvements since 1948: one block criticised in the report for its overcrowding housed 67 women but in 1951, the hospital secretary recalled, it had been occupied by 112 patients and in those days there were bare boards and no curtains at the windows.[8]

Dr Clark, the hospital's geriatrician, blamed the situation on the fact that productive members of the community were being favoured at the expense of old people, who were being sacrificed – something no politician would dare to admit in public. Older people always suffered because they were politically powerless: 'Younger people, who do have the power, are usually either complacent, apathetic or ignorant'.[9]

The group secretary complained that people did not appreciate that the hospitals were transferred after six years of war and that little was done between 1946 and 1948 because of the impending transfer to new authorities. 'Lack of maintenance during the war years resulted in a tremendous backlog of upgrading. Money has never been available in sufficient quantities to deal with these arrears',[10] while the editorial in the local hospital house journal commented:

> Our geriatric wards have, quite simply, failed to keep pace with present day standards. Compare these units with Churchill Square [a new shopping complex in central Brighton] and the modern stand at the racecourse adjacent to Brighton General Hospital. No public outcry was needed to create these symbols of an affluent society. That is the measure of what has gone wrong.[11]

18. Sweeping Away the Old Institutions

The workhouse ... still generates fear, not perhaps so much of the conditions inside, but for the loss of independence that the workhouse symbolised —N.W. Chaplin, Health Care in the United Kingdom (Kluwer Medical, 1982).

I t was not all bad news for East Sussex hospitals in 1971. In May, for example, Eastbourne HMC had been told the regional board had authorised the appointment of five additional nurses to upgrade the group's geriatric staffing. Members also learned that a preliminary meeting had taken place with the board's officer to discuss proposals for a geriatric day hospital.[1] Brighton General Hospital's C Block was going to be adapted to provide 80 beds for geriatric assessment and an associated 50-place day hospital.[2]

However, the most promising news was an announcement in November in the House of Commons by the Secretary of State, Sir Keith Joseph. The government, he told MPs, was allocating a further £118 million 'to speed progress in improving conditions in some of the most vulnerable sectors of the health and personal social services over the next four years'[3] and this included some £45 million that was intended for the NHS. Sir Keith admitted that it would not solve all the problems, but he believed it was enough to make substantial improvements. Events were to prove, however, that the allocation was by no means sufficient to make a major impact on hospital conditions, especially in the long stay sector. There was far too much leeway to make up following the preceding years of neglect and underfunding.

It is open to question, also, whether Sir Keith had given the hospitals a fair share of the money being made available. A third of the £100 million allocation was earmarked for the local authorities and Sir Keith hoped this would enable them to 'sweep away all the former poor law institutions still being used as old people's homes and replace them with modern buildings'. He also hoped it would be possible to replace many of the old and unsatisfactory houses that had been adapted to accommodate elderly people.[4] Thus the allocation was expected to make far greater strides in the residential care sector than in the field of hospital care for the elderly chronic sick. It was never even suggested that for these patients accommodation in unsatisfactory former workhouses would at last be swept away.

Early in 1972, Sir Keith Joseph visited hospitals on the Sussex coast. At Brighton he met 150 nurses at a meeting organised by the Sussex group of the Association of Hospital Matrons at which he discussed 'the need for more resources and services for the elderly and minority groups'.[5] In Eastbourne he reviewed the provision of services by hospitals and the local authority and the discussion also ranged over subjects such as the proposed day hospital, the need for additional beds and the difficulty of recruiting paramedical staff.

It was about his time that at last some positive results emerged from the report on conditions in the geriatric and psycho-geriatric hospitals in the South East Metropolitan region. In February, Dr Irvine wrote to his group secretary saying he had been told the RHB 'has been allocated a large sum of money for improvements in geriatric accommodation, part for new wards, part for minor improvements' and gave details of his requirements – a 'stack' of day rooms which would include lavatories for each of the main wings at St Helen's Hospital. His list also included lifts, additional sanitary facilities and other items for St Helen's, Alexandra House and Battle Hospital.[6]

Three weeks later, however, the true situation became clear. For the present schemes were to be limited to the provision of furnishings and

77. Sir Keith Joseph talks to some of the matrons during his visit to Sussex in 1972.

equipment. 'I think I must make it clear,' the senior administrative medical officer wrote, 'that the sum ... available in 1972/73 is under £100,000 for the entire region and therefore only the most modest needs can be met'.[7]

In June, the board's principal assistant secretary confirmed the details of the special allocation that was being made for geriatric and psycho-geriatric services in the region. For 1972/73 this was to be £90,000; in 1973/4, £730,000; in 1974/75, £990,000 and in 1975/76, £730,000. The medium and large capital schemes in the highest priority group would be included in the four year period, including the £82,000 upgrading of F Block at Brighton General Hospital. The sums remaining would be used for smaller schemes (£340,000) and furniture and equipment (£500,000).

Hastings later learned that it had been allocated up to £6,000 to replace beds and lockers at Battle, Eversfield, St Helen's and Alexandra House. Dr Irvine, commenting on a proposed list of items to be set against the special allocation, said the highest priority was for sanitary annexes at Battle (£10,000). 'It has been asked for for a long time and the female side at Battle is disgracefully sub-standard'. His second and third priorities, a much larger problem, were dayrooms at St Helen's, while his fourth was improved toilets.[8]

Minimum Standards of Care

Evidence that the government was now paying more attention to the problems of elderly people in hospital is provided by the issue of Department of Health circular DS 95/72, Minimum Standards of Care for Geriatric Departments. Commenting on this in a letter to his group secretary in May, Dr Irvine said it was made clear that the standards were the minimum tolerable, but there was a natural fear that the minimum standards might in fact become the norm, especially in groups like Hastings. 'Our own standards are far above these in every particular,' Dr Irvine pointed out, 'but we certainly should not allow them to be reduced to the levels suggested in the memorandum'.[9]

The nursing standards laid down were low, Dr Irvine continued, especially in relation to those to which they had been accustomed at St Helen's Hospital. Even so, wards 9 and 10 did not meet the standards and there was considerable variation in the long stay wards: Eversfield and Alexandra House were well above the minimum, Battle was considerably below.

Dr Irvine also referred to some of the practical difficulties which were encountered: 'The crucial problem is the constraint placed upon nurse allocation by the demands of teaching duties and to a lesser extent by the reluctance of permanent staff to move freely from one ward to another.' Thus there was a situation where some wards were overstaffed even by British Geriatric Society standards while others were 'starved'. Moreover, at times a fluctuating supply of learners to the unit placed a strain on the permanent staff.

Dr Irvine, who noted that there was no day space whatsoever on five of the wards, disagreed with the recommendation that it should be one sixth of the ward space:

> In my view, day space in any geriatric ward, except for those who are acutely ill, should constitute at least 50% of the space allocated to the beds.

And with regard to long-stay wards, added:

> The staff ... are well aware of the need to give them a homely atmosphere and at present our long stay wards do the group great credit.[10]

He also argued that if the wards were to be kept short of nurses, they must be supplemented by an adequate number of domestics and helpers to ensure good rehabilitation.

The administrator of one of the long stay hospitals (Battle) also sent his observations to the group secretary. He said the lockers on the wards were not adequate for all the personal clothing of those patients who were able to dress, that he had requested additional cupboard space in his estimates but his requests had not been met. Whilst the decorative state of the wards was 'quite good', the furniture, especially in the day rooms, was neither homely nor modern 'but does seem quite appropriate to the patients' condition. He added that the curtains were 'bright and cheerful' but more personal clothing was needed for the patients'.[11]

Additional funding

During the early 1970s it would appear that a brighter future for geriatric patients was emerging. Standards of care were being laid down and more money was being made available. However, the financial allocations to the hospitals were not always what they seemed.

In 1971, for example, there were initial reports of an allocation of £200,000 for Brighton hospitals, but the benefits that would accrue to geriatric patients prove to be somewhat limited. The £200,000 referred to was in fact the allocation for all capital developments in the Brighton

& Lewes group. The main item in the programme, it emerged later, was for improvements at the main acute hospital, The Royal Sussex County, costing £100,000. Only £50,000 had been allocated to Brighton General. A scheme to improve the sanitary annexes at Newhaven Downs Hospital costing about £13,000 was placed on the reserve list to be undertaken if funds became available later in the year. This led to a protest by Brighton's building sub-committee to the RHB.

Nevertheless, Brighton HMC's long-stay annexe fared better than the one in the Mid-Sussex group. Following the receipt of the RHB report, in which he acknowledged the group had come out rather well, the chairman visited Cuckfield Hospital and Pouchlands and suggested that there was a need for more acceptable bed spacing in some wards at the latter. However this would have meant a reduction in the bed complement and the regional board, when advised of the need for additional accommodation, said this could not be given a high priority because of needs elsewhere in the region.

The other problem with the capital allocations was that the additional funding was not always being used to the greatest possible effect in the hospital sector. For example, there was no guarantee that all the additional money would be spent as the government intended. How many of the schemes to benefit the geriatric services would have proceeded even if the funding had not been forthcoming is not known. It seems likely that some at least which had already been planned were then charged to the new allocation, and the original funding reallocated to other schemes, perhaps in the acute sector. Certainly the Department later exercised firmer central control over the major schemes.

Secondly, the practice of regional boards of not notifying details of financial allocations to the individual hospital management committees until midway through the financial year – sometimes even later – with the proviso that money must be spent by 31 March meant that allocations were not always spent as wisely as possible. In Brighton, for example, where furniture and equipment to the value of £27,000 had been placed on order, there were difficulties because additional funds had been made available to HMCs throughout the country. As a result the suppliers' order books had rapidly filled up and many of the items were simply not available within the time span allocated. An allocation of £20,000 to Brighton for surgical equipment, ward furniture and wall washing was also subject to a March 31 deadline. In the spring of 1974, the problem was further compounded firstly because of world-wide shortages of raw materials – including cotton, plastics, electrical steel, copper, silver, silver-plate and glass – and later because British industry was working a three day week.

Further indications of the inadequacy of the capital allocations were evident in Brighton when in 1973 the HMC received an allocation of nearly £250,000 for capital works but only £14,000 of this was made available to the geriatric services – for sanitary annexes at Newhaven Downs Hospital. The proposed upgrading of Brighton General's J Block was delayed until March 1974 and for F Block until 1975.

The nurses

In the circumstances, it is perhaps not surprising that some nurses in Brighton felt there was no room for complacency. They complained that in the provision of equipment the group was perpetuating two standards of care: one for general areas, another for geriatrics.[12] On the other hand, there was evidence of attempts to change attitudes and stimulate interest in geriatric care which could be considered to be equally important. A study day held at Eastbourne's All Saints Hospital in 1971 attracted an audience of 70 including staff from local authority welfare homes and private old people's homes. The following year, 300 trained nurses visited Newhaven Downs Hospital where four study days were held to discuss the problems of the elderly at home and in hospital.

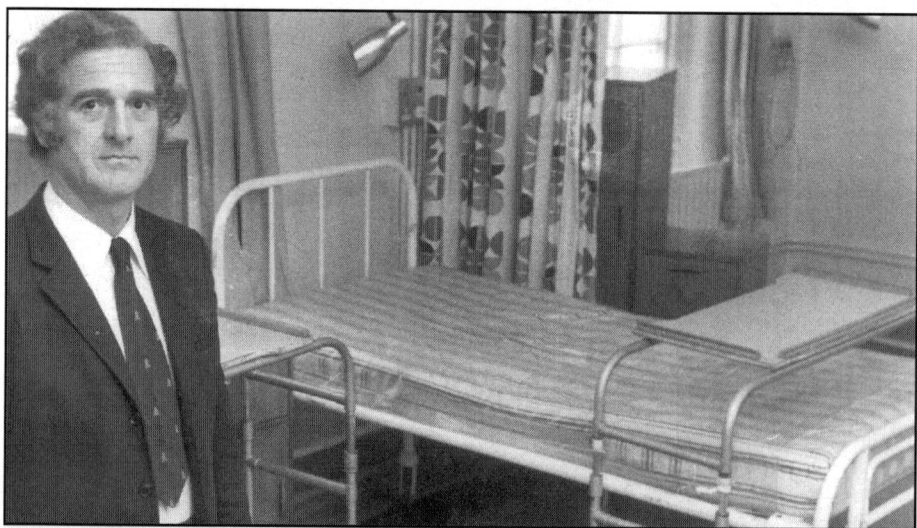

78. *Group Secretary Robert Alderton with unstaffed beds at Brighton General Hospital in 1974.*

A significant contribution to the debate on standards of care was also made by Brighton's group secretary. He forwarded a copy of a poem said to have been found in the locker of a patient after she died in a Scottish geriatric hospital to the editor of his group's house journal.

All members of the staff [he wrote] who have dealings with patients, particularly in the elderly age group, should ponder on what this old woman wrote, in which I feel there is a great deal of underlying truth ... it is rather like the practice which some nurses seem to engage in of tying up old ladies hair with pink bows on the top of their heads, which I think is an indignity which should not be perpetrated upon them.[13]

The poem, *A crabbit old woman wrote this*, (See Appendix) was reprinted in church magazines. A reprint in the local evening newspaper brought many letters of appreciation and was later reprinted in the parent Westminster Press Group papers throughout the country, and even in New Zealand. Under the title *Kate*, it reappeared five years later when it was used by the Open University in its accompanying *Ageing Population* course book.

Nevertheless, in spite of the allocation of more money, the attention to training and attitudes and the evidence of wide public interest and concern, the shortage of nursing staff continued to be a somewhat intractable problem causing one national newspaper to comment: 'why improve a geriatric hospital if no-one can be found to run it?'[14]

In Eastbourne, for example, shortly after Sir Keith Joseph's visit in 1972, a shortage of nursing auxiliaries meant it was not possible to open a new ward at All Saints Hospital. In Hastings, later in the year, Dr Irvine explained to his group secretary that he had closed beds because of 'inadequate nursing resources' and accused everyone of 'burying their heads in the sands of the geriatric population explosion'.[15] In Mid-Sussex, the HMC expressed concern over the nursing staff position at Pouchlands Hospital arising from the introduction of the 44-hour week. And the Brighton group's house journal, in the final month before health service reorganisation in 1974, pictured on the front page its group secretary at Brighton General Hospital in a ward of unmade beds which had been closed because of a shortage of about twenty nurses which meant, the group secretary explained, 'those remaining had to 'be pushed just that bit harder'.[16]

Part III

1974-2008:
The Reorganised NHS

19. The Unchanging Legacy

Public Assistance institutions continued to be known as 'the workhouse'. Death within their walls carried the stigma of humiliation. Everyone knew the horrors of the workhouse, but it was not until World War II that social investigators confirmed that popular mythology was founded in fact — Charles Webster, 'The Elderly and the Early National Health Service.

It should come as no surprise that, despite the ending of the poor law in 1948, numbers of older people still entertained a fear of the workhouse in the early 1970s. The abolition of the boards of guardians in 1930s provided an opportunity to sever the links between poor law and hospitals. Almost without exception in East Sussex, the local authorities failed to take advantage of this. In the minds of those living through the period under local authority control, images of the workhouse still remained. In the early years of the NHS every former workhouse that became a hospital in the county still contained wards housing the elderly chronic sick, still feared as a place from which there was no return – only final discharge, after time spent in often Spartan conditions, via the mortuary to the cemetery or crematorium.

Where the previous decades of NHS control under local management committees had failed to resolve the problem, the question after 1974 was would the NHS, as it moved towards the celebration of its first fifty years, finally eradicate the former workhouses and their memories? Inevitably, with the passing of the years, the numbers of older people fearing life in the workhouse would decline. That in itself would no longer be a problem. The workhouse buildings, however, were to take longer to die. The reorganisation of the NHS in 1974 was the first of three major organisational changes that were to take place during the remainder of the twentieth century. The local hospital management committees were replaced by county-wide area health authorities with local district management teams responsible not only for general hospitals but for psychiatric hospitals too. Their remit also included community services such as district nursing, dentistry and chiropody. Regional health authorities controlled the funding allocated by the government. The area health authorities controlled the purse strings within their areas; the district management teams determined the priorities between the competing claims of the various hospital and community services.

What did the future hold after 1974 for hospital care of the elderly, especially in long-stay wards and hospitals? In many respects the legacy to the newly reorganised service was similar to that to the NHS in 1948. Much of the evidence for this assessment is contained in the annual reports of the Hospital Advisory Service (HAS). These reports show, despite greater public awareness and the willingness of governments to make extra funds available, how little real progress was made.

The Cinderella services

From the outset, the HAS was concerned with all three Cinderella services – mental illness, mental handicap and elderly care. Reflecting Crossman's preoccupation with the problems of mental handicap, the main emphasis was on that area of care. Two of the four HAS teams that were set up were concerned with mental handicap services and it was intended that they should visit every mental handicap institution within two years. Moreover, these teams got down to work much more quickly. By the time the geriatric and chronic sick team assembled for its first visit in August 1970, they had already visited nearly 50 mental handicap hospitals. It was not until 1972 that a second team for geriatrics was established, although this was only short-lived and soon disbanded 'because of the need to ease the pressure of work ... [involved in] the reorganisation of the National Health Service.'[1] The team was not reinstated until two years later in September, 1974.

The first annual report of the HAS noted that there had been little change in many geriatric and chronic sick hospitals since the publication of the report prepared by Dr Boucher fifteen years before. According to the HAS: 'In many areas those concerned are standing by and watching the tide of frail elderly engulfing first the chronic sick, then geriatric, and eventually acute facilities as well'.[2] Although the teams found little evidence of 'deliberate cruelty' they told the Secretaries of State that 'a measure of neglect is common'. This was 'seldom the fault of the staff working on the ward, but is an inevitable result of a situation where too few staff are trying to care for far too many patients in badly equipped premises'.[3]

The HAS discovered that at first there was little evidence of additional sums of money or of greater interest in elderly care. As a result 'staff and patients in many geriatric wards feel they are seriously underprivileged[4] and when 'tangible improvements' were later observed, these were 'fairly obvious in the field of mental handicap, less so in the geriatric field'. There was a 'very considerable gap between generally accepted policies and the reality of the service as patients find it'.[5] In the 1971 report, there were criticisms of the lack of consultation at ward level over upgradings which, in any event, only consisted of 'a coat of paint and new floor covering'. Other necessary improvements, especially those requiring more space, were ruled out 'on the grounds of cost or a dreaded reduction in the bed complement.'[6] Two years later, 'many converted mansions and workhouses' were still being used and in some instances little or nothing had been done 'to create the conditions which modern geriatric practice demands'.[7]

The final report for the period referred to visits to three different regions in which just over one half of the hospitals for geriatric patients were built before the beginning of the century and only 18 per cent since 1950 and commented, tellingly:

> It is distressing after 25 years of the National Health Service to find much of the geriatric service still housed in quite unsuitable accommodation – old fever hospitals, sanatoria and workhouses, in some instances using ex-workhouse accommodation vacated when new welfare accommodation has been built nearby.[8]

The report acknowledged that much money had been spent trying to upgrade buildings, but reiterated that it was often not possible to overcome their basic unsuitability without major reconstruction. As a result, staff were constantly hampered by lack of space and facilities.

The national picture

Further evidence of the scale of the use of old, unsuitable buildings immediately prior to NHS reorganisation, was provided in an adjournment debate in the House of Commons in 1975. This was prompted by the deaths of several elderly patients in Lancashire following their transfer in December 1973 from Bury to Rossendale Hospital, eight miles away. An official inquiry concluded that in the case of five patients who died a contributory factor may have been 'badly fitting windows and skirting boards, uncontrolled ventilation and draughts affecting the heating of the area, inadequate furnishing and equipping of the area for the patients and insufficient qualified medical and nursing cover'.[9]

According to the MP who raised the matter in the Commons, the deferment of all capital schemes in November 1973 because of the economic crisis which had meant a loss of £80,000 in hospital improvements in Bury although earlier in the year a visiting medical team had commented with regard to one of the buildings, 'It would appear impossible for us to believe that anything but a complete demolition could in any way make this accommodation better' and with regard to others: 'The windows were very poorly fitted, with significant and in some cases visible cracks permitting the ingress of uncontrolled air ... some attempts had been made over the years to seal off the cracks with adhesive tape – but this was temporary and unreliable,'[10] which was regarded 'as the understatement of the year' relating as it did to a very cold period in December:

> It is a credit to the nurses who tried to fill the gaps and cracks with what sheets and blankets they could while the old ladies were in the hospital. These windows, however, had been reported as being in need of repairs since 1960. Fourteen years later they were in part responsible for the deaths of the old ladies.[11]

Referring to the general situation in the region, the MP said that 14 per cent of geriatric patients were accommodated in former workhouses built before 1850, 20 per cent in accommodation built between 1850 and 1899 and 26 per cent in hospitals built between 1900 and 1918. In one hospital, again a former workhouse, 80 patients died in 1964 while awaiting admission. In 1965 115 patients died; in 1971, 185; in 1973, 236. In 1974, 283 people were awaiting admission to this one hospital. He continued:

> If the measure of a civilised society is the care of its aged and infirm, the way in which we in Britain take care of them is seriously wanting when we consider that 49.25 per cent – almost half – of the accommodation for our old people is in old poor law hospitals... Only 4 per cent are in new hospitals.[12]

All the available evidence suggests that not only was a large proportion of hospital accommodation for the elderly contained in these very old and unsuitable buildings, but that the elderly chronic sick often occupied, in the words of the earlier Manchester RHB report, the very worst accommodation within them. Wells, for example, who carried out the research for her doctoral thesis between 1972 and 1974, selected for her purpose a 1,200 bed teaching hospital in the north. There had been a hospital on the site since the 1850s and part of the workhouse built then was still in use for geriatric care. Although the structure dated from 1864, the wards had been upgraded in 1972/73. A second one storey building used for geriatric care was situated just across the road. This had been constructed for government office use during the Second World War and converted in 1964. However, three of the hospital's continuing care (long stay) wards were situated in a third building of three storeys which was part of the original workhouse opened in 1855. According to Wells, this showed evidence of structural deterioration due to recent nearby building operations.

> Its entire fabric was stark and in poor repair with dim lighting, holes in the walls, drab colouring, uneven floors, loose window frames, and leaking ceilings...[13]

Fairhurst's research for her sociological study of the rehabilitation of elderly patients was carried out between 1975 and 1977 in a 100 year old hospital in which many changes had taken place since 1948. Two wards had been upgraded shortly before but two others remained 'dark and oppressive'. The baths and toilets were wedged beside each other in an extremely small room thus necessitating 'great feats of manoevrability for two members of staff to attend to a patient'. These wards had been scheduled for upgrading but had been deferred because of cuts in government expenditure.[14]

Even the establishment of minimum standards was not an unqualified success. In the report for 1973, the HAS commented that these had been achieved 'in some, but not by any means all, of the geriatric hospitals' and that too often unsuitable furniture and fittings had been provided because of lack of consultation with the staff.[15] In 1974 the criticism went even deeper: thinking in terms of minimum standards had led sometimes to harm rather than good. For example, hospitals having achieved the minimum congratulated themselves and lost the wish for any further progress.

What was also revealed by the HAS visits was that in levels of care, as in buildings and equipment, there were two distinctly different standards. These were graphically described by two team members in a paper in *The Lancet* in 1973. The authors had visited over 50 hospitals during a six month period and in their opinion 'there still exist widely different trends within the general framework of standards of care'.[16]

> Patients are on the whole given security and affection in hospitals, and there is little or no evidence of cruelty in their management. They can nevertheless be targeted in small inconspicuous ways which ultimately deny them occupation, identity and dignity.[17]

Many of the examples given have a familiar ring. Patients nursed in beds with high cot sides, toileting in the wards without screens for privacy, early wakening (at 6 am) for a wash and a cup of tea. The use of bibs,[18] women not being given knickers to wear and sitting with bare buttocks on mats on their chairs. Patients dressed from common pools of clothing, including some of dead patients from the same ward. Nurses putting patients back to bed at 3pm, drab and dull dayrooms, nurses talking to each other rather than to patients, restricted visiting and so forth. The nurses agreed the practices were wrong, the authors said, and could find little reason for them except perhaps shortage of staff 'although staffing allocation in good practising hospitals is no greater'.[19]

The paper was referred to by Adams in his presidential address to the British Geriatrics Society in April, 1974. It was, he said, 'a timely reminder of the risks of complacency, and one of them is that we ourselves might drift into narrow specialism at the expense of long-stay standards'.[20] Moreover, the paper provided more information than was generally available as a result of the HAS visits. At this time, very few details were leaked to local newspapers. Access to these could have provided information of the kind referred to in the 1975 adjournment debate. One report, for Brighton, which is available, is especially useful because it makes possible an assessment of the progress made since the publication of the SEMRHB report in 1970.

Progress in East Sussex

The HAS team visited every geriatric hospital in East Sussex, with visits to the three units in Brighton taking place in October 1975. The introduction to the report noted there was an overwhelming demand for services to meet the needs of the elderly population. It praised the Brighton service for its 'excellent leadership and unstinted efforts behind the improvements of the last eight years' adding there were features to be proud of within the various units but that *there was still a great deal to be done.*

The team was concerned about the disparity of standards between hospitals (Pouchlands compared unfavourably with Newhaven Downs) and 'more disturbingly within the same hospital'[22] (Brighton General Hospital: Ward A4 compared very unfavourably with C Block).

The detailed comments on **Brighton General Hospital** included references to overcrowding in much of the accommodation, the drab appearance of the hospital entrance 'with an old wooden letter box and usually an accumulation of paper sacks containing soiled linen. It has poor lights, poor furniture and no receptionist, and the impression given to patients and visitors is most unsatisfactory and unwelcoming'. Although the wards had been upgraded and in some the accommodation was excellent, Ward A4 was 'a repainted Dickensian conglomerate of small side wards with small day rooms. This badly maintained ward is on the third floor opposite the offices of the District Management Team (which are of a much higher standard of decor!).' J Block was noted to be in the middle of an extensive improvement scheme 'but it was disappointing to note that on completion two wards would still be without day rooms and thus unsuitable for present-day geriatric care'.[23]

The team was also critical of the tendency for patients to remain in bed during the day. Several of those who were up were in night attire and many returned to bed by 4 pm, even in the assessment ward. In one block indwelling urethral catheters were in frequent use and plastic pillow cases were in widespread use. On other wards faulty showers and bedpan washers were seen. An excessive use was made of cot sides at night with patients left unsupervised while nurses gathered in kitchens or offices, frequently making unnecessary noise. On some wards, breakfast for the following morning was prepared before midnight.

At **Newhaven Downs Hospital** conditions were said to be good. 'The nursing staff looked smart, and this is obviously a happy unit with good team spirit'.

> There is full consultation with ward staff regarding the selection of nursing aids and equipment, and the bathrooms are well designed and equipped. A great deal of thought has been given to the improvement effected so far in both the structure and ward decor.[24]

However, there was a lack of a personal laundry service for patients' clothing about which there were 'many complaints'.[25]

Pouchlands Hospital was said to be pleasantly situated and in a reasonable state of repair. The nurses were commended for their high standard of care 'despite difficulties'. All wards were overcrowded and had poor sanitary annexes. There was no privacy when commodes were used in the ward or side by side in a sluice. No variable height beds had been provided. Nurse staffing was found to be at 'dangerously low levels' at certain periods during the day and sometimes at night there was only one nursing auxiliary caring for sixteen patients while one ward was supervised by occasional visits by staff from another ward.

The report tended to confirm the earlier finding by Norton that conditions were often better in the smaller hospitals, worse in those with more than 200 beds, and the prevailing view that conditions for elderly care were often most acute 'in the two extremes of rural areas and city centres'.[27] It showed, too, that poor conditions could be overcome to provide a reasonably satisfactory service, as at Newhaven, where it was later decided to take part in a pilot study with King Edward's Hospital Fund for London on conditions in elderly long stay units which offered an opportunity to assess the effect of facilities at the hospital. The subsequent report summarised the improvements that had been made since 1974:

> Until two years ago the two wards together contained 75 beds, had very unsatisfactory plumbing and no separate day accommodation for the patients. Upgrading has reduced the number to 69 [actually 65], given an adequate number of modern and accessible geriatric bathrooms and lavatories and two superb day rooms with wide views leading respectively from the east and west sides of each ward. In addition to the four new day rooms a large occupational therapy room was built on the ground floor. The four day rooms are carpeted and have windows on three sides. They are in front of the hospital so that the patients enjoy a bird's eye view of the town, harbour and railway station as well as being able to observe all the comings and goings of hospital life.[28]

One of the more interesting conclusions to emerge from this detailed report is that there were few comments by patients on environmental conditions unlike many staff who made suggestions for possible change; the patients and their visitors most frequent comment was on the care and kindliness of staff, particularly the nurses. In many ways this reinforced earlier findings that patients are reluctant to complain but are always ready to express their appreciation.[29]

Inappropriate care

The modest achievements at Newhaven are in some way a measure of shortcomings which 25 years of NHS control had failed to solve. So too are the activities of bodies like the King's Fund. In 1975, the Fund published *Living in Hospital*[30] which attempted to help those caring for people in long term care to cater for their social rather than medical needs. An exhibition, *The Growing Needs of Growing Old*, was held at its central London centre from February until May. The survey of old people living in hospitals[31] was followed in 1980 with two well attended seminars at the Hospital Centre in London.

Also in 1975, the Royal College of Nursing published its report[32,] compiled in conjunction with the British Geriatrics Society and funded by the Department of Health. This reflected the concern that although a great deal of information was available about the medical, nursing, social, remedial and other aspects of the care of elderly patients, there were still

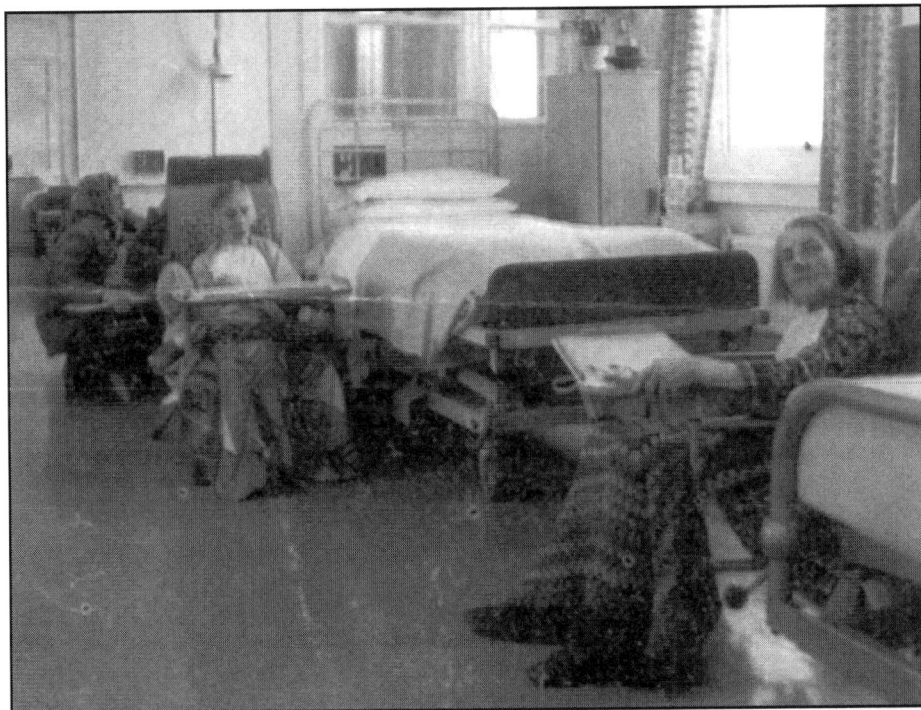

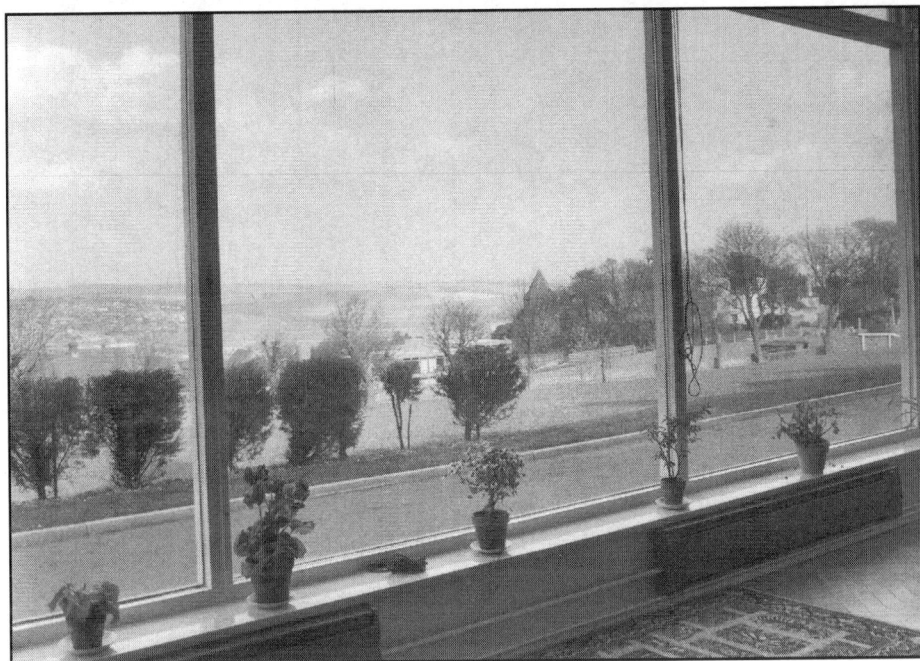

79. One of the generally unsuitable wards at Pouchlands Hospital where cubicles had been formed to provide a little privacy. 80. A new dayroom at Newhaven Downs Hospital that gave uninterrupted views over the town towards the Downs beyond.

hospitals where 'despite the fact that staff are concerned, kind, and have the best intentions, patients are treated inappropriately, inadequately or inhumanely'.[33]

One result of the publication of the RCN report was the establishment by the DHSS in March 1976 of a working group which was given the task of evolving a programme for improving the standards of geriatric care. Another was the implementation of a recommendation that regional conferences should be set up to be followed by seminars in regions, areas and districts. These were intended to provide forums for discussion on the improvement of care of the elderly in the light of the principles expressed in the report. In the introduction to one of these regional seminars, the chairman commented:

> The increasing number of elderly people in hospital has not led, as one might have hoped, to a corresponding increase in sympathy and concern for their plight – rather the reverse. As a result, the quality of care for the elderly sick is often not all that it might be. Progress in safeguarding patients' well being as individuals has lagged behind improvements in scientific investigation and treatment.[34]

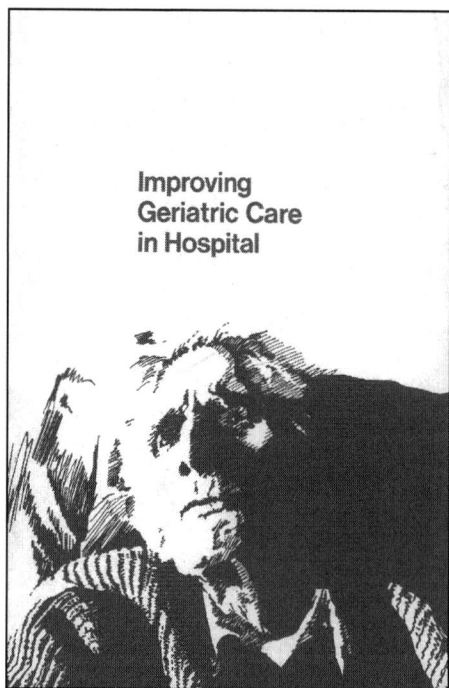

Improving
Geriatric Care
in Hospital

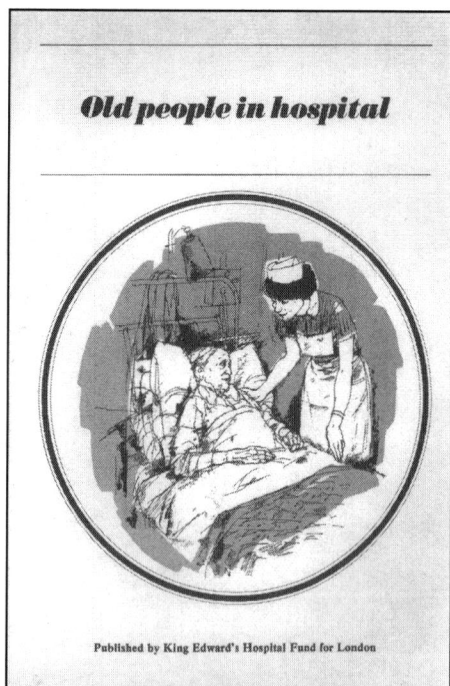

Old people in hospital

Published by King Edward's Hospital Fund for London

81 and 82. The booklet published in 1976 by the Royal College of Nursing and the British Geriatric Society that acknowledged that patients could be treated inadequately or inhumanely and the 1979 publication by the King's Fund describing a survey of opinions of patients, visitors and staff in six geriatric hospitals.

20. Farewell to the Workhouse

*Pleasant, purpose built physical surroundings, good staffing levels and a limitless supply of money will not necessarily produce a high standard of nursing care. The answer lies in choosing nurses of high calibre ... nurses with the **right attitude** — Editorial, British Journal of Geriatric Nursing, November/December 1984.*

In the 1980s it became clear that many hospitals had failed to recognise what most residential homes had already realised, that traditional nursing attitudes, developed in the climate of acute and life threatening illness, were not necessarily appropriate in caring for elderly people.[1]

In 1986, the BMA was still arguing that nursing homes and long-stay wards should present a more personalised and homelike environment and the 1987 report by the HAS (now the NHS Health Advisory Service and DHSS Social Service Inspectorate) commented:

> The quality of long-term care offered to elderly people in hospital is generally very poor. There is a growing contrast with the individual personal care provided in many local authority homes ... in hospitals the 'traditional' care is still prevalent.[2]

In the twelve districts visited by the HAS teams this care included the recurrent and unnecessary use of restraint by means of chairs fitted with trays or through the use of cot sides. Long-stay wards consistently offered environments unable to provide privacy (especially in dressing, washing and use of the toilet), homely surroundings, personal space and possessions or adequate furniture. None had a comprehensive personalised clothing service. Catering was often provided according to the needs of the institution rather than the resident patients with the last meal of the day being served as early as 5pm. Impersonal ward routines for bed times, waking times and even visiting times were widely observed.[3]

The HAS visit to the Brighton District

Brighton hospitals were among those visited by the HAS in 1986. At Brighton General they found three long-stay wards, one of 24 beds for women, one of 19 beds for men and a mixed sex ward of 34 beds. During the couple of years preceding the inspectors' visit a number of developments had taken place at the hospital. £120,000 had been spent on internal redecoration and other improvements. These included, as a first step, double glazing the windows on the top floors of the exposed C, D and E blocks. In 1985, thanks to a £170,000 development, Lancing Ward had been converted to a 24-bedded unit (complete with lift) for rehabilitating elderly orthopaedic patients. Despite this, the inspectors maintained that basic limitations of the structure meant that no ward was appropriate for its function.

The section of the report on long-stay care referred in detail to Pouchlands and Newhaven Downs as well as Brighton General Hospital. At the latter the three wards were named as Jevington (formerly J) Block, the top floors were named Fletching Ward 3 and Hollingbury Ward 3. At Newhaven, there were 65 predominantly female patients. Pouchlands had 28 beds in 'a mainly mental handicap hospital due to close in two years.'[4] Standards of care were said to be 'kindly and compassionate but over-protective and out of date'[5]. There was a failure to provide appropriately for the comfort, dignity, choice and privacy of old, incapacitated people.

According to the report, all the long-stay wards had been allowed to become overcrowded, day space was inadequate and nursing had been reduced to repetitive drudgery. The burden of long-stay care had effectively been handed, without assistance, to nurses who had little or no assistance from other disciplines. However, this was not always the case.

At Pouchlands Hospital, for example, the reference to kindly, compassionate, over-protective and out-of date nursing might well have been leavened by a reference to the efforts of those same staff to broaden the horizons of patients who might otherwise have been confined largely to

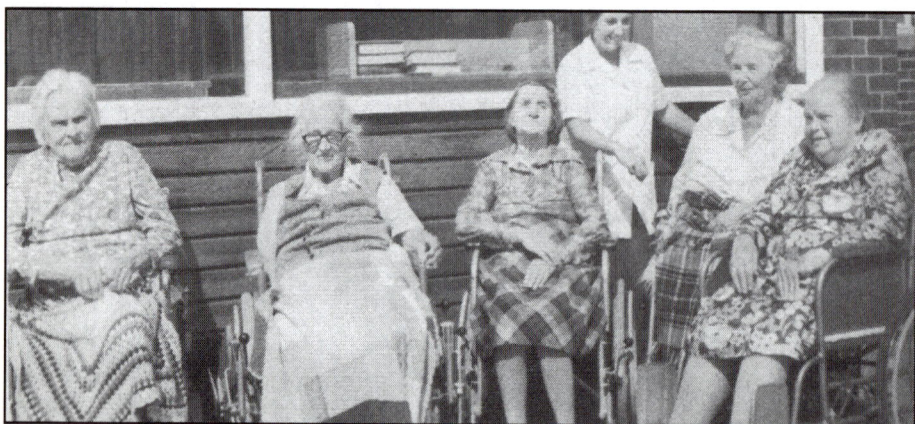

83. Physiotherapy helper Shirley Bowes with the elderly ladies who made the first day trip from Pouchlands Hospital to Dieppe.

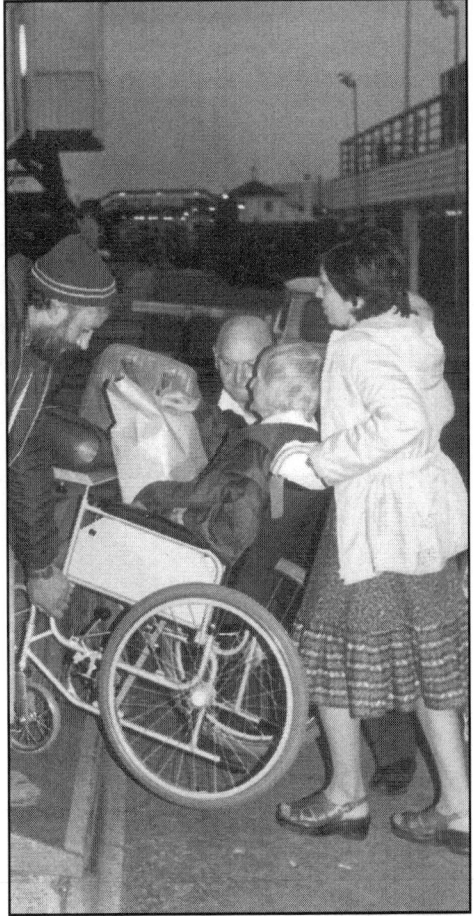

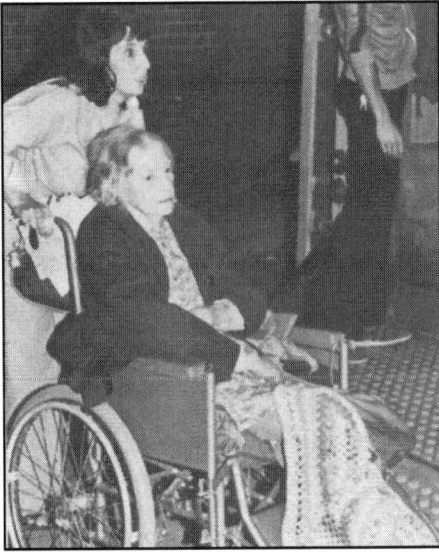

84. *A Pouchlands patient is wheeled aboard the ferry at Newhaven in 1978.*

85. *A helping hand for nursing officer Evelyn Clear as she pushes a wheelchair patient from Newhaven Downs Hospital up the ramp of the ferry to France in 1981.*

86. *Staff and volunteers with long-stay patients enjoying the day out in Dieppe.*

the four walls of their wards. It was at Pouchlands in 1976 that thanks to the enthusiasm of a physiotherapy helper five elderly wheelchair-bound patients were taken on a trip that must have been viewed with some trepidation by those in authority. The idea for the outing, a day trip across the channel to Dieppe, was born when patients in the occupational therapy department had been trying their hands at continental cooking. It was so successful that it became an annual event for patients not only at Pouchlands but from Newhaven as well. It is not clear how many trips were made but there is certainly evidence that both hospitals participated five years later in 1981 thanks to staff and volunteers and the support of the leagues of hospital friends.

The friends also provided minibuses to Newhaven Downs and Brighton General Hospitals. In the years leading up to the HAS visit, outings to the races, pubs and shopping trips were being reported at all three hospitals. At a conference, *Who Cares for the Elderly*, held at Brighton General's

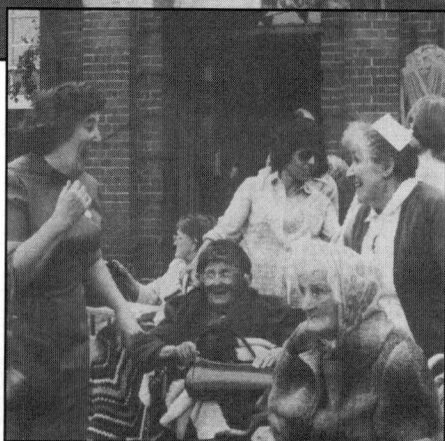

87. *The presentation of an ambulance to Brighton General Hospital by the League of Hospital Friends that enabled staff to take patients on shopping trips and other outings.*

88. *Away from the wards ... Nursing officer Katie Plasins welcomes patients from Newhaven to the Pouchlands Hospital midsummer fayre in 1981.*

Postgraduate Medical Centre in 1985, a sister from one of the continuing care wards described the outings enjoyed by her patients and gave an example of community interest with regular visits being made by a young family living nearby, including toddlers. She also spoke about the value of animals to elderly patients, not only birds and fish; they had even experimented with a dog on the ward. That experiment had failed, she admitted, but they might try again one day.[6] What this nurse-organised conference illustrated was that many nurses were alive to the problems posed by geriatric care. A questionnaire sent to fifty nurses of all grades asked them to imagine what patients might feel – who were incontinent and incapable of coherent speech but with full mental faculties. Asked what improvements were needed on Brighton General's fourteen wards for the elderly they replied that they wanted to give more individual attention. A maximum of twenty patients to a ward was suggested. More space was needed, more dayrooms, more entertainment and more community help.

The final contribution to the conference was by a clinical nurse manager. He presented the results of a survey of 154 of the hospital's patients to support his argument that that long-stay beds at the hospital should go and, as the HAS inspectors were to recommend in their report a year later, be looked after in health authority nursing homes in the community where they could lead a more normal life. 'Is tender loving care enough? Are we being fair to our elderly people by keeping them in a long-stay geriatric unit?'[7]

By the end of 1986, life was undergoing a fundamental change for the remaining 28 patients in what was by then known as the continuing care unit for the elderly

89. *A patient at Pouchlands tries her hand at the spinning wheel, one of the new activities designed for patients during the final days at the hospital.*

at Pouchlands. A key worker system, recommended by the HAS in its report, was introduced making each nurse responsible for the physical and social wellbeing of two or three residents. A residents' committee was formed. Social evenings and barbecues were held with cooperation from the catering and occupational therapy departments. As a result 'a more relaxed and democratic relationship between residents and staff has begun to take shape ... team leaders and key workers are also finding that working at Pouchlands is now more interesting and fulfilling.'[8] Two years later, further developments were reported, including a monthly flower club held in the occupational therapy department and extended activities that included spinning.

Meanwhile, the residents were continuing to enjoy their trips outside the hospital. On one notable occasion in 1988 six of them were taken to Lewes railway station. There they were given the privilege of welcoming the Princess of Wales on her arrival to open the town's new magistrates' courts.

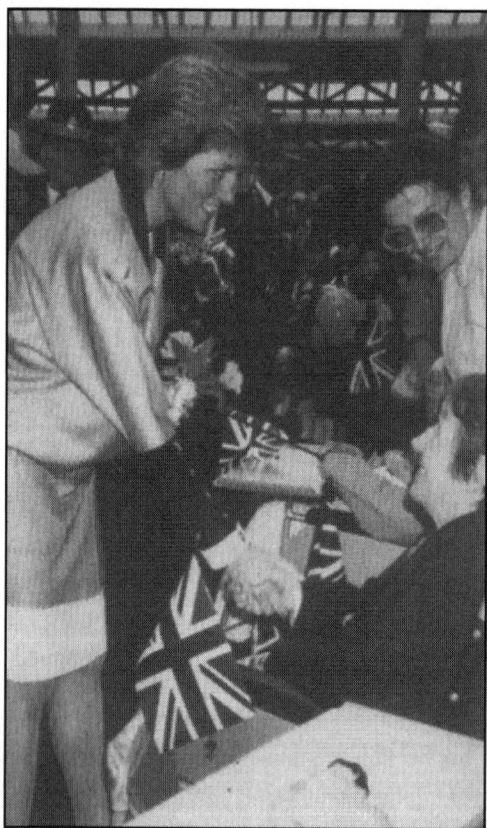

Soon, however, all the residents were to leave the hospital for good. In 1991 Pouchlands became the first of the former East Sussex workhouses to close. Mental handicap patients were moved to new homes in the community and the elderly continuing care unit was replaced by a new NHS purpose-built nursing home, Meadow Lodge, adjacent to the Lewes Victoria community hospital. Meadow Lodge was one of the first NHS nursing homes to be built in the country. At the opening the chairman of

90. *Welcome to Lewes. Six Pouchlands residents welcomed the Princess of Wales on her visit to the county town. Here a smiling Princess talks to resident Mrs Kathleen Watkins while nursing auxiliary Anne Tattum looks on.*

the health authority said it would provide a domestic atmosphere and surroundings in which even the most frail and dependent residents could maintain their dignity and individuality. 'Everyone living in Meadow Lodge has freedom of choice, privacy when they need it and company when they want it – as well as continuing high standards in nursing care.'[9]

The health authority saw the new facility as a model for the future in the district and even, perhaps, nationally. A proposal to convert Newhaven Downs Hospital into an NHS nursing home had earlier been referred to in the 1986 HAS report and strongly supported by the inspectors. However the plan met considerable opposition locally which was being voiced even as Meadow Lodge opened.

At Newhaven, the inspectors were critical of the minimal amount of intermittent and holiday care provided. Fifteen years or so before, both had in fact been a feature of the services provided there. Holiday care for two or three weeks enabled relatives to take a break for an annual holiday. Intermittent care was based on a 'six weeks in/six weeks out' basis, with effectively, two patients sharing one bed: while one was in hospital for six weeks, the other spent six weeks at home, the pair changing places at the end of the six week period. These schemes were seen as a way of breaking down the image of a place where people were admitted only to die. They also possessed other practical advantages. For example, the hospital secretary explained: 'On the one hand elderly patients are able to retain their links with home and family. On the other they do not burden their relatives with an unrelieved heavy nursing problem'.[10]

According the first report of the Brighton Health District Planning Team for the Care of the Elderly, some 40 to 50 patients participated in the district in its 'six weeks hospital, six weeks home' programme, so the numbers appear to have declined during the following ten years. Possibly the nursing staff situation at Newhaven was one of the contributory factors. This was described by the HAS inspectors as 'difficult', despite introduction of an early morning 'twilight shift' of nursing auxiliaries. Domestic services were also found to be poor.[11]

St Mary's Hospital was the next former workhouse to close. In fact its closure was proposed as early as 1961 when the regional authority decided that Eastbourne would best be served by a new, single hospital. The scheme, due to get off the ground in 1975, suffered a delay, like most other capital projects in the country, by the oil crisis in 1974. When the

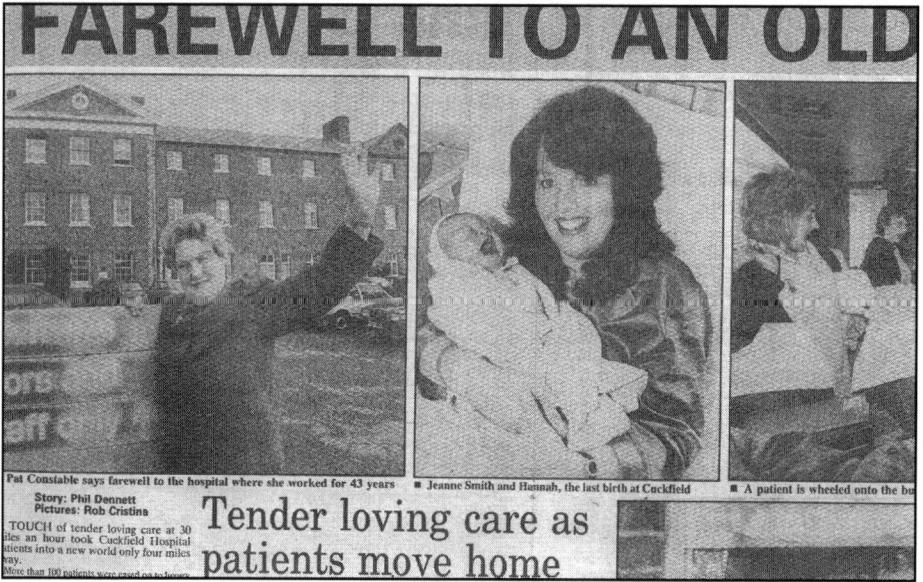

FAREWELL TO AN OLD

Pat Constable says farewell to the hospital where she worked for 43 years ■ Jeanne Smith and Hannah, the last birth at Cuckfield ■ A patient is wheeled onto the bu

Story: Phil Dennett
Pictures: Rob Cristins

TOUCH of tender loving care at 30
miles an hour took Cuckfield Hospital
patients into a new world only four miles
way.
More than 100 patients were eased on to houses

Tender loving care as patients move home

91. Farewell to an old friend ... how the press reported the closure of Cuckfield Hospital.

first phase of the new hospital opened in 1976, long-stay patients from St Mary's were transferred to the former voluntary hospital, Princess Alice.

During the planning process of Phase 2 of the Eastbourne development for 1982/83 it seemed likely that the hospital would, after all, be upgraded and continue to 'soldier on' through the rest of the century and beyond. However, after intensive local lobbying, the regional authority decided to proceed with the original single hospital proposal and the last patient from St Mary's was transferred to the new Eastbourne District General Hospital in October 1989. The following February the site was purchased for redevelopment to provide executive style housing and in April the work of demolition began.

The former Cuckfield Institution was the next to close. As a result of the boundary changes in 1974, Cuckfield had been placed over the administrative county border into West Sussex. However it remained closely linked with Pouchlands Hospital which continued to supply the long-stay beds. With the prospect of a new hospital being built in Haywards Heath, few changes took place at Cuckfield until 1991 when the former workhouse was closed and its patients transferred to the new Princess Royal Hospital.

Despite these successes, there were still four former workhouse hospitals operating in the county as the end of the twentieth century

92. *Battle Hospital, described as 'an exemplar of the style of building in 1841, pictured some time after its closure.*

93. *Not all the buildings at Battle Hospital were so imposing as the front entrance.*

94. *The old St Helen's Hospital pictured in 1994, shortly after its closure.*

95. *St Helen's Hospital. The rear of the 1838 building as it appeared in January 1995.*

approached. However, East Sussex was by no means alone in continuing to provide care for what were formerly known as the elderly chronic sick in former workhouse accommodation. Results of a study of the South West Thames region published in 1991 show that 23 of the 34 wards were housed in pre-war buildings. All had been upgraded, but the quality varied from 'near luxury to the bare minimum'. Four departments had admission wards in huts that had been built during the Second World War. In some wards standards of upkeep and decoration were 'a disgrace to a civilised nation' although others were imaginatively colour co-ordinated and immaculately clean. Half the nurses interviewed were critical of their ward environment; two stated they worked in a neglected building that was falling down.

The HAS visit to the Hastings district

It was in 1991 that Hastings, ironically the acknowledged leader of geriatric care in the county prior to 1974, was the subject of a highly critical HAS report. At a time when the regional health authority had made cuts of almost £27 million in capital expenditure in order to balance its books, the HAS reported that conditions in the district's three

96. *The end of an era at Battle Hospital was the subject of a full page story in a county newspaper.*

hospitals were so poor they should be closed. Eversfield Hospital was said to be quite unsuitable for the residential care of physically and mentally frail old people. The building was a fire hazard, while the neglect of the small garden and paths prevented patients from being taken outside.

> The wards are poor, badly maintained, overcrowded and poorly furnished. The toilets and bathrooms are just acceptable. There is little privacy for patients. At least half the patients are incontinent.[12]

Battle Hospital, described as a 150 year-old former workhouse listed for its historic importance, was 'a good exemplar of a style of building in 1840 but is wholly inappropriate for modern-day care of elderly people'. Wards were overcrowded; toilets, bathrooms and sitting rooms were poor and privacy was 'not readily available'.[13] There was a high level of incontinence and a smell of urine at night in some wards. The staff were devoted professionals, the inspectors said, but appeared to have 'accepted the environment they work in and no longer see it for what it is.'[14] The report recommended an immediate reduction of 14 beds and the replacement of the hospital 'in the near future'.

At St Helen's, due to be replaced by phase two of the new DGH, still in the design stage, the wards were of very poor standard, overcrowded, cluttered with furniture; where there were no dayrooms, patients sat by their beds. There was a distinct absence of privacy.[15]

It was not only the fabric of the buildings that was criticised. The inspectors were critical of the way Hastings health authority had been run and the quality of care in some areas. They were particularly concerned with the quality of nurse management. They found a shortage of nurses in all areas and recommended a fundamental review of nursing roles.

In addition to the financial cuts imposed by the regional authority, it seems likely that St Helen's and the other hospitals in the locality would also have suffered financially from the usual blight while the new hospital, in this case the Conquest, was under construction.

Activities at St Helen's were scaled down and when the Conquest opened in 1992 only 40 in-patients and the day hospital attenders remained. Finally, in March 1994, following the provision of portable ward accommodation at the Conquest, the remaining patients and the day hospital facility were transferred.

It was not until 1998 that Battle Hospital finally closed its doors. The building stood empty for a time until the site was sold and developed for

97. *A grim reminder ... the House block at Newhaven Downs Hospital in 2008, the last remaining evidence of the old workhouse.*

98. *New building, new look ... Newhaven Downs House opened in 1996.*

private accommodation named Thatcher Place, after the original architect of Stone House, Frederick Thatcher.

Final days at Newhaven and Brighton

Meanwhile, in the Brighton area, one of the two remaining former work-houses, Newhaven Downs Hospital, had also closed. It had not been a smooth process. A plan to build a 48-place NHS nursing home on the site was unveiled at a public health authority meeting in the April 1989. A suggestion that a day hospital should also be included depended on the sale of the remainder of the five acre site when building work was completed. From the outset the proposal was met with controversy. Some health authority members felt the new unit would be too large and create 'a ghetto for old people' where they would be in danger of 'a very insti-tutional regime'.[16]

A campaign by the town council and other local groups to include a casualty unit on the site that had the backing of the community council (CHC) proved to be a major stumbling block. The health authority warned that if the CHC did not agree to the scheme as it stood, it was unlikely to go ahead. In fact the scheme was deferred when the CHC put in place a counter proposal for a 22-bedded home with a day hospital and using a local Guinness Trust building for 26 elderly patients. The town mayor added to the delay calling the plan fundamentally unsound because

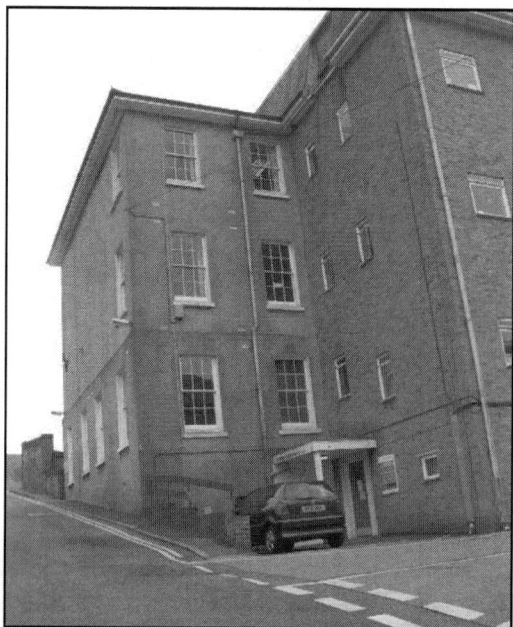

99. *J Block at Brighton General, currently home to the headquarters of South Downs Health NHS Trust.*

it lacked the inclusion of a casualty and emergency service for the town. The mayor, a local GP, later told a public meeting 'a nursing home is not what [the patients] want'[17] while fears of possible traffic congestion if houses were built in the grounds were raised.

However it was national economic conditions that finally put paid to the scheme. Falling land and property prices had upset plans for hospital developments throughout the south-east, and the Downs scheme was no exception. Locally the sale of sites at Pouchlands and the Hove School of Nursing were affected. The outlook was so bleak that major schemes at the Royal Sussex County Hospital were put back for a year. In view of the inevitable delay, the health authority agreed to redecorate some of the wards and corridors at the Downs.

In 1992 South Downs NHS Trust became responsible for the management of the hospital. Within three years new plans had been approved and the necessary funding obtained. In 1995 when the number of patients had been reduced from 65 to 40, one half of the infirmary building was closed and demolished. The following year, staff and patients moved into a new building, Newhaven Downs House, its name chosen following consultation with staff and local residents.

The remaining buildings on the site were later demolished to make way for new facilities for day hospital care for elderly people with physical and

100. *Lancing Ward patients and staff enjoyed the improved conditions in their new home on Brighton General's D2 ward.*

mental health problems and a polyclinic. Newhaven Downs House later became known as Newhaven Rehabilitation Centre, admitting patients from the Brighton area.

Only the listed original building remained on site, with plans approved for its conversion to private apartments. Considerable preparatory work was undertaken. All the windows were replaced and the building was made dry and water tight. In 2009, however, because of the prevailing economic and financial situation, progress had clearly stalled, leaving the building standing empty and looking neglected, a reminder still of its early grim origins.

The closure of Brighton General Hospital, at least as a provider of in-patient accommodation, took much longer to achieve. In April 1990, the health authority announced the closure of Jevington Block where the 60 elderly patients were living in what was described as cramped conditions. The patients were transferred into residential nursing homes where it was believed they would enjoy a better quality of life although the nursing staff expressed doubts about nursing home staffing levels.

In 1998 the Homeward Unit, which four years earlier had earned an accolade as a centre of excellence, was closed. The staff and patients were transferred to a new base, ironically in the former workhouse at Southlands Hospital. To be fair, the wards at Southlands had undergone a

101. A Nightingale ward at Brighton General in 2003. Hopes that these wards would be replaced in a new clinical block were dashed when funding was not made available.

£45,000 facelift with larger bathrooms, fully independent disabled access, new furniture and equipment, a gym and a dining area.[18]

In September 1999 the hospital's laundry building was gutted by fire. When it was demolished shortly afterwards South Downs Health, which was responsible for the site, announced that all remaining services would be removed over the following five to ten years. Next in line for demolition, the authority announced, would be Lancing and Keymer blocks. Lancing Ward was transferred for six months to the Royal Sussex County Hospital before returning to the converted late Victorian Dyke 2 Ward, which had been adapted as a 23-bedded rehabilitation unit.

In 2002, the future of the hospital plans were unveiled that promised to give the General a new lease of life. Staff were told about an £11 million project to replace the Nightingale wards in blocks C, D and E. Using the old laundry site, it was planned to construct a new 'systems' building that

102. Sign of the times ... Brighton General in 2009 provides a range of services including stop smoking and falls prevention clinics and children's services, but no wards for elderly in-patients.

could be built in six months. With three storeys at the front and two at the back, the slate roofed building would contain four-bedded and single bedded bays with en suite facilities for 41 patients on the first floor and 42 on the second. The new block had an anticipated life of 20 years.

By the end of the year, however, no funding had been approved for the upgrading of the Nightingale wards although design work on a £1.2 million scheme to upgrade the original building, A Block, was under way As a result, it was intended to provide improved facilities for the dermatology department, that had been on the stocks for two years, together with plastic surgery clinical areas.

Within a few weeks, however, the hopes of replacing the Nightingale wards had been dashed. Unable to secure the necessary funding, the recently formed Brighton and Sussex University Hospital NHS trust could only promise 'to struggle against the deteriorating fabric and invest what money we can in maintaining those buildings until they close.'[19]

Towards the end of 2004 the future of Brighton General featured in a consultation document, *Best Care, Best Place*, containing proposals for the delivery of health care in central Sussex. This suggested that all acute care would be removed, leaving only outpatient and day care services and possibly a polyclinic on site.

During the summer of 2004, following the transfer of elderly patients in Edburton 2 to a community setting and other wards to the Royal Sussex County Hospital, the number of wards was reduced from seven to two. The remaining wards based in Cuckmere block catered for older people making the transition from hospital to home, focusing on respiratory illness and orthopaedic rehabilitation. This was intended to be a temporary arrangement but another three years passed before plans to close the block and transfer the patients were announced. Not everybody was happy with the proposal to move most of the patients to Newhaven Rehabilitation Centre despite the far superior accommodation. There were concerns about the distance to be travelled from Brighton by relatives and staff. Again the move was intended to be a temporary one until patients were able to return to Brighton and Hove.

Nevertheless, on 12 December 2007, the patients were transferred to Newhaven and the last of the former workhouses in East Sussex finally closed its wards to the elderly of Brighton. Most of the buildings still stood, many of them transformed inside, serving new purposes, owing little to the legacy of their workhouse past.

Afterword

The fear of the workhouse was very real for many old people. The principal reasons for this probably varied with the passage of time: the Spartan conditions and brutality of the nineteenth century, the knowledge that once admitted, husbands would be separated from wives, the stigma attached to the poor law and, above all, the fear that admission, especially for the elderly chronic sick, meant they would never see the outside world again. For them, Dante's inscription of the gates of hell seemed all too appropriate: Abandon all hope, ye who enter here.

When I undertook the original research more than twenty years ago on which this book is largely based, the general belief seemed to be that workhouse history ended with the abolition of the guardians in 1930. The books that chronicled the story following 1930 were, in the main, concerned with the development of residential care. The development of services for the elderly chronic sick who had occupied the poor law infirmaries was largely neglected, so my aim was to trace this development and the rise of geriatric medicine which accompanied it. I had intended to cover the period from 1930 to 1982, the year in which the second major reorganisation of the NHS took place and also the year in which I decided to take early retirement from the service. I was unable to do this because the Thatcher government decreed that part-time Ph.D. and D.Phil. students should no longer have an unlimited time to submit their theses and set a deadline of six years. In any event, by then my results of my research until 1974, the date of the first NHS reorganisation, totalled 120,000 words – 30,000 more than the prescribed upper limit.

When I came to write this book, however, it was 1974 that provided the source of inspiration. It was around that time that I saw for myself first hand evidence that the fear of the workhouse still existed. In the following years, of course, there would inevitably be fewer and fewer older people who had lived through the Thirties. As they died, so would the fear of the workhouse. But even if the fear died, the unacceptable physical conditions existing in the former workhouses remained. Until these hospitals were closed, the conditions under which elderly patients were nursed, especially in the long-stay wards, would remain a legacy of their workhouse origins.

That is why the book also tells the continuing story, of necessity in rather less detail, of the East Sussex hospitals that began life as nineteenth century workhouses. Amazingly, it is only relatively recently that the curtain has come down on what should have been the final act – the discharge of the last remaining elderly patients from Brighton General Hospital.

Anyone reading the book, however, must surely see that it was not just the physical conditions in hospitals that were the problem. From the publication of *Sans Everything* onwards, it is abundantly clear that the question of the attitudes towards older patients, and the too frequent examples of neglect and passive cruelty, that continued to give rise for concern. And, regrettably, those attitudes haven't changed. Unlike the workhouses, they haven't withered and died.

The previous pages chronicle events of the final seventy years of the twentieth century. The first decade of the twenty-first century demonstrates all too clearly that these abject failures in geriatric care persist, despite the demise of the workhouses.

In 2001 the launch of the National Service Framework for Older People promised, among other things, the establishment of Older People's Champions. At ward level, this would have meant appointing and training nurses who would act as advocates for their patients' views, needs and preferences. An important task – admittedly not an easy one – would be to challenge age discrimination and poor practice.

It is not clear how enthusiastically this proposal was taken up. It appears that four years passed before Brighton gave the matter consideration – even then only to be overtaken by events – the screening of the secretly filmed BBC Panorama programme, *Undercover Nurse*, which revealed harrowing scenes of the care, or lack of it, on the Royal Sussex County Hospital's Peel and Stewart ward. At the time some claimed that similar scenes could have been filmed at any one of a number of hospitals. Events were to prove them right.

In April 2006 the Department of Health publication *A New Ambition for Old Age* set out the priorities for the next phase of the NSF for Older People. This described how some staff still demonstrated deep-rooted negative attitudes towards older people. It recommended that each NHS authority should nominate a member of staff to take responsibility for promoting and protecting the dignity of older people. Prior to this, the British Geriatric Society (BGS) had already brought together a multi-agency committee that included, among others, Age Concern England, Help the Aged and the Royal College of Nursing. This group then chose toilet access and used behind closed doors as a marker of human rights and dignity. The BGS then launched its campaign named *Behind Closed Doors* (using the toilet in private) at the House of Lords.

Then, in November 2006, five years after the introduction the NSF Framework and its attendant Older People's Champions, the Department of Health launched its *Dignity in Care* campaign. This aimed to create a care system 'where there is zero tolerance of abuse and disrespect of adults' and also to improve the quality of care in NIIS hospitals, community services and care homes. People were encouraged to sign up as Dignity Champions and were offered a *Toolkit for Action*.

There was not much evidence of early success of this attempt at 'winning the hearts and minds, changing the culture of care services'. On the contrary, 2007 saw mounting evidence of failings in the care of older people in some NHS hospitals.

In July a report by the joint parliamentary committee on human rights claimed that vulnerable elderly people were being subjected to abuse, neglect, discrimination and ill-treatment in hospitals and care homes that should be looking after them. Many old people, it warned, were facing maltreatment ranging from physical neglect so severe that they were left lying in their own faeces or urine, and to malnutrition and dehydration through lack of help with eating.

In September, the Healthcare Commission issued a report highlighting how mixed sex wards and attitudes among some staff contributed to a culture of neglect. A survey of 23 NHS trusts that had self-certified themselves as meeting national dignity in care standards revealed that only five actually did so. Eight trusts received formal warnings, ten others were told to make improvements.

In October, an investigation by the *Observer* newspaper revealed that elderly people were being forced to use embarrassing portable commodes or to wear incontinence pads rather than being taken to the toilet. The report was published only days after news that large numbers of old people had died of the *C. difficile* infection in hospitals controlled by Maidstone and Tunbridge Wells NHS Trust. Staff had allowed (even encouraged) patients to go to toilet in their beds. According to the report, the level of dirt and neglect had contributed to two outbreaks of the infection.

In May 2008, Sir Michael Parkinson was named as the Government's ambassador to promote a drive to ensure patients lived with dignity and respect in hospitals and care homes. He related his own experience and told how he had complained about the treatment his 95-year old mother had received – but fearing repercussions he was fearful about leaving her alone.

'I came across an extraordinary mixture of care. Some nurses were utterly dedicated and wonderful. But there were others who treated it as a job and a bit like they were a jailer, treated people in their care as inmates. There were distressing signs of elderly people being left weeping who were still there half an hour later, and that's obviously not right.'

The new NHS Constitution published in January this year included the right for all patients to be treated with dignity and respect. Recently a news report from the Department of Health Care Networks announced that in the third year of their Dignity in Care campaign 79% of patients survey said they were 'always' treated with the dignity and respect, and that this 'small but significant increase' on the previous year 'demonstrates that Dignity is still very much at the heart of the NHS.'

The fact remains, however, that these figures show that 21% – one patient in every five – is still *not* always treated with dignity and respect. As I write, there comes still more evidence that vulnerable and elderly people are not always receiving appropriate care and basic dignity in UK hospitals. A dossier submitted this week by the Patients' Association to the Quality Care Commission highlights sixteen cases of patients who died who had been left lying in faeces and urine and had not received the help they needed to eat and drink.

Despite *Sans Everything* in 1965, the later campaigns by the British Geriatrics Society, the King's Fund, the British Medical Association and the Royal College of Nursing in the 1970s, and the reports by the Health Advisory Services in the following years, the neglect and abuse of older people in NHS hospitals continues.

There is no room for complacency.

Harry Gaston,
Newhaven,
August 2009.

Appendix

A crabbit old woman wrote this

What do you see nurses, what do you see?
Are you thinking when you are looking at me –
A crabbit old woman, not very wise,
Uncertain of habbit, with far – away eyes,
Who dribbles her food and makes no reply
When you say in a loud voice –
"I do wish you'd try."
Who seems not to notice the things that you do,
And forever is losing a stocking or shoe.
Who unresisting or not, lets you do as you will,
With bathing and feeding, the long day to fill.
Is that what you are thinking, is that what you see?
Then open your eyes, nurse, you're not looking at me.

I'll tell you who I am as I sit here so still;
As I use at your bidding, as I eat at your will,
I'm a small child of ten with a father and mother,
Brother and sisters, who love one another.
A young girl of sixteen with wings on her feet,
Dreaming that soon now a lover she'll meet;
A bride soon at twenty – my heart gives a leap,
Remembering the vows that I promised to keep;
At twenty – five now I have young of my own,
Who need me to build a secure, happy home;
A woman of thirty, my young now grow fast,
Bound to each other with ties that should last;
At forty, my young sons have grown and are gone,
But my man's beside me to see I don't mourn;
At fifty once more babies play round my knee,
Again we know children, my loved one and me.
Dark days are upon me, my husband is dead,
I look at the future, I shudder with dread,
For my young are all rearing young of their own,
And I think of the years and the love that I've known.

A Lingering Fear

I'm an old woman now and nature is cruel —
'Tis her jest to make old age look like a fool.
The body it crumbles, grace and vigour depart,
There is now a stone where I once had a heart;
But inside this old carcase a young girl still dwells,
And now and again my battered heart swells.
I remember the joys, I remember the pain,
And I'm loving and living life over again.
I think of the years all too few — gone too fast,
And accept the stark fact that nothing can last.

So open your eyes, nurses, open and see
Not a crabbit old woman, look closer — see ME !

When this poem was published, for the third time, following the furore following the screening of the BBC TV programme *Undercover Nurse* with its allegations of ill-treatment of elderly patients on a ward at the Royal Sussex County Hospital, two readers of the *Brighton University Hospitals' Bulletin* wrote to the editor enclosing *A Nurse's Reply*, which the magazine later also published.

What do we see, you ask, what do we see?
Yes, we are thinking when looking at thee!
We may seem to be hard when we hurry and fuss,
But there's many of you, and too few of us.
We would like far more time to sit by you and talk,
To bath you and feed you and help you to walk.
To hear of your lives and the things you have done;
Your childhood, your husband, your daughter, your son.
But time is against us, there's too much to do -
Patients too many, and nurses too few.
We grieve when we see you so sad and alone,
With nobody near you, no friends of your own.
We feel all your pain, and know of your fear
That nobody cares now your end is so near.
But nurses are people with feelings as well,
And when we're together you'll often hear tell
Of the dearest old Gran in the very end bed,
And the lovely old Dad, and the things that he said,

We speak with compassion and love, and feel sad
When we think of your lives and the joy that you've had,
When the time has arrived for you to depart,
You leave us behind with an ache in our heart.
When you sleep the long sleep, no more worry or care,
There are other old people, and we must be there.

So please understand if we hurry and fuss -
There are many of you,
And so few of us.

Both poems were by then freely available and has been widely read on the Internet. Research by another nurse reader, Claire Anderson, came up with the name Liz Hogben as the author of the reply, although Bruni Abbott of the former Prince Henry's Hospital, Melbourne, Australia is sometimes cited as the author.

Notes

Preface

1. Mid Sussex Hospital Management Committee (HMC) Minutes, 3 June 1952, WSCRO HM 11/1/1
2. Gaston, Harry. 'A Garden Fete this Summer', *Hospital and Social Service Journal*, 8 May 1959, p. 467
3. Clark, A.N.G. 'Looking back...', *Age and Ageing*, 1999, 28, p.585
4. Surtees, John. *Barracks, Workhouse, and Hospital: St Mary's, Eastbourne 1794-1990*, Eastbourne Local History Society, 1992, p.41
5. Gaston, Harry. *Workhouse to Hospital: The development of hospital services for the elderly chronic sick at Newhaven and other East Sussex public assistance institutions, 1930-1948*, The Open University, 1984, (Unpublished). (2)
6. Gaston, Harry. *After the Workhouse; The development of hospitals for the elderly chronic sick, with particular reference to the former public assistance institutions in East Sussex, 1991*, Doctoral thesis, University of Sussex. (Unpublished).(3)
7. Gaston, Harry. *Out of the Shadows: A history of Newhaven Downs 1836-1996*, South Downs Health NHS Trust, 1997. (1)

Introduction. The Fear of the Workhouse

1. Carder, Timothy. *The Encyclopaedia of Brighton*, East Sussex County Libraries, 1990, section 215 (a) and (b).
2. Opitz, Leslie. 'Cuckfield: A Village and a Hospital', *Sussex Garland*, December 1988, p. 16
3. Surtees, J. *op .cit.* p. 18
4. Valentine, Don. *St Helen's Hospital, Hastings (1837-1994): Paupers to Pacemakers*, Rosewell Publishing, 2000, p. 3
5. Gaston, (1) *op. cit,* p. 4
6. Hastings Union consisted of the parishes of All Saints, Fairlight, Guestling, Holy Trinity, Ore, Pett, St Andrew, St Clement, St Leonards, St Mary Bulverhythe, St Mary-in-the-Castle, St Mary Magdalen, St Matthew and St Michael-on-the-Rock. The original fourteen parishes comprising Battle Union were Ashburnham, Battle, Bexhill, Brightling, Catsfield, Crowhurst, Dallington, Ewhurst, Hollington, Mountfield, Penshurst, Seddlescombe, Westfield and Whatlington. 23 parishes comprised the original Steyning Union: Aldrington, Ashurst, Beeding, West Blatchington, Botolphs, Bramber, Coombes, Edburton, Hangleton, Henfield, Hove, Kingston-by-Sea, Patcham, Portslade, Poynings, Preston, Shermanbury, New and Old Shoreham, Sompting, Southwick, Steyning and Woodmancote.
7. Felix Driver in *Power and Pauperism, The Workhouse System 1824-1884*, Cambridge University Press, 1993, p.1 quotes the *Social Science Review* 1865, which published an unflattering portrait of the 'English Bastile',

the Union Workhouse (by which name the post 1834 workhouses were known), whose critics believed that the disciplinary regime of the austere forbidding institutions crushed the unfortunate inmates under a huge apparatus of rules and regulations, that constantly reminded them of their powerless, degraded status as paupers.

8. Checkland, S.G. and E.O. (eds.), *The Poor Law Report of 1834*, Penguin 1974, p. 430
9. Leslie, Kim. *Sussex. Tales of the Unexpected, Five Centuries of County Life*, West Sussex County Council, 2008, p. 96
10. Anstruther, Ian. *The Scandal of the Andover Workhouse*, Alan Sutton, 1984, quotes pp. 30/31 PRO M.H. 32/9 q.p., a report by William Henry Toovey Hawley, Assistant Poor Law Commissioner for Sussex.
11. Comprehensive details of the punishments for misbehaviour by paupers in 1871 are given in Gooch, Janet, *A History of Brighton General Hospital*, Phillimore, 1980, pp. 20-23.
12. Quoted in Gaston (1), *op cit*, pp. 7-8
13. Quoted in White, Rev. John. *Southlands, Workhouse and Hospital*, League of Friends of Southlands Hospital, 1990. pp, 9-10
14. Quoted in Surtees, *op cit*, p.23
15. Quoted in Longmate, Norman, *The Workhouse*, PBS Book Club edition, n.d., p. 121 (Republished in 2003 by Pimlico with a new Foreword by the author).

1. The Survival of the Guardians

1. McIntyre, S. 'Old Age as a Social Problem', in Dingwall R. *et al* (eds), *Health Care and Health Care Knowledge*, Croom Helm, 1977, p.47
2. Ministry of Health. *On the State of the Public Health*, Annual Report of the Chief Medical Officer, 1928, HMSO, 1929.
3. *ibid.*
4. *Sussex Daily News*, 28 March 1930.
5. *Eastbourne Herald*, 29 March 1930.
6. *Brighton & Hove Herald*, 6 April 1930.
7. *ibid.*
8. *Sussex Daily News*, 1 April 1930.

2. The East Sussex Inheritance

1. Bell, C.V.R. *A History of East Sussex County Council, 1889-1974*, Phillimore, 1975, p. 55
2. ESCRO C/C11/68/56 and 69/1.
3. Keat, Euan, *Cuckfield General Hospital, A review, 1845-1949-1991*, published in aid of the League of Friends of Cuckfield and Mid Sussex Hospitals, n.d.
4. *Eastbourne Herald*, 29 March 1930.
5. Lester, A.M. 'The Evolution of St Mary's Hospital', *Gazette*, Vol. 2 1976-1980, No.1 (1976), published by Eastbourne Postgraduate Medical Centre.
6. Webb, S. and B. *The Breakup of the Poor Law: Being Part One of the*

Minority Report of the Poor Law Commission, Longmans Green, 1909, pp. 3 and 574.

7. ESCRO C/C11/66/56
8. *ibid.*
9. ESCRO C/C11/69/1
10. Quoted in Gaston, *Out of the Shadows, op. cit,* p. 26

3. Farewell to the Poor Law

1. ESCRO C/C11/64/1 Minutes of the Poor Law Organisation Committee, 4 June 1929.
2. ESCRO C/C11/66/56 Joint memorandum by the County Medical Officer of Health, the County Architect and the County Public Assistance Officer on the utilisation of Public Assistance Institutions in East Sussex, September 1931.
3. ESCRO C/C11/64/1 Memorandum on the Survey of Poor Law Instiutions by R. Ashleigh Glegg, CMOH., June, 1929.
4. ESCRO C/C11/69/1. Report by the CMOH to the Committee on Hospital Accommodation, March 1935.
5. ESCRO C/C11/64/1 ESCC. Report of the Committee on Hospital Accommodation, 8 October 1935.
6. *Eastbourne Herald,* 29 March 1930.
7. *ibid.*
8. ESCRO DE/A7/9 Eastbourne CB. Minutes of the Sanitary and Public Health Committee, 22 January 1934.
9. ESCRO. DE/A7/9 Eastbourne BC San & PHC Minutes, 17 December 1934.
10. ESCRO. R/C50/1 Eastbourne BC PAC Minutes, 21 January and 5 February 1935.
11. At Brighton, where there had been less pressure to provide a separate entrance, a second entrance was eventually provided at the rear of the hospital. However, the main entrance remained in Elm Grove, which was still being used by applicants for the reception centre for present day 'vagrants' as well as by hospital patients almost sixty years later in 1991.
12. ESCRO DE/A7/9 Eastbourne CB. Minutes of the San & PHC,18 February 1935.
13. General hospitals £2 14s 6d per week, poor law hospitals £1 18s 3d, poor law institutions £1 2s 2d. The current cost of St Mary's (then a PLI) was £1 18s 8d - because the hospital part, according to the Borough Treasurer, 'has already been developed far beyond the hospital work usually carried out in a Poor Law Institution'.
14. ESCRO DE/A7/10 Eastbourne CB. Minutes of the San & PHC, 15 March 1935.
15. ESCRO RC/50/2 Eastbourne CB PAC Minutes, 24 September 1936. [original emphasis]
16. ESCRO. R/C50/2 Eastbourne CB PAC Minutes, 23 March 1939.

17. *ibid.*, 21 November 1939.
18. Hastings CB. PAC Minutes, 7 November 1930.
19. ESCRO RS/10/51.Brighton CB. Minutes of the PAC House Sub-Committee, 8 April 1931.
20. *ibid*, 23 January, 1935.
21. ESCRO RS/11/14. Brighton CB, Extract from the proceedings of the Health Committee, 29 November 1934.
22. *The Lancet*, 2 April 1932, p. 733.
23. *ibid.*
24. ESCRO RS/11/14 Brighton CB Health Committee proceedings, *op cit.*
25. ESCRO RS/10/45 Brighton CB. Minutes of a joint meeting between representatives of the House Sub-Committee and the Health Committee, 18 January 1935.
26. ESCRO RS/10/54 Brighton CB. Minutes of the House Sub-Committee, 25 September 1935.

4. Institutional Life

1. Paris, R. 'Christmas Day in the Workhouse', *Sussex Life*, December 1988, p. 16
2. Gaston, *Out of the Shadows, op. cit.*, pp. 28-9
3. Frankie Gee (aged 92), in an interview with the author, 19 April 2008.
4. White, Rev. T. *Southlands Workhouse and Hospital, op. cit.*, p.36
5. Aranovitch, B. *Give it Time: An experience of hospital 1928-1932*, Deutsch, London, 1981, p. 71
6. Gilbert, M. 'Growing up geriatric', *The Guardian*, 23 December 1966, p. 10
7. Paris, *op. cit.*
8. Valentine, *op. cit.*, p. 29
9. Hastings PAC, M&H Minutes, 25 September 1930.
10. Eastbourne CB PAC Minutes, 6 November 1933.
11. ESCRO HH 9/1 Battle Institution House Visitors' Reports, 6 February 1934.
12, *ibid*, 28 July 1932.
13. Surtees, *op cit*, p. 79
14. ESCRO RS 11/14 Brighton CB PAC minutes, 1 December 1936.
15. *ibid.*
16. ESCRO RS/11/15 Brighton CB PAC House Committee Minutes, 21 October 1938.
17. ESCRO HH9/1 House Visitors' Reports, 29 March 1943.
18. ESCRO RS/11/15 21 October 1938, *op. cit.*
19. *ibid.*
20. Hastings, PAC, M&H Minutes, 25 September 1930
21. 'The not-so-good old days at Pouchlands', *op. cit.*
22. Aranovitch, B. *op cit.*, p. 71
23. *ibid.*

24. *ibid.*
25. Paris, *op. cit.*
26. ESCRO C/C11/66/6 East Sussex CC PAC Minutes, 30 December 1932
27. *ibid.*
28. *ibid.*, 28 December 1932
29. ESCRO HW1/3 Southlands Hospital, Visitors Reports, 13 April 1934.
30. *ibid*, 30 July 1934.
31. ESCRO G7/33/5 Newhaven Institution, Master's Half Yearly Reports, 30 January 1934, 30 June 1939.
32. ESCRO C/C11/66/7 East Sussex CC PAC minutes, 28 March 1939.
33. ESCRO RS 10/53 Brighton CB PAC Minutes, 14 March 1934.
34. Aranovitch, B. *op cit*, p.63
35. ESCRO HW 1/3 Southlands Hospital, House Visitors Report Book, 13 April 1934.
36. *ibid*, 30 July 1934.
37. ESCRO RS 10/52 Brighton CB PAC House Committee minutes, 28 October 1931.
38. Hastings CB PAC Management & House Committee minutes, 26 June 1930.
39. *ibid*, 12 January 1933.
40. Hastings CB PAC Management & House Sub-Committee minutes, 8 April 1930.
41. Hastings CB St Helen's Hospital, Medical Officer's Report Book, 23 October 1930.
42. The medical officer's report book (*ibid*) contains several references to problems with mental patients in 1931 and 1932.

5. The Chronic Sick and their Nurses

1. Gilbert, M. *op cit.*
2. Vaizey, J. *Scenes from Institutional Life*, Faber and Faber. London, 1959, p.7. Vaizey later went on to write *National Health*, Martin Robertson, Oxford, 1984, in which, perhaps not surprisingly, he argued in favour of more home -based care and that 'many hospitals *ought* to be and *will* be closed'. (p.vii)
3. Banks, A. Leslie. 'Care of the Aged and Infirm', *Nursing Times*, 27 October 1945, p. 698.
4, Nisbet, W.H. *The Care of the Elderly, with special reference to the Foresthall Institution, Glasgow*, unpublished M.D. thesis, University of Glasgow, 1952, p. 97–8.
5. *ibid.*
6. Amulree, Lord. 'The Care of the "chronic" sick', *Nursing Times*, 10 May 1947, p. 304
7. Abel Smith, B. 'A History of the Nursing Profession,' *op cit*, p. 139.
8. *ibid*, pp. 139-140.
9. ESCRO C/C11/66/5 East Sussex CC PAC Minutes, 27 November 1934.

10. ESCRO G7/32/2 Newhaven Institution, Medical Officer's Report Book, 27 March 1936, 22 April 1938.
11. ESCRO C/C11/66/10 East Sussex CC PAC Minutes, 25 October 1946.
12. ESCRO C/C11/66/10 East Sussex CC PAC Minutes, 13 May 1947.

6. The Casuals at the Gates

1. Gaston, *Out of the Shadows, op cit*, p. 31
2. Valentine, *op cit*, p. 7
3. Gaston, *op cit*, p. 30
4. ESCRO HW 1/3 House Visitors' Report Book, 19 February 1935.
5. ESCRO G7/32/2 Medical Officer's Report Book, 25 October 1935.
6. Gooch, *op cit*, p. 123
7. ESCRO HW/1 *op cit*.

7. The Second World War

1. ESRO C/C11/66/7, ESCC PAC minutes, 26 September 1939, supplementary report to the county council, 28 April 1939.
2. *ibid.*, PAC minutes 30 May 1939.
3. PAC supplementary report, 28 April 1939, *op cit*.
4. ESCRO G7/33/4. Newhaven Institution, Master's Journal, 19 July 1940.
5. ESCRO G7/32/3. Newhaven Institution, Medical Officer's Report Book, 21 June 1940.
6. *ibid.*, 18 September 1942.
7. ESCRO HH9/1 Battle Institution, House Visitors Reports, 29 March 1943.
8. *ibid*, 7 December 1944.
9. ESCRO G7/33/3 Newhaven Institution, Medical Officer's Report Book, 20 October 1940.
10. *ibid.*, December 1942.
11. *ibid.*, 18 May 1944.
12. *ibid*, 18 October 1940.
13. ESCRO G7/33/4 Newhaven Institution, Master's Journal, 15 November, 1940.
14. ESCRO HH9/1 Battle Institution, House Visitors Reports, 29 March 1943.
15. Newhaven Institution, Medical Officer's Report Book, *op cit.*, 20 June 1941.
16. ESCRO C/C55/149 File 'West Hylands (Cuckfield) Transfer to Canadian Army.'
17. Titmuss, R, *Problems with Social Policy*, HMSO, 1950, pp 488-9.

8. Aftermath: Towards the NHS

1. Gray, A.M.H. and Topping, A. *Hospital Survey: The Hospital Services of London and the Surrounding Area.* (London, HMSO, 1945, p. ii).
2. Gray and Topping, *op cit*, p. v.
3. *The Hospital Surveys: The Domesday Book of the Hospital Surveys.*

(Nuffield Provincial Hospitals Trust, Oxford, 1946, p. 3).

4. *The Lancet*, 2, 24 November 1945, p. 681
5. *British Medical Journal*, 1, 2 February 1946, p. 170
6. The quotation is taken from the report for the Yorkshire region.
7. *The Hospital Surveys*, *op cit*, pp. 15-16
8. Smith, N.Ross 'Memorandum on a National Health Service: An Alternative Scheme', *BMJ, Supplement*, 21 October 1944, p. 86
9. Kelly, P.M. 'The White Paper - and a Suggested Plan'. *BMJ Supplement*. 3 June 1944, p. 130
10. A.L.W. in obituary published in *The Lancet*, 17 September 1960.
11. Warren, M.W. 'Care of the Chronic Sick: A case for treating the chronic sick in blocks in a general hospital, *BMJ*, 2, 1943.
12. Howell, T. 'Origins of the British Geriatric Society'. *Age and Ageing*, vol. 3, no. 2, May 1974, p. 69
13. Adams, G.F. 'Eld Health: Origins and Destiny of British Geriatrics', *Age and Ageing*, vol.4, no. 2, May 1975, p. 66
14. Howell, T. 'Origins of the British Geriatric Society', *op cit*, p. 71
15. Adams, 'Eld Health', *op cit*.
16. Amulree, Lord. 'Twenty-five Years of Geriatrics', *British Journal of Clinical Practice*, vol. 25, no. 3, March 1971, p. 97
17. 'Care of the Chronic Sick and Aged'. *BMJ*, 1, 20 April 1946, p. 617
18. *ibid*.
19. *ibid*.
20. 'Care of the Chronic Sick'. *BMJ*, 2, 28 September 1946, p. 464
21. Institute of Hospital Almoners, 'Memorandum of the Chronic Sick', 1946.
22. 'Care of the Chronic Sick', *BMJ*, 1946 *op cit*.
23. Institute of Almoners, *op cit*.
24. Report (1947) of the Committee on the Care and Treatment of the Elderly and Infirm'. *BMJ, Supplement*, 21 June 1947, p. 133
25. Nuffield Foundation. 'Old People', (Cumberlege, Oxford, 1947).
26. *ibid*, p. 63
27. *ibid*.
28. BMA Report, 1947, *op cit*.
29. *ibid*, pp. 133-4
30. *ibid*, p. 135
31. *ibid*, p. 137

9. The Years of Make Do and Mend

1. *The Times*, 25 November 1946.
2. Abel-Smith, B. 'Present and Future Costs of the Health Service: The Economic Evidence to the Guillebaud Committee'. *The Lancet*, 28 January 1956, p. 199
3. Roberts, N. 'Our Neglected Hospitals – Ten Years of Tinkering', *The Guardian*, 9 September 1959, p. 6

4. Hadfield, S.J. 'A Field Survey of General Practice, 1951-2', *BMJ*, 26 September 1953, p. 696.
5. Thomas, J.S. 'The General Practitioner and the Health Visitor,' *BMJ*, 31 October 1953, p. 965
6. *BMJ*, 24 February 1951, p. 422.
7. *ibid*, 25 June 1949, p. 1134
8. Boucher, C.A. *Survey of Services available to the Chronic Sick and Elderly 1954-1955*, London, HMSO, 1957, p. 5
9. *ibid*, p.16
10 *ibid*, p. 17
11. Hughes, T. 'The Care of Old People,' *Medical World*, vol. 81, 1954, p. 296-6
12. Boucher, *op cit*, p. 27
13. Boucher, *op cit*, p. 28
14. *ibid*, p. 48
15. Quoted in Honigsbaum, F. 'The Division in British Medicine', London, Kogan Page, 1979, p. 309
16. National Health Service, H.M.(57)86: Geriatric Services and the Care of the Chronic Sick, Ministry of Health, 7 October 1957.

10. Brighton's Two Kinds of Care

1. Gaston, H. 'Workhouse to Hospital'. *Brighton Health Bulletin*, No 226, June 1988, p. 11
2. *Evening Argus* (Brighton) 4 May 1971.
3. ESCRO HB 72/2 Brighton & Lewes HMC. Group 1 House Committee minutes, 1 May 1951.
4. ESCRO HB 72/2 Brighton & Lewes HMC. Group 1 House Committee minutes 23 April 1957, 28 January 1958, 23 June 1959.
5. ESCRO HB 73/2 Brighton & Lewes HMC Brighton General Hospital Medical Staff Committee minutes, 15 March 1951.
6. ESCRO HB1/1. Brighton & Lewes HMC. Minutes, 1 October 1954.
7. *ibid*.
8. ESCRO HB 1/1, HMC Minutes, 1 October 1954.
9. ESCRO HB 72/2 Brighton & Lewes HMC Group 1 House Committee minutes, 26 June 1956.
10. ESCRO HB 72/2 Brighton & Lewes HMC Group 1 House Committee minutes, 24 September 1957.
11. ESCRO HB1/1. Brighton & Lewes HMC. Minutes, 1 October 1954.
12. Gaston, H. 'A Fete This Summer?' *Hospital and Social Services Journal*, 8 May 1959, pp. 467-8
13. Gaston, '*Out of the Shadows*', *op cit.*, p. 52.

11. Overcoming the Problems at Hastings

1. ESCRO HH15/2. Hastings HMC Minutes, 29 April 1949.
2. ESCRO HH 40/3 Hastings HMC File: Hospital Plan 1948-50, 3 August 1949.

3. *ibid*, 20 March 1950.
4. ESCRO HH 40/4 Hastings HMC File: Battle Hospital Conversion for Chronic Sick, 3 November 1949.
5. *ibid*, minutes of sub-committee to consider question of patient and staff accommodation, 23 December 1949.
6. ESCRO HH 15/3 Hastings HMC Minutes, 28 April 1950.
7. ESCRO HH 15/3 Hastings HMC, Report by Mr S.J. Lock MAOT, 28 June 1950.
8. ESCRO HH 15/4 Hastings HMC, Second Annual Report, 1 July 1949-30 June 1950.
9. ESCRO HH 15/4 Hastings HMC Minutes, 26 June 1951.
10. ESCRO 40/62 Hastings HMC Geriatric Services Correspondence, 8 June 1959.
11. ESCRO HH 15/12 Hastings HMC Minutes of the Geriatric Sub-Committee, 1 December 1959.
12. *ibid*.
13. ESCRO HH 15/12 Hastings HMC Minutes of the Geriatric Sub-Committee, 1 December 1959.
14. *ibid*, 22 April 1965.
15. *ibid*, 15 June 1965.
16. *ibid*, 14 June 1965.
17. *ibid*, 18 February 1966.

12. Eastbourne: A Desperate Search for Nurses

1. ESCRO HE 86/1 Eastbourne HMC Minutes, 21 July 1948 and 25 August 1948.
2. *ibid*, 21 December 1948.
3. *ibid*, 29 August 1949.
4. ESCRO HE 88/1 Eastbourne HMC Medical Staff Committee minutes, 24 April 1950 and 8 May 1950.
5. ESCRO HE 88/1 Eastbourne HMC General Medical Committee minutes, 9 December 1952.
6. ESCRO HE 86/1 Eastbourne HMC minutes, 3 December 1954 and 12 December 1956.
7. ESCRO HE 88/1 Eastbourne HMC GMC minutes 8 November 1955
8. *ibid*, 14 January 1958.
9. ESCRO HE 86/1 Eastbourne HMC GMC minutes 14 April 1959.
10. ESCRO HE 86/2 Eastbourne HMC minutes, 3 February 1960.
11. *ibid*, 6 April 1960.
12. *ibid*, minutes of the annual general meeting, 9 December 1960.
13. *ibid*, 5 December 1962.
14. *ibid*, annual general meeting, 7 December 1962.
15. ESCRO HE 87/10 Eastbourne HMC, All Saints House Committee minutes, 8 December 1961.

16. *ibid*, 1 June 1962.
17. *ibid*, 4 September 1964.
18. ESCRO HE 87/10 Eastbourne HMC, All Saints HC minutes, 10 October 1970 .
19. *ibid*, 11 December 1970.

13. Mid Sussex: A New General Hospital and an Old Workhouse

1. WSCRO HM 1/1/1 Mid-Sussex HMC minutes, 4 April 1950.
2. *ibid*.
3. 'The not-so-good old days at Pouchlands', *Brighton Hospitals Bulletin*, Summer 1982, p. 4
4. WSCRO HM 1/1/1 Mid-Sussex HMC minutes, 2 September 1952.
5. Gaston, H. 'A Garden Fete This Summer?' *Hospital and Social Service Journal*, 8 May 1959, p. 467
6. 'People in the News', *Brighton Hospitals Bulletin*, June 1978, p. 10
7. Townsend, P. *The Last Refuge, A Survey of Residential Institutions in England and Wales*, Routledge & Kegan Paul, 1962, pp. 506-9
8. Miller, H. *Medicine and Society*, London, Oxford University Press, 1973, p. 34

14. Press, Pressure Groups and Hospital Scandals

1. Rudd, T.N. 'Hospital Geriatrics – the Mechanism of Success', B*ritish Hospital and Social Services Journal*, 21 July 1967, p. 1360
2. Robb, B. (ed). *Sans Everything: A Case to Answer*, Nelson, 1967.
3. Cohen, G.L. *What's Wrong With Hospitals?* Harmondsworth, Pengiun Books, 1964, p.7
4. *ibid*. p.187
5. *ibid*.
6. Robb, B. 'Sans Everything – and after', *Nursing Times*, 24 April 1975. p.644
7. House of Lords debate, 7 July 1965, cols 1396-1399.
8. *ibid*.
9. H of C, written answer 2 August 1965, cols. 224-5.
10. *Sunday Times*, 4 June 1967, p.11-12.
11. Robb. *Sans Everything, op cit.*, p. 3
12. *ibid*, p. 5-6
13. *The Times*, 20 June 1968, p. 3
14. *ibid*, 28 October 1967, p. 3; 22 July 1967, p. 23
15. Woodford-Williams. E. 'Misery in our Midst.' *British Medical Journal* 19 August 1967, p. 484
16. *Brighton Hospitals Bulletin*, July 1967, p. 3
17. *The Times*, 3 July 1967, p. 8
18. *ibid*, 12 October 1967, p. 2
19. *ibid*, 8 February 1968, p. 3
20. WSCRO HM 1/1/2 Mid-Sussex HMC minutes, 4 July 1967.

21. *ibid.*
22. *ibid,* 4 June 1968.
23. WSCRO HM 3/3/18 Mid-Sussex HMC, letter from the group secretary to the secretary of the RHB, 9 August 1968.
24. WSCRO HM 3/3/18 Report by Miss Marchant on standards of staffing and nursing care at Pouchlands Hospital, enclosed with the group secretary's letter, *op cit,* 9 August 1968.
25. *ibid.*
26. In fact a committee of inquiry was set up by the management committee just one year later to investigate allegations concerning the care and treatment of mentally subnormal patients (WSCRI H/1/1/2, Mid Sussex HMC minutes, 2 September 1969) and a Hospital Advisory Service team which visited in 1970 noted 'The hospital has recently had two inquiries resulting from allegations of ill-treatment … these incidents resulted in a lowering of morale and made for despondency among nursing staff. The hospital now appears to by recovering from this setback and I formed the impression that the standard of patient care was good. … (ESCRO HC 76/2, Pouchlands Hospital quoted in a memorandum from the group secretary).
27. WSCRO H 1/1/2 Mid-Sussex HMC minutes, 19 December 1968 and 4 February 1969.

15. The Unpopular Patient

1. Stacey, F. *The British Ombudsman,* Oxford, Clarendon Press, 1971, p.9-10
2. Cited by Mrs Robb in 'The Hospital Advisory Service,' *Nursing Times,* 24 April 1975, p.646
3. ESCRO HE 86/2. Eastbourne HMC minutes, 5 July 1967.
4. *ibid,* 2 August 1967.
5. Boorer, D. 'The study of attitudes – a vital problem for all nurses', *Nursing Times,* 26 August 1971, pp 1045-1047
6. *ibid.*
7. Stockwell, F. *The Unpopular Patient* published as 'The study of Nursing Care Project Reports.' 1972. The Royal College of Nursing, Series 1, Number 2, 1972, an investigation in the series 'The Study of Nursing Care' administered by the Royal College of Nursing and the National Council of Nurses of the United Kingdom and financed by the DHSS.
8. *ibid.,* p. 48
9. *ibid.,* p. 52
10. *ibid.,* p. 53
11. Baker, D.E. *Attitudes of Nurses to the Care of the Elderly.* Unpublished Ph.D. thesis, University of Manchester, 1978.
12. Fairhurst, E. *Sociological Study of the Rehabilitation of Elderly Patients in an Urban Hospital.* Unpublished Ph.D. thesis, University of Leeds, 1981, p.326-327.

13. Fielding, P. *An Investigation of Student Nurses' Attitudes Towards Old People in Hospital.* Unpublished Ph.D. thesis, University of Southampton, 1982, p. 288
14. Fielding, p. 291, quotes student nurses who rejected a career in geriatrics because they said such nursing was depressing, too heavy or too routine.
15. Manchester Guardian, 6 March 1943, *op cit.*

16. Ancient Monuments and General Dickensia

1. Norton, D., McLaren, R. and Exton-Smith, A.N. *An Investigation of Geriatric Nursing Problems in Hospital,* London, The National Corporation for the Care of Old People, 1962.
2. Norton, D. *Hospitals of the Long-stay Patient: a Study of their Practical* Nursing Problems and Solutions, Oxford, Pergamon Press, 1967.
3. 'Where to Nurse the Elderly?', *The Lancet,* 9 March 1968, pp. 517-18
4. *ibid,* p. 518
5. *Birmingham Regional Hospital Board, 1947-1966,* Birmingham, Birmingham RHB, 1966.
6. *The Times,* 21 June 1961.
7. *Guardian,* 21 June 1961.
8. Report to Birmingham RHB ... op cit., p. 174
9. *ibid.,* p. 177
10. *ibid.,* p. 188
11. Roberts, N. 'Decrepit Hospital Buildings'. *Guardian,* 10 September 1959.
12. *ibid.*
13. Brocklehurst, J.C. et al. *The Development of Services for the Elderly and Elderly Confused in the South-East Metropolitan Hospital Region,* London, SEMRHB, 1970.
14. *Guardian,* 3 May 1971; *Sunday Express,* 2 May 1971.
15. Brocklehurst, *op. cit.,* p. 108
16. *Eastbourne Gazette,* 26 June 1968, p. 2
17. ESCRO HE 88/2 Eastbourne HMC General Medical Committee minutes, 10 October 1967.
18. ESCRO HE 86/2 Eastbourne HMC minutes, 1 November 1967.
19. *Eastbourne Gazette,* 19 June 1968 p. 1
20. ESCRO HH 40/64 Hastings HMC letter from the management side secretary of the Whitley Council, 2 October 1969.
21. The Ely Hospital Inquiry (1969) was the result of allegations by a nursing assistant published in the *News of the World* in 1967. Ely, a former public assistance institution, was a mental subnormality hospital and the first of a series of psychiatric and mental subnormality hospitals where scandals resulted in inquiries during the following 15 years. See, for example, J.P. Martin, *Hospitals in Trouble,* Blackwell, 1984.
22. ESCRO HH 40/64 Hastings HMC Letter from the SAMO to the group secretary, 4 July 1969.

23. *ibid.*
24. *ibid,* letter from group secretary to Dr Irvine, 13 August 1969.
25. *Sunday Express,* 7 June 1970, p. 1
26. ESCRO HB 1/2 Brighton & Lewes HMC minutes, 9 October 1970.
27. *ibid.*
28. 'Geriatrics are human, too!', *Brighton Hospitals Bulletin,* No. 44 December 1970, p. 6
29. *ibid.*
30. Whitehead, T. *In the Service of Old Age,* Harmondsworth, Penguin Books, 1970. In a review *The Lancet* (18 April 1970, p. 817) commented: 'No-one reading this book can remain complacent, excusing himself for doing nothing to improve the care of the elderly on the ground that resources are inadequate'.
31. Geriatrics well cared for, say nurses', *Brighton Hospitals Bulletin,* No. 45, January 1971.

17. Sussex Hospitals Under the Microscope

1. ESCRO HH 40/65 Hastings HMC, Letter from the secretary of the RHB to all group secretaries, 16 April 1971.
2. *ibid,* SEMRHB News and Information (press release) 20 April 1971.
3. *Evening Argus* (Brighton), 3 May 1971, p. 1
4. *ibid.,* 4 and 5 May 1971
5. *Brighton Hospitals Bulletin,* No. 49, May 1971, pp. 1, 3 and 8.
6. Brocklehurst *et al, op cit.,* p. 131
7. *Evening Argus,* 3 May 1971, p. 12
8. *ibid.*
9. *ibid.*
10. *Brighton Hospitals Bulletin,* No. 49, p. 1
11. *ibid,* p. 2

18. Sweeping Away the Old Institutions

1. *Brighton Hospitals Bulletin,* No. 76, March 1974, p. 1
2. ESCRO HE 86/3 Eastbourne HMC minutes, 5 May 1971.
3. *Brighton Hospitals Bulletin,* December 1971, p. 11.
4. House of Commons statement, 22 November 1971, col. 957.
5. *ibid,* col. 958.
6. *Brighton Health Bulletin,* no. 58, p. 4
7. ESCRO HH 40/65 Hastings HMC. Letter from Dr Irvine to Mr A.C. Wright, 29 February 1972.
8. *ibid,* letter from ASMO, RHB to A.C. Wright, 21 March 1972.
9. *ibid,* letter from Dr Irvine to the group secretary, 30 May 1972.
10. *ibid.*
11. *ibid.*
12. *ibid.*

13. *Brighton Health Bulletin,* no. 61, Summer 1972, p. 6
14. *ibid.,* no. 68, May 1973, p. 7
15. Quoted in *Brighton Health Bulletin,* No. 54, Christmas 1971.
16. ESCRO HH 40/66 Hastings HMC, letter from Dr Irvine to the group secretary.

19. The Unchanging Legacy

1. *HAS Annual Report,* 1973, covering letter sent with the report to the Secretaries of State (for Health and for Wales) by Dr Baker and his successor, Dr Woodford-Williams.
2. *ibid,* 1969-70, p. 22
3. *ibid.,* preface, p. iv
4. *ibid.,* 1971, p. 5
5. HAS Annual Report 1972, Introduction by Dr Baker, p. 1. An example of the way mental handicap services were able to forge ahead is given in Ham's study of policy making in the Leeds region. Capital expenditure on these services increased from £460,000 in 1969/70 to £1.2m in 1970/71 and £1.17m the following year which were due in part, Ham says, to the priority that Crossman asked boards to give to mental handicap. Developments included the erection of what were later to be known as Crossman units, prefabricated buildings with a lifespan of 10-15 years to mitigate the worst cases of overcrowding. See: Ham, C. *Policy-making in the National Health Service: A Case Study of the Leeds Regional Hospital Board,* Macmillan, 1981, p. 113
6. *ibid,* 1971, p. 7
7. *ibid,* 1973, p. 16
8. *ibid,* 1974, p. 6
9. H of C., 12 May 1975, col. 216
10. *ibid.,* col. 210
11. *ibid.*
12. *ibid.*
13. Wells, T.J. *Problems in Geriatric Nursing Care: A Study of Nurses' Problems in Care of Old People in Hospitals,* Edinburgh, Churchill Livingstone, 1980, pp. 5-6
14. Fairhurst, E. *Sociological Study of the Rehabilitation of Elderly Patients an Urban Hospital,* unpublished Ph.D. thesis, Leeds, 1981, p. 7
15. *HAS Report, 1973, op cit.,* p. 16
16. Haliburton, P.M. and Wright, W.B. 'Variations in Standards of Geriatric Hospital Care'. *The Lancet,* 9 June 1973, pp. 1300-1302.
17. *ibid.,* p. 1300
18. In 1979, there were campaigns to ban the use of plastic bibs for elderly patients in Exeter and Brighton. Withdrawing the bibs, it was argued, afforded greater dignity to the patient. The Brighton campaign, which was taken up local press and radio, was launched in the *Brighton Health Bulletin,* June 1979, p. 11

19. *ibid,* p. 1301

20. Adams, G.F. 'Eld Health'. *BMJ,* 28 September 1974, p. 790

21. *Hospital Advisory Service Report on Brighton Health District,* December 1975, p. 11

22. *ibid.,* p. 23

23. *ibid.,* p. 38

24. *ibid.,* p. 43

25. *ibid.*

26. *ibid.,* p. 41

27. *BMJ,* Supplement, 8 May 1971, p. 89

28. Report on the survey by the King's Fund Centre on conditions for long stay elderly patients at Newhaven Downs Hospital by Mrs Jean Mandeville, October 1977, p. 21.

29. Hospital Advisory Service Annual Reports 1972, p. iv; 1974, pp.14–15. See also *The Hospital,* vol. 66, no. 11, November 1970, p. 369 for comments on the Scottish survey which found patients in general hospitals 'were reluctant to say they were other than "very satisfied" generally with their stay in hospital' and that some insisted they would never make a complaint under any circumstances.

30. Elliott, J.R. *Living in Hospital: The Social Needs of People in Long-term Care,* London, King Edward's Hospital Fund, 1975.

31. Raphael, W. and Mandeville, J. *Old People in Hospital,* King Edward's Hospital Fund, 1979. The hospitals which participated in the survey were Cheam Hospital, North Cheam; Newhaven Downs Hospital, Newhaven; Queen's Hospital, Croydon; St Andrew's Hospital, Chippenham; St. John's Hospital, London; Staines Hospital.

32. Royal College of Nursing, *Improving Geriatric Care in Hospital,* 1975.

33. *ibid.,* p.7

34. South East Thames Regional Health Authority, *Improving the Care of the Elderly, Report of a Seminar,* 2 August 1977, Croydon, SETRHA, 1977.

20. Farewell to the Workhouse

1. Young, J. 'The Case for Small Nursing Units' in Shegog, R.F.A., *The Impending Crisis of Old Age,* Nuffield Provincial Hospitals Trust/OUP, 1982, p. 130; Stevenson, O. *Age and Vulnerability: A Guide to Better Care,* Arnold, 1989.

2. HAS, *Annual Report,* June 1987, p. 14

3. *ibid.*

4. NHS HAS, DHSS Social Services Inspectorate. *Report on Services for Elderly People Provided by Brighton Health Authority and the Social Services Department of East Sussex County Council,* May 1986, pp. 17-18

5. *ibid.*

6. 'Who cares for the elderly conference calls for far-reaching changes',

Brighton Health Bulletin, March 1985, p. 6.

7. *ibid*, p. 7.
8. Marter, Elizabeth. 'A new life for Pouchlands old folk', *Brighton Health Bulletin*, October 1986, p. 7.
9. 'Meadow Lodge is a model of care', *Brighton Health Bulletin*, January 1990, p. 2
10. Gaston, H. 'Newhaven's hospitals – past and present', *Newhaven Church Parish Magazine*, June 1972.
11. NHS/DHSS Report, *op. cit.*, pp. 28-9
12. *The Guardian*, 19 September 1991, p. 4
13. *ibid.*
14. *ibid.*
15. *ibid.*
16. 'Nursing home for Newhaven', *Brighton Health Bulletin*, May 1989, p. 2.
17. 'Nursing home is no nearer', *Brighton Health Bulletin*, February 1990, p. 2.
18. Southlands Hospital, admittedly the most modern of the former East Sussex public assistance institutions, is the only one still to be admitting elderly patients towards the end of the first decade of the 21st century. In 2008, there were plans to move Brighton and East Sussex patients to a new rehabilitation unit at the Princess Royal Hospital at Haywards Heath. (This eventually opened in January 2009). Elderly care cases were to be moved to Worthing Hospital this finally severing links with the former workhouse which was to continue providing acute care.
19. 'Brighton General's new ward hopes dashed', *BSUH Bulletin*, February 2003, p. 3

Select Bibliography

General

Abel Smith, Brian. A *History of the Nursing Profession*, Heinemann, 1982.

Anstruther, Ian. *The Scandal of the Andover Workhouse*, Alan Sutton, 1984.

Aranovitch, B. *Give it Time: An experience of hospital 1928-1932*, Deutsch, 1981.

Crowther, M.A. *The Workhouse System 1834-1929 – the history of an English social institution*, Batsford, 1981.

Elliott, J.R. *Living in Hospital: The Social Needs of People in Long-term Care*, London, King Edward's Hospital Fund, 1975.

Fowler, Simon. *Workhouse: The People, The Places, The Life Behind Doors*. The National Archives, 2007.

Longmate, Norman. *The Workhouse*, Pimlico, 2003.

Norton, D., McLaren, R. and Exton-Smith, A.N. *An Investigation of Geriatric Nursing Problems in Hospital*, London, The National Corporation for the Care of Old People, 1962.

Norton, D. *Hospitals of the Long-stay Patient: A Study of their Practical Nursing Problems and Solutions*, Oxford, Pergamon Press, 1967.

Raphael, W. and Mandeville, J. *Old People in Hospital*, King Edward's Hospital Fund, 1979.

Robb, Barbara. *Sans Everything, A Case to Answer*, Nelson, 1967.

Royal College of Nursing, *Improving Geriatric Care in Hospital*, 1975.

Vaizey, J. *National Health*, Martin Robertson, Oxford, 1984.

Vaizey, J. *Scenes from Institutional Life*, Faber and Faber, London, 1959.

Sussex

Bell, C.V.R. *A History of East Sussex County Council, 1889-1974*, Phillimore, 1975.

Gaston, Harry. *Out of the Shadows: A history of Newhaven Downs 1836-1996*, South Downs Health NHS Trust, 1997.

Gooch, Janet. *A History of Brighton General Hospital*, Phillimore, 1980.

Keat, Euan. *Cuckfield General Hospital, A review, 1845-1949-1991*, published in aid of the League of Friends of Cuckfield and Mid Sussex Hospitals, n.d.

Leslie, Kim. *Sussex. Tales of the Unexpected, Five Centuries of County Life*, West Sussex County Council, 2008.

Raphael, W. and Mandeville, J. *Old People in Hospital*, King Edward's Hospital Fund, 1979.

Surtees, John. *Barracks, Workhouse, and Hospital: St Mary's, Eastbourne 1794-1990*, Eastbourne Local History Society, 1992.

Valentine, Don. *St Helen's Hospital, Hastings (1837-1994): Paupers to Pacemakers*, Rosewell Publishing, 2000.

White, Rev. John. *Southlands, Workhouse and Hospital*, League of Friends of Southlands Hospital, 1990.

Index

Bold figures refer to illustrations, titles of books and magazines are in italics